NEWS/400
TECHNICA
REFERENC_
SERIES

Bryan Meyers
series editor

MW01174175

Desktop
Guide to
AS/400
Programmers'
Tools

by Dan Riehl

Library of Congress Cataloging-in-Publication Data

Riehl, Dan, 1953-
    Desktop guide to AS/400 programmer's tools/ by Dan Riehl.
        p.   cm.—(NEWS 3X/400 Technical Reference Series)
    Includes bibliographical references.
    ISBN 1-882419-14-6
    1. IBM AS/400 (Computer) — Programming I. Title. II. Series.
QA76.8.125919R43 1995
005.2'45—dc20   94-48576
                                                                      CIP

Published by DUKE PRESS
DUKE COMMUNICATIONS INTERNATIONAL
Loveland, Colorado

Copyright © 1995 by Dan Riehl

This book was printed and bound in Canada.
First Edition, Second Printing: October 1997

ISBN 1-882419-14-6

ISBN 1-882419-11-1 (*NEWS/400* Technical Reference Series)
2 3 4 5 6 WL 1 0 9 8 7

Acknowledgments

Several people contributed to the form and content of this book. Their diligent and creative efforts appear on every page. My sincere thanks to all.

Editor	Sharon Hamm	(Duke Communications)
Co-Editor	Dave Bernard	(Duke Communications)
Production	Sharon Hamm	
	Jan Caufman	(Duke Communications)
Technical Editor	Bryan Meyers	(KOA Kampgrounds of America)
Cover Design	Steve Adams	(Duke Communications)
Technical Assistance	Gordon Hof	(Gumbo Software)
	Brock Ward	(IBM)

Table of Contents

Section 3: Screen Design Aid (SDA)

Section 4: Report Layout Utility (RLU)

Section 5: File Compare and Merge Utility (FCMU)

Section 6: Interactive Source Debugger (ISDB)

Foreword

When I recall my first several months as a computer programmer, I have a vivid memory of the exhilarating feeling I had when I could get a program to compile correctly — and then again, when it ran and actually did the work it was supposed to do. What a good feeling that was!

I remember trying to figure out how to make the computer do the things that others said couldn't be done. Sometimes they were right; but other times I did find a solution. I was just learning, but learning was an exciting adventure!

If you are an experienced AS/400 programmer, much of the information in this book may not be new. But... I guarantee that, even so, there is much learning "to be had" between these covers. Have you ever created complex PDM user-defined options? What's the easiest way to center a field on your SDA work display? How do you create a subfile in a window with SDA? What shortcuts are available in SEU?

I have included in this Desk Reference the latest and greatest tools available with OS/400 V3R1. These V3R1 tools include the new File Compare/Merge Utility (FCMU) and the Interactive Source Debugger (ISDB). If you do not yet have V3R1, you can read about these tools in anticipation of being able to use them. These exciting new tools come packaged in the base support of the Application Development Toolset/400 Licensed Program Product that also includes the other tools covered in this book: PDM, SEU, SDA, and RLU.

Where I have presented new features of OS/400 V3R1 in the sections on PDM, SEU, SDA and RLU, those features are shown in red print. Again, if you are not using V3R1 or later, you can see what's in your programming future. *Not* highlighted in red are the full sections discussing the utilities introduced with V3R1: FCMU and ISDB.

My goal has been to make this book valuable for both the AS/400 beginner and the more experienced AS/400 programmer. Most of the tools are presented in a tutorial format, which is helpful for beginners. I have included valuable charts and tables as a ready reference for your programming needs, whatever your level of expertise.

My sincere desire is that this book will give you a comprehensive knowledge of the AS/400 programmers' tools; and that you consider that knowledge to be both valuable and useful. For those of us who spend 7 to 10 hours a day in front of a computer terminal kicking out new programs and fixing old ones, learning must continue to be exciting. We must have a mind-set that by improving our knowledge we improve ourselves.

Learning *is* an exciting adventure!

Dan Riehl
December 1994

Section 1

Programming Development Manager (PDM)

Introduction to PDM
and the Object Hierarchy

Chapter 1

Programming Development Manager (PDM) is a programming environment that provides access to AS/400 functions through a standard list interface. PDM is not a part of the OS/400 base operating system; it is a part of an IBM licensed program product called Application Development Toolset/400 (ADTS/400). The ADTS/400 product also includes programming tools such as the AS/400 Source Entry Utility (SEU) and the AS/400 Report Layout Utility (RLU). Almost every AS/400 that is used for program development will contain the ADTS/400 product.

PDM is not an end-user tool. Rather, it provides specific functions to increase AS/400 programmers' and system administrators' productivity. PDM makes it easy to perform functions such as copying files, moving objects from one library to another, compiling programs, and displaying the contents of a library.

The AS/400 Object-Based Architecture

To appreciate PDM's usefulness, you need to understand something about the AS/400's *object-based* architecture. Basically, everything that exists on the AS/400 is called an object. An object is simply a unique entity that is identified by its attributes or characteristics.

There are many types of objects on the AS/400. Figure 1.1 lists some of the AS/400 object types and their associated abbreviations.

Figure 1.1 Some AS/400 Object Types

Object Type	AS/400 Abbreviation
Command	*CMD
Data area	*DTAARA
Data queue	*DTAQ
File	*FILE
Job description	*JOBD
Journal	*JRN
Journal receiver	*JRNRCV
Library	*LIB
Message file	*MSGF
Message queue	*MSGQ
Output queue	*OUTQ
Program	*PGM
Subsystem description	*SBSD
User profile	*USRPRF

Object Attributes

One of the object types is the program (*PGM). Any program that can be created on the AS/400 will be a *PGM type object. However, you can have an RPG program, a CL program, a COBOL program, and so on. On the AS/400 each of these different types of programs has different attributes. The program object's attributes determine how the AS/400 will run a particular type of program.

As another example of object attributes, consider the object type *FILE. The AS/400 supports many different file types. For example, there are database files, display files, printer files, and source physical files. Each of these different types of files has different attributes. For instance, a database file can be used to store data, but a display file cannot. While both a database file and a display file are *FILE type objects, they have different attributes.

Figure 1.2 lists some attributes of AS/400 *FILE and *PGM type objects.

Figure 1.2 Object Attributes

Object Type	Object Attributes	
*FILE	DSPF	(Display File)
	PRTF	(Printer File)
	PF-SRC	(Source Physical File)
	PF-DTA	(Data Physical File)
	LF	(Logical File)
*PGM	RPG	(RPG program)
	CLP	(CL program)
	CBL	(COBOL program)
	SYSC	(System C program)

AS/400 Libraries

Any given AS/400 object is stored within a library. You can think of a library as a directory that allows you to find the objects that it contains. The concept of an AS/400 library is very similar to that of a directory on your personal computer's hard disk drive. From the DOS prompt on a PC, you can type the DOS command DIR to get a listing of all of the files and programs in a directory. Likewise, on the AS/400, you can use the command DSPLIB (Display Library) to get a listing of all the objects (files, programs, etc.) in a particular AS/400 library.

Just as files and programs are AS/400 objects, an AS/400 library is also an object. There is a difference, however, in that a library is a special kind of object used to hold other objects.

On the AS/400, IBM has supplied one special library, named QSYS, with some unique characteristics. The QSYS library contains many files, programs, and other objects that make up much of the OS/400 operating system. Some object types can only be stored in the QSYS library. These include user profile objects, communication line description objects, and — strangely enough — library type objects. QSYS is the only library that can contain a library type object. On a personal computer's hard disk drive, you can create a subdirectory within a directory. However, on the AS/400 you cannot create a sublibrary within a library, unless the library is the IBM-supplied library QSYS. Every library object that is created on the AS/400 will be created in the library QSYS. Figure 1.3 illustrates the AS/400 object architecture.

Figure 1.3 AS/400 Object-Based Structure

```
Library QSYS
Contains Libraries and other objects, such as
Object name   Object Type    Object attribute
QADSPOBJ      *FILE          PF-DTA
QCMD          *PGM
QSAVSYS       *DTAARA
QGPL          *LIB
MYLIBRARY     *LIB
```

Breakout of MYLIBRARY

```
Library MYLIBRARY
Cannot contain another library, but can contain
other objects such as
Object name       Object Type     Object attribute
MYPROGRAM         *PGM            CLP
MYDATA            *FILE           PF-DTA
QCLSRC            *FILE           PF-SRC
QRPGSRC           *FILE           PF-SRC
MYSCREEN          *FILE           DSPF
MYREPORT          *FILE           PRTF
```

File Members

Just as AS/400 libraries can contain objects, certain AS/400 files can contain members. To contain members, an AS/400 *FILE type object must have an object attribute of PF-DTA (data file), LF (logical file), or PF-SRC (source file).

On the AS/400, a file itself does not contain data records; rather, it is the member within the file that contains the records. A file can have one member, or it can have many members. All the members within a file will have the same format (i.e., length and data fields), but each member will have its own name. A file can actually be created with no members at all, in which case the file is incapable of holding data records. Typically, files are created with no members only when the file will be used to define the characteristics of data elements and data structures. Figure 1.4 shows three PF-DTA files. The first (FILEA) has no members and therefore can hold no data. The second (FILEB) has one member capable of holding data. The third (FILEC) has four members that can hold data.

Figure 1.4 File Members

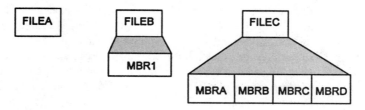

The PF-DTA Attribute

AS/400 *FILE type objects with the attribute PF-DTA are database files. PF-DTA is an abbreviation for "Data Physical File." If you needed to create a file on the AS/400 to hold customer names and addresses, you would create a PF-DTA file. After creating the file, you would create a member within that file to hold the actual data records. Normally, PF-DTA files have only one member, which holds all the data records for the file. Figure 1.5 illustrates the structure of a typical data physical file named CUSTMAST, with one member, also named CUSTMAST. The member CUSTMAST contains five data records.

Figure 1.5 Data Physical File

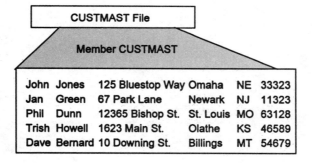

The PF-SRC Attribute

Files with the attribute PF-SRC are typically used to hold multiple members that contain data records consisting of source statements. PF-SRC is an abbreviation for "Source Physical File." If you need a place to store the source statements for an RPG program or for a CL program, you will create a source physical file, or simply add a member to an existing source physical file. Figure 1.6 illustrates a typical source physical file named QCLSRC. QCLSRC here contains three members. The first member (PGM1CL) contains four records, the second member (PGM2CL) contains five records, and the third member (PGM3CL) contains three records.

Figure 1.6 Source Physical File

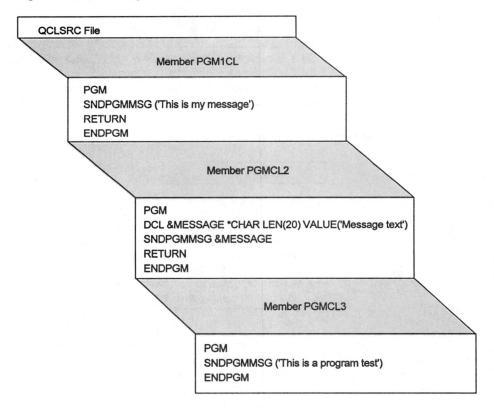

QCLSRC File

Member PGM1CL
```
PGM
SNDPGMMSG ('This is my message')
RETURN
ENDPGM
```

Member PGMCL2
```
PGM
DCL &MESSAGE *CHAR LEN(20) VALUE('Message text')
SNDPGMMSG &MESSAGE
RETURN
ENDPGM
```

Member PGMCL3
```
PGM
SNDPGMMSG ('This is a program test')
ENDPGM
```

PDM as a Navigation Tool

Figure 1.7 illustrates the three levels of the AS/400 object hierarchy: the library level, the object level, and the member level.

Figure 1.7 The Object Hierarchy

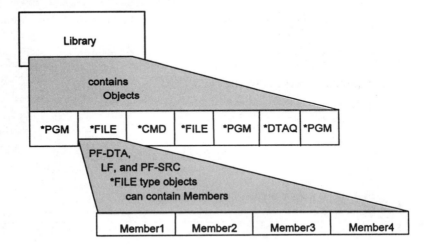

PDM is the programmer's environment used to navigate through the various levels of the AS/400 object-based architecture. PDM allows you to go easily from one level to the next. For instance, you can start at the library level, then drop down to the object level. From the object level, you can either go back up to the library level or drop down to the member level.

Accessing PDM

You can access PDM from your workstation in a number of ways. You can go through an AS/400 menu, such as the PROGRAM menu, and select the PDM menu option. You can also go to any command line and use the IBM-supplied commands that are a part of PDM. The IBM-supplied commands for accessing PDM are

STRPDM (Start PDM)

WRKLIBPDM (Work with Libraries Using PDM)

WRKOBJPDM (Work with Objects Using PDM)

WRKMBRPDM (Work with Members Using PDM)

The STRPDM Command

When you type the command STRPDM on a command line, you are presented with the PDM Main Menu shown in Figure 1.8. You can choose from any of the four options shown.

Figure 1.8 PDM Main Menu

```
                    AS/400 Programming Development Manager (PDM)
    Select one of the following:

        1. Work with libraries
        2. Work with objects
        3. Work with members

        9. Work with user-defined options







    Selection or command
    ===> _____

    F3=Exit        F4=Prompt              F9=Retrieve      F10=Command entry
    F12=Cancel     F18=Change defaults
```

Selecting option 1 (Work with libraries) in effect executes the same function as the PDM command WRKLIBPDM. Option 2 (Work with objects) has the same effect as using the WRKOBJPDM command. And option 3 (Work with members) has the same effect as typing in the command WRKMBRPDM. The menu options 1, 2, and 3 simply provide access to the PDM commands in a menu format. As you become comfortable with how PDM works, you will rarely use the STRPDM command. Instead, you will simply use the commands WRKLIBPDM, WRKOBJPDM, and WRKMBRPDM. We will discuss the PDM menu option 9 (Work with user-defined options) later.

Working with Libraries Using PDM

Chapter 2

When you select option 1 from the PDM Main Menu, you are presented with the display shown in Figure 2.1. Here, you must specify which libraries you wish to work with. In this example we have chosen to work with all the libraries that start with the letters ST, but we could have chosen from any of the options listed, such as *LIBL, *ALLUSR, *USRLIBL, and so on. If you are uncertain about what these library options mean, you can position the cursor on the Library field and press the HELP key. The HELP text will explain the different options.

Figure 2.1 The Library Selection Display

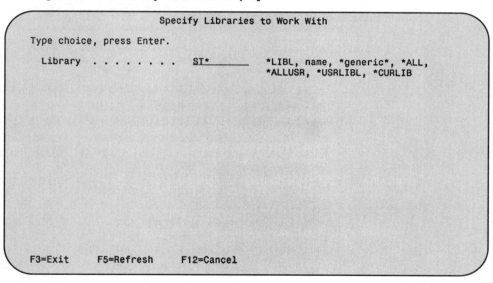

```
                        Specify Libraries to Work With

   Type choice, press Enter.

       Library . . . . . . . .   ST*          *LIBL, name, *generic*, *ALL,
                                              *ALLUSR, *USRLIBL, *CURLIB

















   F3=Exit      F5=Refresh      F12=Cancel
```

After you press the Enter key from the display shown in Figure 2.1, PDM shows you the PDM screen for working with libraries. The libraries listed on the display are determined by your selection on the previous screen. Figure 2.2 shows the Work with Libraries Using PDM screen that resulted when we selected all libraries that start with the letters ST. The same display is presented when you enter the command WRKLIBPDM LIB(ST*) on a command line.

Figure 2.2 The Work with Libraries Using PDM Display

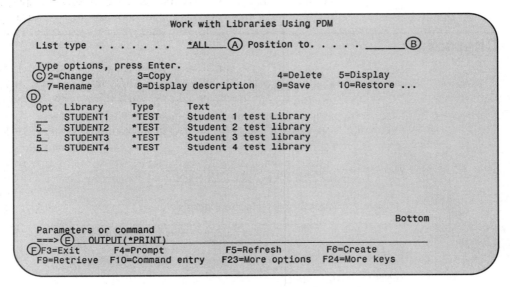

The Work with Libraries Using PDM display shows a list of all the libraries that you selected. At (A) on this display you are shown the list type; here, the list type is *ALL. The other types of lists are *LIBL and *ALLUSR. Here, *ALL means you are being presented with a list of *ALL libraries that match the list criteria (*ALL starting with ST).

At (B) is a field that allows you to position the list starting at a particular library. This is especially useful for cases in which the list contains more libraries than will fit on one page of the display. If you wanted to have the listing start at library STUDENT4, you would simply enter the characters STUDENT4 into the field. This field only appears on the display when the libraries are presented in alphabetical order (i.e., it would not be seen if you originally specified the library to work with as *LIBL. In that case, the libraries would be presented in the order they appear on the job's library list, not alphabetically.)

At (C) you are shown a list of valid options that you can enter next to the list entries to cause some operation to be performed to the corresponding library. For instance, if you wanted to display the contents of a library, you could place the number 5 in the option (Opt) field of an entry on the list, and press the Enter key.

You will notice that in the list of valid options defined at (C), there is an ellipsis (...) after the option for 10=Restore. This tells you that there are more options than will fit on the screen at one time. You can see the additional options by pressing the F23 (More options) key. The valid options from the Work with Libraries Using PDM display are shown in Figure 2.3. *Note*: All of these options cannot fit on the display at one time. So even if these options are not currently shown in area (C) of your display, they are still valid. Any exceptions to this are noted in Figure 2.3.

There is a CL command to correspond to most PDM options. The PDM environment provides a user-friendly front end to let you execute CL commands that act upon the system's objects. You do not need to know the AS/400's Control Language to use the PDM options; PDM is executing the CL commands for you that correspond to the option you select.

Figure 2.3 Valid Options with WRKLIBPDM

Option	Operation	CL Command Used by PDM
2	Allows you to change the type and text of a library.	CHGLIB
3	Copy the contents of a library to another library.	CPYLIB
4	Delete a library. Option is only valid when list type is *ALL or *ALLUSR.	DLTLIB
5	Display a list of the objects within a library.	DSPLIB
7	Rename a library.	RNMOBJ
8	Display a description of the library.	DSPOBJD
9	Save the contents of a library to backup media or to a save file.	SAVLIB
10	Restore the contents of a library from backup media or from a save file.	RSTLIB
12	Go to the Work with Objects Using PDM screen. This option allows you to navigate down one level in the object hierarchy. When option 12 is	WRKOBJPDM

Option	Operation	CL Command Used by PDM
	selected, you can work with the objects within the library that option 12 is selected for.	
13	Allows you to change the text associated with a library.	CHGOBJD

The following options are only valid when the list type is *LIBL or *USRLIBL. There are no corresponding CL commands executed when these options are selected.

Option	Operation
20	Move this library to a different place within the job's library list. The target of the move is identified by option 21 or option 22.
21	Place the library identified with option 20 ahead of this library on the list.
22	Place the library identified with option 20 behind this library on the list.
23	Remove this library from the library list.

At (D) in Figure 2.2 is the list of libraries you have selected to work with. From left to right within this list are columns Opt, Library, Type, and Text.

The Opt field is used for entering PDM options. Here, you can enter any of the options discussed in the preceding section, as well as certain user-defined options that we will discuss later.

The Library column identifies the library name for this list entry.

The Type field indicates whether the library is a *TEST or *PROD type library. This entry is used to specify what type of data resides in this library (e.g., test data). However, a library's type is only taken into account when you are using the AS/400 debug facility.

The Text field shows the descriptive text that is associated with this library.

It is possible to alter the placement and contents of the list entries using function keys. For instance, if you press F11 (Names only), only the Opt field and Library columns are displayed within the list. Since less information is displayed about each individual library, more libraries can fit on one page of the display. If you then press F11 again, the display will revert to its default display shown in Figure 2.2. The display will be slightly different when the list type is *LIBL or *USRLIBL.

At (E) in Figure 2.2 you can see that the display also includes a command line. You can use this command line as you would any other AS/400 command line. The F4 (Prompt) key is available, as is the F9 (Retrieve) key. However, another function of the command line is presented within PDM. When an option is entered next to an entry in the list, you can use the command entry line to enter command parameters and their values. Figure 2.2 shows an example of using option 5 (Display) on three list entries at the same time, and the command line contains the CL command parameter OUTPUT(*PRINT). The reason you can place a command parameter on the command line is that when PDM performs the operations you specify, it is actually executing the CL commands listed in Figure 2.3. The command executed when you select option 5 from PDM is the CL command DSPLIB. One of the command parameters for the DSPLIB command is OUTPUT. So by placing 5 in the Option field for the libraries STUDENT2, STUDENT3, and STUDENT4, and placing OUTPUT(*PRINT) on the command line, you are telling PDM to execute three CL commands:

```
DSPLIB LIB(STUDENT2) OUTPUT(*PRINT)
DSPLIB LIB(STUDENT3) OUTPUT(*PRINT)
DSPLIB LIB(STUDENT4) OUTPUT(*PRINT)
```

At (F), Figure 2.2 shows the function keys that are valid within PDM. In the lower right-hand corner of the figure, you can see that the F24 key is displayed. Since the PDM display does not have enough room to show you all the valid function keys, the F24 key is available to show you the additional function keys that are allowed. All the function keys listed are always valid, even if they are not currently displayed on the screen. Figure 2.4 lists the function keys that are available within the WRKLIBPDM display.

Figure 2.4 WRKLIBPDM Function Keys

Function Key	Function	Operation
F1	Help	Provides additional information. This key is cursor sensitive; place the cursor at the location in question before pressing F1.
F3	Exit	To exit from PDM.
F4	Prompt	Invokes the AS/400 prompt facility.
F5	Refresh	Refreshes the display screen.
F6	Create	Prompts you for the CRTLIB command. (Only valid when list type is *ALL or *ALLUSR)
	or	
	Add to list	Allows you to add a library to your job's library list (Only valid when the list type is *LIBL or *USRLIBL)

Function Key	Function	Operation
F9	Retrieve	Retrieves commands previously entered on the command line. Using F9 can help reduce the number of keystrokes when you are entering CL commands.
F10	Command entry	Calls the IBM-supplied program QCMD. This program presents an extended AS/400 command line, which allows you to use different functions than are available from the PDM command line.
F11	Display names	This is a toggle switch that allows you to flip back and forth between two different "views" of the list of libraries.
F12	Cancel	Return to the previous display; do not process any options on the current display.
F13	Repeat	If you type a PDM option next to a list entry and then press F13, that option will be copied into the Opt field for all subsequent list entries. List entries previous to the one you selected are not affected.
F16	User options	Allows you to change your user-defined options for PDM.
F17	Subset	Allows you to select a subset of the currently displayed list entries. The subsetted list will then be displayed, instead of the full list. If you are working with a large number of entries, this allows you to specify a smaller list of entries.
F18	Change defaults	This option allows you to tailor PDM for your special needs.
F21	Print the list	This option will print the entries of the current list.
F23	More options	Allows you to see other options that are valid within this PDM display.
F24	More keys	Allows you to see descriptions of other function keys that are available within PDM.

Working with Objects Using PDM

Chapter 3

When you select option 2 from the PDM Main Menu, you are presented with the display shown in Figure 3.1. Here you must specify which objects you wish to work with, and the library in which the objects reside. In this example, we have chosen to work with all the objects in library STUDENT1. If you were only interested in working with a certain subset of the objects within the STUDENT1 library, the Name, Type, and Attribute fields on the display let you specify your selection criteria. For example, if you only wanted to work with objects whose name starts with the letter L, you could type L* into the Name field; or, if you only wanted to work with objects whose object type is *FILE, you could enter *FILE into the Type field.

Figure 3.1 The Object Selection Display

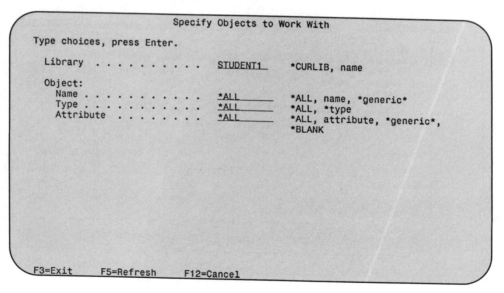

```
                        Specify Objects to Work With

 Type choices, press Enter.

    Library . . . . . . . . . .    STUDENT1     *CURLIB, name

    Object:
      Name . . . . . . . . . .    *ALL         *ALL, name, *generic*
      Type . . . . . . . . . .    *ALL         *ALL, *type
      Attribute  . . . . . . .    *ALL         *ALL, attribute, *generic*,
                                               *BLANK














 F3=Exit     F5=Refresh     F12=Cancel
```

Instead of using the PDM main menu to access the Work with Objects Using PDM display, you may find it easier, and faster, to simply use the command WRKOBJPDM. When you type the WRKOBJPDM command on a command line and press the F4 (Prompt) key, you will see the same display as in Figure 3.1. The only difference is that the library name that is displayed will contain the default value *PRV. This means that the default for the WRKOBJPDM command will always be to work with the library that you worked with previously using WRKOBJPDM. In effect, if you usually work with only one library (such as STUDENT1), you only need to type the command WRKOBJPDM on a command line and press the Enter key. No library name needs to be specified.

After pressing the Enter key from the display shown in Figure 3.1, or after typing the command WRKOBJPDM, you'll see the PDM screen for working with objects. The objects listed on the display are determined by your selection on the previous screen, or by selections performed using the WRKOBJPDM command. Figure 3.2 shows the Work with Objects Using PDM screen that resulted when we selected the library STUDENT1. The same display is presented when you enter the command WRKOBJPDM LIB(STUDENT1) on a command line, or when you place option 12 (Work with) next to the STUDENT1 library entry on the Work with Libraries Using PDM display.

Figure 3.2 The Work with Objects Using PDM Display

```
                        Work with Objects Using PDM
                                                          (B)
        Library . . . . (A) STUDENT1      Position to . . . . . . . . _____
                                          Position to type . . . . . _____


        Type options, press Enter.
           2=Change       3=Copy      4=Delete    5=Display    7=Rename
           8=Display description      9=Save      10=Restore   11=Move ...

        Opt   Object      Type    Attribute   Text
              PGM1        *PGM    RPG         Print a product Master List
        __    STUDENT1    *OUTQ               STUDENT1 outq for class
        __    OPLF001A    *FILE   LF          Order Header by Order Number
        __    OPLF001B    *FILE   LF          Order header for RPG class
        __    OPLF001CA   *FILE   LF          Invoiced order header records
        __    OPLF001D    *FILE   LF          Invoiced order header records
        __    OPLF003A    *FILE   LF          Product Mast by Prod number for inq
        __    OPLF003B    *FILE   LF          Product Mast by Prod Number for upd
                                                                        More...

        Parameters or command
        ===>
        F3=Exit          F4=Prompt          F5=Refresh        F6=Create
        F9=Retrieve      F10=Command entry  F23=More options  F24=More keys
```

The Work with Objects Using PDM display shows a list of all the objects that you selected. The objects are listed in alphabetical order within object type. (A) on this display shows you the library name that is currently being displayed. This field is input capable, so you can overtype the library name with a different library name to work with the objects within another library.

At (B) are two fields that allow you to position the list starting at a particular object, and/or position the list at a particular object type within the library. This is particularly useful for cases in which the list contains many objects of different types. If you wanted to have the listing start at a file with the name of OPPF004, you would simply enter the characters OPPF004 into the 'Position to' field, and place the object type *FILE in the 'Position to type' field.

The rest of the Work with Objects Using PDM screen is similar to the Work with Libraries Using PDM screen. All the function keys are the same, but the list of options from which you can choose is different.

Within the list of objects, PDM displays columns for the object name, the object type, the object attribute, and the object text. Because a library can contain several different types of objects, the type and attribute are displayed to provide you with additional information about each object.

Figure 3.3 details the options available on the Work with Objects Using PDM screen. You will notice in the figure that, in certain cases, PDM can use several different CL commands when processing an option number. The command that PDM uses is dependent upon the object type you selected. For example, when option 2 (Change Object) is placed next to an object, PDM examines the object type and the object attribute to determine the appropriate command to execute that will change that object. If the object type is *PGM, the CHGPGM (Change Program) command is used; if the object type is *FILE, and the object attribute is PF-DTA, the CHGPF (Change Physical File) command is used, and so on.

Some options are only valid for certain object types. For example, option 15 is the Copy file option. This option is only valid for certain *FILE type objects. The figure shows any such restrictions.

Figure 3.3 Valid Options for WRKOBJPDM Display

Option	Operation	CL Command Used by PDM
2	Change certain attributes of an object.	CHGPF CHGPGM etc.
3	Create a duplicate object.	CRTDUPOBJ
4	Delete an object.	DLTF DLTPGM etc.
5	Display information about an object or display the contents of an object.	DSPFD DSPPGM DSPDTAARA etc.
7	Rename an object.	RNMOBJ
8	Display an object's description.	DSPOBJD
9	Save an object to backup media or to a save file.	SAVOBJ SAVSAVFDTA
10	Restore an object from backup media or from a save file.	RSTOBJ
12	Work with an object. If the object type is *FILE and the object attribute is PF-DTA, LF, or PF-SRC, the Work with Members Using PDM screen will be displayed. This option lets you navigate down one level in the object hierarchy. When option 12 is selected, you can work with the members within the file that option 12 is selected for.	WRKPGM WRKF etc. WRKMBRPDM
13	Change the text associated with an object.	CHGOBJD
15	Copy selected records or members from one file to another file. (This option is only valid for *FILE type objects with an attribute of DKTF, LF, PF-DTA, and PF-SRC.)	CPYF CPYSRCF
16	Run an object. If the object type is *CMD, the command will be executed. If the object type is *PGM, the program is called. If the object type is *QRYDFN, the query is run.	CALL CHGDTA RUNQRY
18	Change the data in a file using the Data File Utility. This option is only valid when the object type is *FILE and the attributes PF-DTA or LF, or when the object type is *PGM and the attribute is DFU.	UPDDTA STRDFU OPTION(3)

Option	Operation	CL Command Used by PDM
25	Find a selected character string within members of a file. This option is only valid when the object type is *FILE and the attribute is PF-DTA or PF-SRC. (While this is a similar function as that provided by the FNDSTRPDM command, no CL command is executed to perform this function.)	(None)
26	Create a program object from *MODULE objects. This is used in the ILE environment.	CRTPGM
27	Create a service program from *MODULE objects. This is used in the ILE environment.	CRTSRVPGM
34	New for V3R1. Start the Interactive Surce Debugger for this program. This is valid only for the object types *PGM and *SRVPGM.(See Section 6 for an examination of the STRISDB command.)	STRISDB, or call ILE debugger
54	New for V3R1. Start the Compare Physical File Member command for this file. This is only valid for an object type *FILE, with attributes of PF-SRC or PF-DTA.(See Section 5 for an examination of the CMPPFM command.)	CMPPFM

All the function keys available from the Work with Libraries Using PDM screen can also be used from the Work with Objects Using PDM screen. However, there is one function key that works a little differently here than it does on the WRKLIBPDM display; that is the F6 (Create) key. When you are working with objects, and you select the Create function key, you are asked to supply the object type. Each type of object is created with a different command (CRTPF, CRTLF, CRTDTAARA, etc.), so PDM will ask you for the object type before presenting you with a prompt to actually create an object. An additional function key, F14, is also available on this display. When you press F14, the list will display the size of each object — i.e., the amount of storage (in bytes) — that it takes to hold the object on disk.

Working with Members Using PDM

Chapter 4

The lowest level in the object hierarchy that PDM provides access to is file members. You will recall that only objects with an object type of *FILE can contain members. Other objects such as programs and data areas do not. PDM provides three ways for you to access the Work with Members Using PDM display: 1) from the PDM Main Menu, you can select option 3 (Work with members); 2) from the Work with Objects Using PDM display, you can place option 12 next to a *FILE object; and 3) you can use the WRKMBRPDM command from any command line.

Figure 4.1 shows the display if you select option 3 from the PDM Main Menu. Here, you specify the name of the file and its library. You

Figure 4.1 The Member Selection Display

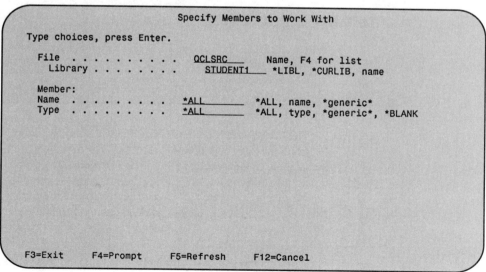

```
                         Specify Members to Work With
    Type choices, press Enter.

        File  . . . . . . . . . .     QCLSRC___    Name, F4 for list
          Library . . . . . . . .      STUDENT1__  *LIBL, *CURLIB, name

        Member:
        Name  . . . . . . . . . .     *ALL_____   *ALL, name, *generic*
        Type  . . . . . . . . . .     *ALL_____   *ALL, type, *generic*, *BLANK




    F3=Exit      F4=Prompt      F5=Refresh      F12=Cancel
```

can also specify which members of the file you wish to work with using the Name and Type fields.

When the Work with Objects Using PDM screen is displayed, you can drop down to the member level of the object hierarchy by typing option 12 next to a *FILE type object that has an attribute of PF-DTA, LF, or PF- SRC (Figure 4.2). You will notice in the figure that one of the *FILE type objects has an attribute of PRTF. Although this is a *FILE type object, you cannot use PDM to Work with members in this file; a PRTF file cannot contain members. In this figure, we select to work with the members of the source file QCLSRC in the STUDENT1 library. In effect, you are executing the WRKMBRPDM FILE(STUDENT1/QCLSRC) command.

Figure 4.2 Accessing Work with Members Using PDM with Option 12

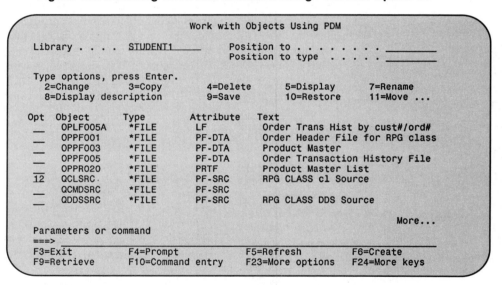

The Work with Members Using PDM display in Figure 4.3 shows a list of all the members that you selected. The members are listed in alphabetical order and, as in the other PDM displays, you can change position within the list by entering data into the 'Position to' field. At (A) on this display, you are shown the file name (and the library) whose members are currently displayed. You can overtype these fields with a different library name or file name to work with the members of another file.

At (B) is the listing of members. The type and text fields are both input capable, so you can modify them from this display. The rest of the

Figure 4.3 Work with Members Using PDM for a PF-SRC File

```
                         Work with Members Using PDM

   File . . . . . Ⓐ QCLSRC
     Library . . . .    STUDENT1        Position to . . . . . _____

   Type options, press Enter.
     2=Edit         3=Copy        4=Delete       5=Display    6=Print
     7=Rename       8=Display description        9=Save       13=Change text ...

   Opt  Member  Ⓑ  Type     Text
    __   BCL810      CLP__    DSPLSTSAV CPP_____
    __   CLRMSGCL    CLP__    Clear *PRV Message queue_____
    __   DSPMSGCL    CLP__    Display Messages..remove SFL rec not found___
    __   OPCLO10     CLP__    CUSTOMER REPORT RPG CLASS_____
    __   RPGINIT     CLP__    initial program_____
    __   SLTCO00     CLP__    Select Job CL Pgm_____
    __   SLTCO01     CLP__    Select Job CL pgm_____
    __   SLTCO02     CLP__    Select Job CL Pgm_____

                                                              More...
   Parameters or command
   ===>_____
   F3=Exit       F4=Prompt              F5=Refresh         F6=Create
   F9=Retrieve   F10=Command entry      F23=More options   F24=More keys
```

Work with Members Using PDM screen is similar to the other PDM screens. As with the other PDM screens, all of the function keys are the same, but some of the options are different.

PF-DTA and PF-SRC Differences

When you used the Work with Objects Using PDM screen, you saw that, depending upon the object type, certain options are valid and others invalid. When you use the Work with Members Using PDM display, there are also some differences based upon whether you are working with members of a PF-DTA file or members of a PF-SRC file. Some options are only valid when you are working with a PF-SRC file member; others are only valid when you are working with a PF-DTA file member. In fact, the Work with Members Using PDM screen is slightly different depending on the file type. Figure 4.4 shows how the screen looks when you select a PF-DTA file, compared with the PF-SRC file shown in Figure 4.3.

PF-DTA files normally have only one member. The date that the member was last changed is listed instead of the Type field that was listed in Figure 4.3. Also, there are a reduced number of options you can use when you are working with the members of a PF-DTA file compared to when you are working with a PF-SRC file.

Figure 4.4 Work with Members Using PDM for a PF-DTA File

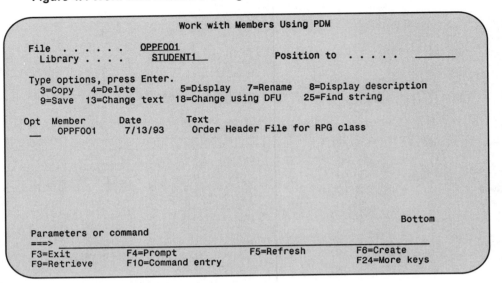

```
                        Work with Members Using PDM

   File . . . . . .   OPPF001
     Library . . . .    STUDENT1              Position to . . . . .   _____

   Type options, press Enter.
     3=Copy    4=Delete      5=Display   7=Rename   8=Display description
     9=Save  13=Change text  18=Change using DFU   25=Find string

   Opt  Member    Date       Text
    _    OPPF001   7/13/93    Order Header File for RPG class




                                                                 Bottom
   Parameters or command
   ===>_____
   F3=Exit           F4=Prompt              F5=Refresh       F6=Create
   F9=Retrieve       F10=Command entry                       F24=More keys
```

Figure 4.5 lists the valid options when you are working with members using PDM. You will notice that the options are different based upon the type of file that you select (i.e., PF-DTA or PF-SRC). In the figure, N/A is shown when a particular option is not available for that file type.

Figure 4.5 Valid Options for WRKMBRPDM Display

Option	Operation	CL Command Used by PDM	
		PF-SRC	**PF-DTA**
2	Start SEU to edit a member.	STRSEU OPTION(2)	(N/A)
3	Copy a member.	CPYSRCF	CPYF
4	Remove a member.	RMVM	RMVM
5	Display the data in a member.	STRSEU OPTION(5)	DSPPFM
6	Print a member.	STRSEU OPTION(6)	(N/A)
7	Rename a member.	RNMM	RNMM
8	Display member description.	(None)	(None)
9	Save the file of which this is a member. (*Note*: A member can only be saved when the file itself is saved).	SAVOBJ	SAVOBJ
13	Allows you to change the text associated with a member.	CHGPFM	CHGPFM

Option	Operation	CL Command Used by PDM	
		PF-SRC	**PF-DTA**
14	Compile an object using this source member as input to the compiler. This option is only valid for PF-SRC members; the compiler used is dependent upon the source type. For example, if the source type is RPG, the RPG compiler will be used. If the source type is CL, the CL compiler will be used, etc.	CRTRPGPGM CRTCLPGM CRTDSPF etc.	(N/A)
15	Create a *MODULE object from the source member.	CRTRPGMOD CRTCLMOD etc.	(N/A)
16	Allows you to run a procedure specified within a member. This option is only valid for PF-SRC members; the command used to run the procedure is dependent upon the source type field. For example, for a source type of REXX, the STRREXPRC will be used; for an OCL36 type source member, STRS36PRC will be used.	STRREXPRC STRS36PRC STRBASPRC QSYS38/EXCBASPRC	(N/A)
17	Change using SDA. This option allows you to start the AS/400 Screen Design Aid tool for a member. This option is only valid for PF-SRC members with a source type of DSPF (display file), DSPF36 (System/36 display file), or DSPF38 (System/38 display file).	STRSDA	(N/A)
18	Change using DFU. Allows you to use the Data File Utility to add/change or delete records from a file. This option is only valid for PF-DTA file members.	(N/A)	UPDDTA
19	Change using RLU. This option allows you to start the AS/400 Report Layout Utility tool for a member. This option is only valid for PF-SRC members	STRRLU	(N/A)

Option	Operation	CL Command Used by PDM	
		PF-SRC	PF-DTA
	with a source type of PRTF (printer file).		
25	Allows you to find a selected character string within the member (no CL command executed).	(None)	(None)
54	New for V3R1. Compare the selected member with another member. (See Section 5 for an examination of the CMPPFM command.)	CMPPFM	CMPPFM
55	New for V3R1. Merge the selected member with other members. This option is valid for all PF-SRC members. (See Section 5 for an examination of the MRGSRC command.)	MRGSRC	(N/A)

When you are using the WRKMBRPDM display, all the function keys that are available on the other 'Work with' PDM displays are available. However, the WRKMBRPDM display changes the function of one function key (F14) and adds a new one (F15). The F14 key that is available on the WRKMBRPDM display allows you switch between displaying the last changed date of the member and the member type. The new F15 function key allows you to sort the entries on the list in either name or last-changed-date sequence.

Customizing Your PDM Defaults

Chapter 5

When you start PDM, certain defaults affect the way PDM acts. Each PDM user can individually personalize those defaults. From any PDM screen, you can press the F18 (Change defaults) function key to display the screen shown in Figure 5.1. For additional options, you can Page Down to the display in Figure 5.1A.

Figure 5.1 Changing the PDM Defaults

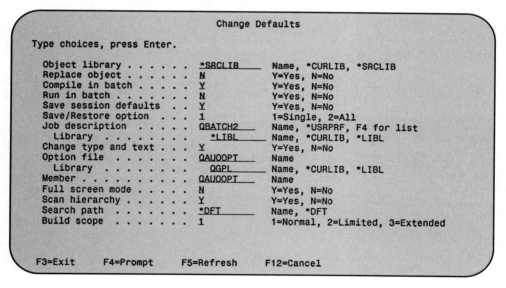

```
                              Change Defaults

   Type choices, press Enter.

         Object library . . . . . .    *SRCLIB      Name, *CURLIB, *SRCLIB
         Replace object . . . . . .    N            Y=Yes, N=No
         Compile in batch . . . . .    Y            Y=Yes, N=No
         Run in batch . . . . . . .    N            Y=Yes, N=No
         Save session defaults  . .    Y            Y=Yes, N=No
         Save/Restore option  . . .    1            1=Single, 2=All
         Job description  . . . . .    QBATCH2      Name, *USRPRF, F4 for list
            Library . . . . . . . .    *LIBL        Name, *CURLIB, *LIBL
         Change type and text . . .    Y            Y=Yes, N=No
         Option file  . . . . . . .    QAUOOPT      Name
            Library . . . . . . . .    QGPL         Name, *CURLIB, *LIBL
         Member . . . . . . . . . .    QAUOOPT      Name
         Full screen mode . . . . .    N            Y=Yes, N=No
         Scan hierarchy . . . . . .    Y            Y=Yes, N=No
         Search path  . . . . . . .    *DFT         Name, *DFT
         Build scope  . . . . . . .    1            1=Normal, 2=Limited, 3=Extended


   F3=Exit      F4=Prompt     F5=Refresh     F12=Cancel
```

Figure 5.1A Changing the PDM Defaults, Page 2

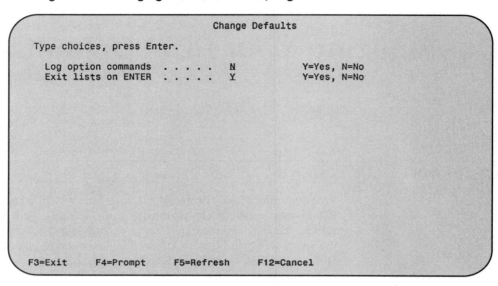

```
                              Change Defaults

  Type choices, press Enter.

     Log option commands  . . . . .   N              Y=Yes, N=No
     Exit lists on ENTER  . . . . .   Y              Y=Yes, N=No













  F3=Exit      F4=Prompt      F5=Refresh      F12=Cancel
```

On this display, you can change your individual PDM defaults. Figure 5.2 provides information about the meaning of each PDM default.

Figure 5.2 PDM Default Meanings

Prompt	Meaning
Object library	Specifies the library that you wish to compile your objects into when you use option 14 (Compile). Specifying *SRCLIB indicates that objects are always created in the same library in which the source member is stored.
Replace object	Specifies whether or not to replace an existing object when a compile (option 14) is successful.
Compile in batch	Specifies whether compile (option 14) operations are to execute in batch. Specifying 'N' indicates interactive compiles.

Prompt	Meaning
Run in batch	Specifies whether 'Run' and 'Call' processes will run interactively or in batch.
Save session defaults	Specifies whether or not your PDM session defaults are to be saved for your next PDM session. This also enables the *PRV capability.
Save/Restore option	Specifies, on multiple save/restore requests, whether the objects will be saved/restored in one operation (All), or in separate individual operations (Single).
Job description	Specifies which job description object to use when submitting batch jobs.
Change type and text	Specifies whether or not you can change the Type and Text fields on the Work with Members Using PDM display.
Option file	Specifies the name of a file to store PDM user-defined options (Chapter 6).
Member	Specifies the member in the option file to store user-defined options (Chapter 6).
Full-screen mode	Specifies whether or not PDM screens will be displayed in full screen mode, sometimes called "expert" mode, without showing valid options or function keys. More list entries appear on the display in this mode.
Scan hierarchy Search path Build scope	(Used only by IBM's Application Development Manager/400 Licensed Program Product)
Log option commands	Specifies whether or not commands executed through PDM options or user-defined options are written to the job log. If this option is set to Y, you are able to use the F9 key to retrieve the CL commands that PDM has executed for you.
Exit lists on Enter	Specifies whether or not pressing the Enter key on list displays will have the same effect as pressing F12 (Cancel).

Creating User-Defined Options

Chapter 6

In addition to the standard options that are shown at the top of each PDM 'Work with' display, you can create your own user-defined PDM options. These user-defined options let you customize your PDM environment so you can be more productive.

Here are a few of the things you might do with user-defined options:

- Perform additional operations on libraries, objects, and members that are not standard PDM options. For example, PDM does not provide a command to allow you to display the security authorizations in effect for an object. You could create a user-defined option (e.g., DA) that would execute the DSPOBJAUT (Display Object Authority) command. When this special option is placed next to a list entry on the PDM display, the DSPOBJAUT command would be executed for the associated object within the list.

- Allow a shorthand method to call a commonly used program. For example, if several times a day you call a CL program named MYPROGRAM, you could create a user-defined option (e.g., MY) that would call the program any time you enter the option next to any list entry on the PDM display.

- Create a shorthand method to enter a commonly used CL command. For example, the command to see a listing of your spooled output files is WRKSPLF (Work with Spooled Files). Whenever you wish to see a listing of your spooled output files from a PDM 'Work with' display, you need to move your cursor to the command line and enter the command WRKSPLF. Using a PDM user-defined option, you could simply type the letters SP into the option field next to any list entry, and the WRKSPLF command would be executed.

Figure 6.1 shows an example of entering a user-defined option.

Figure 6.1 Using User-Defined Options

```
                      Work with Members Using PDM

   File . . . . . .    QCLSRC
     Library . . . .    STUDENT1         Position to . . . . . _____

   Type options, press Enter.
     2=Edit      3=Copy       4=Delete      5=Display   6=Print
     7=Rename    8=Display description      9=Save      13=Change text ...

 Opt  Member      Type        Text
  __   BCL810      CLP         DSPLSTSAV CPP_____
       CLRMSGCL    CLP         Clear *PRV Message queue_____
  SP   DSPMSGCL    CLP         Display Messages..remove SFL rec not found__
  __   OPCLO10     CLP         CUSTOMER REPORT RPG CLASS_____
  __   RPGINIT     CLP         initial program_____
  __   SLTCO00     CLP         Select Job CL Pgm_____
  __   SLTCO01     CLP         Select Job CL pgm_____
  __   SLTCO02     CLP         Select Job CL Pgm_____

                                                              More...
   Parameters or command
   ===> _____
   F3=Exit       F4=Prompt            F5=Refresh         F6=Create
   F9=Retrieve   F10=Command entry    F23=More options   F24=More keys
```

Any time you are working from a PDM 'Work with' display, you can view and change your user-defined options by pressing F16 (User options). You can also view and change your user-defined options from the PDM Main Menu by selecting option 9, as shown in Figure 6.2.

Figure 6.2 The PDM Main Menu

```
                    AS/400 Programming Development Manager(PDM)
Select one of the following:

    1. Work with libraries
    2. Work with objects
    3. Work with members

    9. Work with user-defined options




Selection or command
===> _____

F3=Exit       F4=Prompt       F9=Retrieve      F10=Command entry
F12=Cancel    F18=Change defaults
```

When you select option 9 from the PDM Main Menu, the system presents the display shown in Figure 6.3. This screen allows you to specify the name of the file that is used to contain your user-defined options.

The AS/400 keeps track of your user-defined options by placing them into a data file. Each PDM user on your system can have his/her own PDM option file. When PDM comes shipped to you from IBM, a sample user-defined option file already exists. The name of this file is QAUOOPT in library QGPL. This option file contains several sample user-defined options for PDM. You can use the IBM-supplied file as a basis for your own PDM option file by simply creating a copy of the file in your library.

When the screen in Figure 6.3 is shown, you can supply the name of your personal PDM option file, or use the IBM-supplied option file shown here. You should note that if you pressed F16 (User options) from a PDM 'Work with' display, the screen shown in Figure 6.4 would not be shown. The screen is only shown when you select option 9 from the PDM Main Menu.

Figure 6.3 Selecting the Option File To Work With

```
                     Specify Option File to Work With

  Type choices, press Enter.

       File  . . . . . . . . .     QAUOOPT      Name, F4 for list
         Library . . . . . . .       QGPL       *LIBL, *CURLIB, name
       Member  . . . . . . . .     QAUOOPT      Name

















  F3=Exit      F5=Refresh      F12=Cancel
```

When you press the Enter key from the screen in Figure 6.3, the system shows the Work with User-Defined Options screen shown in Figure 6.4. In this example, we are working with the IBM-supplied file QAUOOPT in library QGPL.

Figure 6.4 Work with User-Defined Options

```
                    Work with User-Defined Options
 File . . . . . . . :    QAUOOPT         Member . . . . . . :    QAUOOPT
   Library . . . . :      QGPL

 Type options, press Enter.
   2=Change          3=Copy          4=Delete        5=Display

 Opt  Option   Command
  __     C       CALL &L/&N
  __     DJ      DSPJOB
  __     DM      DSPMSG
  __     EA      EDTOBJAUT OBJ(&L/&N) OBJTYPE(&T)
  __     GO      GO &L/&N
  __     JL      DSPJOBLOG
  __     SO      SIGNOFF
  __     WS      WRKSBMJOB

                                                              More...

 Command
 ===>
 F3=Exit           F4=Prompt         F5=Refresh        F6=Create
 F9=Retrieve       F10=Command entry F24=More keys
```

This display shows the PDM user-defined options that are stored within the file named at the top of the display. The list displays several options, such as DJ, DM, JL, SO, and so on. You can use these options whenever you are working from any of the PDM list screens. Next to the option is the command that will execute when you enter this option next to an entry on a 'Work with' list.

Using this display, you can change, copy, or delete the user-defined options listed. You can also create new user-defined options by pressing F6 (Create).

You will notice that some of the command strings contain strange-looking symbols. For example, the option named C will execute the command CALL &L/&N. You probably understand the CALL command, but the &L/&N may be a little confusing. The &L and &N are called *substitution values*. Whenever they appear within a user-defined option, PDM replaces the symbol (i.e., &L) with a value from the list display or with a value from the PDM Options display. For example, if you are working from the Work with Members Using PDM display, and you place the user-defined option C next to a source member named PROGRAM1, the following will occur:

- PDM finds the option C in the user-defined option file.

- PDM substitutes the value from the list PROGRAM1 for the substitution value &N. PDM substitutes the name of the library in which the member resides (for example, STUDENT1) for the substitution value &L.

- PDM executes the command CALL STUDENT1/PROGRAM1.

The use of substitution values differs depending upon which PDM 'Work with' display you are using. For example, the user-defined option C would not work correctly from the Work with Libraries Using PDM display. If it was entered on that display, PDM would try to execute the following command, which would end in an error:

```
CALL QSYS/LIBRARY1
```

Figure 6.5 lists all the PDM substitution values, their meanings, and how the substitution will occur.

Figure 6.5 PDM Substitution Values

Parm	Meaning	Description
&A	Object attribute	From WRKOBJPDM, &A is replaced by the object's attribute. From WRKLIBPDM and WRKMBRPDM, &A is replaced by *NULL.
&B	List type	From WRKLIBPDM using a library list (*LIBL, or *USRLIBL), &B is replaced by X. From WRKLIBPDM using libraries (*ALL, or *ALLUSR), &B is replaced by L. From WRKOBJPDM, &B is replaced by O. From WRKMBRPDM, &B is replaced by M.
&C	Option	&C is always replaced by the user-defined option code.
&D	Change date	From WRKMBRPDM, &D is replaced by the date the member was last changed. From WRKOBJPDM and WRKLIBPDM, &D is replaced by *NULL. You must use this variable in apostrophes (that is, '&D') because the date will contain separator characters, which may be interpreted as arithmetic operators. The format of the date returned is determined by the QDATFMT system value.
&E	Run in batch	&E is replaced by *YES if Y is specified in the "Run in batch" prompt on the Change PDM Defaults display; otherwise, it is replaced by *NO.
&F	File name	From WRKMBRPDM, &F is replaced by the name of the file that contains the member; otherwise, &F is replaced by *NULL.
&G	JOBD library	&G is replaced by the job description library value from the Change PDM Defaults display.
&H	Job description	&H is replaced by the job description value from the Change PDM Defaults display.

Parm	Meaning	Description
&J	Qualified JOBD	&J is replaced by the qualified job description value from the Change PDM Defaults display. The format is LIB/JOBD.
&L	Library name	From WRKLIBPDM, &L is replaced by QSYS; otherwise, &L is replaced by the name of the library that contains the objects or members.
&N	List item	&N is always replaced by the name of the item in the list beside which the option was entered.
&O	Object library	&O is always replaced by the object library specified on the Change PDM Defaults display.
&P	Compile in batch	&P is replaced by *YES if Y is specified in the "Compile in batch" prompt on the Change PDM Defaults display; otherwise, it is replaced by *NO.
&R	Replace object	&R is replaced by *YES if Y is specified in the "Replace object" prompt on the Change PDM Defaults display; otherwise, it is replaced by *NO.
&S	Item type	From WRKLIBPDM, &S is replaced by LIB (without '*'). From WRKOBJPDM, &S is replaced by the object type (without an asterisk). From WRKMBRPDM, &S is replaced by the member type (e.g., CLP or RPG).
&T	Item type (with *)	From WRKLIBPDM, &T is replaced by *LIB. From WRKOBJPDM or WRKMBRPDM, &T is replaced by the object or member type, respectively.
&U	User option file	&U is replaced by the name of the user-defined option file from the Change PDM Defaults display.
&V	User option library	&V is replaced by the name of the user-defined option file library from the Change PDM Defaults display.
&W	User option member	&W is replaced by the name of the user-defined option file member from the Change PDM Defaults display.
&X	Item text	&X is replaced by the text (enclosed in apostrophes) of the item beside which the option was typed.

If you want to create a new user-defined option, you simply press F6 (Create) from the Work with User Options screen. In the following example (Figure 6.6), we'll create a new user option DA. The DA option will display the object authority for an object on the PDM list display.

Figure 6.6 Creating a User-Defined Option

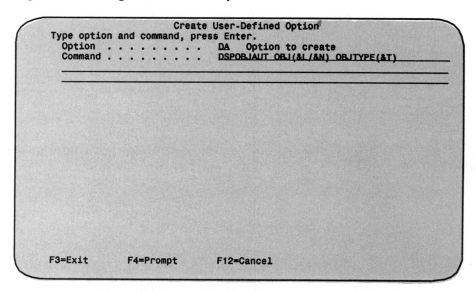

```
                        Create User-Defined Option
    Type option and command, press Enter.
        Option . . . . . . . . .    DA   Option to create
        Command . . . . . . . . .   DSPOBJAUT OBJ(&L/&N) OBJTYPE(&T)




    F3=Exit         F4=Prompt       F12=Cancel
```

We specified DA as the Option, and DSPOBJAUT OBJ(&L/&N) OBJTYPE(&T) as the command to execute. When the option is used from the Work with Objects using PDM display, &L will be replaced with the library name, &N will be replaced by the name of the list entry, and &T will be replaced with the object type.

When you press the Enter key, the new option will be added to the option file specified at the top of the display. Everyone who uses that option file will now have a new user-defined option. Here are some useful examples to get you started:

Option	Command
AJ	WRKACTJOB
CC	CHGCURLIB CURLIB(&L)
DM	DSPMSG
EL	EDTLIBL
PC	CPYTOPCD FROMFILE(&L/&F) TOFLR('&L/&F') FROMMBR(&N)
SJ	WRKSBMJOB
SP	WRKSPLF

The FNDSTRPDM Command

Chapter 7

We have already discussed how PDM can be used to search for text in file members. You can use PDM option 25 (Find string) from the WRKMBRPDM and WRKOBJPDM displays. Entering this option causes the system to search for any occurrence of the character string specified and perform an action, such as displaying the member containing the string, and/or printing a list of all members in which the string was found.

Because option 25 (Find string) is only available within the PDM environment, and because it is a very useful feature, IBM created a special CL command that you can use to perform searches when you are outside the PDM list environment. The command is named FNDSTRPDM (Find String using PDM), and it is shipped as part of the Application Development Toolset/400. You can use the FNDSTRPDM command interactively, or in batch, and you can include it in your programs. A wide variety of command options are available, making this command very flexible and quite powerful.

FNDSTRPDM Command Parameters
STRING('string-to-find')

The required STRING parameter is used to specify the character string you want to locate. You can specify up to 40 characters enclosed in apostrophes.

Example: STRING('COMPANY')

FILE(library-name/file-name)

The required FILE parameter identifies the qualified name of the file whose members are to be searched. The file must be a data physical file or a source physical file. You can use the special values *LIBL and *CURLIB to specify the name of the library in which the file exists.

Example: FILE(*LIBL/QCLSRC)

MBR(generic-member-name)

The required MBR parameter identifies the members within the file that are to be searched. You can specify the special value *ALL to indicate that all the members within the file will be searched. You can alternately specify a generic member name such as PAY*, *APY*, A*P, and so forth. You also can enter the individual names of more than 100 members if you choose to do so.

OPTION(action-option prompt-option)

The required OPTION parameter includes two elements: first, the action to be taken when the string is found; second, an option to control how prompting is handled for the action. You can specify a single value of *NONE to indicate no action is to be taken; you would use this value when a printed list of members or records is all that you want.

action-option

The action options available depend upon the type of file being searched. When a source physical file is being searched, the valid action options are as follows:

Source Physical File Action Options

Value	Action Taken
*EDIT	Invokes an SEU edit session for the member.
*COPY	Copies the member to another member.
*DLT	Removes the member from the file.
*DSP	Invokes an SEU browse session for the member.
*PRT	Prints the member.
*RNM	Renames the member.
*DSPD	Displays a description of the member.
*SAVE	Saves the member to off-line media or to a save file.
*CHGT	Changes some attributes of the member.
*CMPL	Compiles the member.
*SDA	Invokes a Screen Design Aid (SDA) session for the member.
*RLU	Invokes a Report Layout Utility (RLU) session for the member.

When a data physical file is being searched, the valid action options are as follows:

Data Physical File Action Options

Value	Action Taken
*COPY	Copies the member to another member.
*DLT	Removes the member from the file.
*DSP	Displays the member's data, using the DSPPFM (Display Physical File Member) command.
*RNM	Renames the member.
*DSPD	Displays a description of the member.
*SAVE	Saves the member to off-line media or to a save file.
*CHGT	Changes some attributes of the member.
*DFU	Invokes a Data File Utility (DFU) session for the member.

In addition to the predefined special values listed, you can also specify a user-defined option (for both source and data physical files). This capability makes the command very powerful because you can perform any valid OS/400 function on a member when the search string is found. When a user-defined option is specified, the option must exist in your PDM option file.

prompt-option

The prompt option specifies whether or not the user is prompted each time the command in the action-option is performed. The valid values are *PROMPT and *NOPROMPT.

Examples: OPTION(*RNM *PROMPT)

OPTION(*EDIT *NOPROMPT)

COL(from-column to-column)

This optional parameter specifies what columns of the records within the member should be searched for the string. This parameter includes two elements: the from-column, and the to-column. The default value of this parameter is COL(1 *RCDLEN), which specifies that the search will examine all column positions within the record. You can alternately use integers to specify a from and to column.

Examples: COL(40 56)

COL(40 *RCDLEN)

CASE(case-option)

This optional parameter is used to specify whether or not the search operation is case sensitive. For example, if STRING('COMPANY') is specified and CASE(*MATCH) is specified, only occurrences of the exact uppercase string 'COMPANY' will result in a match. If CASE(*IGNORE) is specified, the strings 'company' and 'Company' would also be considered matches for the search operation. The default value of this parameter is CASE(*IGNORE).

PRTMBRLIST(member-listing-option)

This optional parameter specifies whether or not a member listing is generated when the search is performed. If PRTMBRLST(*YES) is specified, a listing will be generated containing one line per member that contained the search string. If PRTMBRLST(*NO) is specified, no listing is generated. The default value for this parameter is PRTMBRLST(*NO).

PRTRCDS(number-to-print print-format mark-option overflow-option)

This optional parameter specifies whether, and how, records containing the search string are printed. The parameter consists of four elements: number-to-print, print-format, mark-option, and overflow-option. You can also use the single value *NONE to indicate that individual records are not to be printed. PRTRCDS(*NONE) is the parameter default.

number-to-print

This element specifies how many records are to be printed from a source member when the search string is found. Only records containing the search string will be printed. You can specify either the value *ALL, meaning that all records containing the search string are printed, or a number from 1 through 99999.

print-format

This element specifies the printing format of the records containing the search string. The allowable values for this element are *CHAR, *HEX, and *ALTHEX. *CHAR specifies character format. *HEX indicates a hexadecimal format in which character values are printed above the hexadecimal values for the record contents. *ALTHEX indicates a hexadecimal format in which the character representation is listed to the right of the hexadecimal values.

mark-option

This element determines whether or not to print asterisks (*) above the search string in the printed report. This makes it easy for you to locate the search string. You can specify this element as either *MARK or *NOMARK.

overflow-option

This element specifies whether records printed should be folded or truncated when they are longer than the width of a printed page. The value *FOLD will cause the entire long record to be printed on multiple lines. The value *TRUNCATE will cause a long record to be contained on one line only; certain record positions will not be printed for long records.

Example: `PRTRCDS(*ALL *HEX *MARK *FOLD)`

This example will print all records in HEX (over/under) format. The string will be marked by asterisks, and the entire record will be printed, regardless of its length.

PARM(appended parameters)

This optional parameter lets you specify additional parameters that will be used in conjunction with the value specified on the OPTION parameter. For example, if you are searching CL source members for a string, and the members are to be recompiled when they are found, you can specify additional parameters for the CRTCLPGM command.

```
Example:  FNDSTRPDM STRING('PRODLIB')        +
                    FILE(TESTLIB/QCLSRC)     +
                    MBR(*ALL)                +
                    OPTION(*CMPL *NOPROMPT)  +
                    PRTMBRLST(*YES)          +
                    PARM('AUT(*EXCLUDE)')
```

In this example, the programs are to be compiled with AUT(*EXCLUDE).

Section 2

Source Entry Utility (SEU)

Introduction to SEU

Chapter 8

Source Entry Utility (SEU) is a full-screen editor that is used to manipulate the text stored within an AS/400 source file member. The text usually consists of source language statements that you'll use later to compile a program or other object, but SEU can also be used to edit any textual material. While SEU is by no means a full-function word processor, you can use SEU for maintaining such things as program documentation or a personal phone book.

SEU is not a part of the OS/400 base operating system, but instead is a part of an IBM licensed program product called Application Development Toolset/400 (ADTS/400). Almost every AS/400 used for program development and maintenance will contain the ADTS/400 product.

Using SEU, you can enter or modify the source statements that you will use to create a CL program, an RPG/400 program, a COBOL/400 program, an externally described file, and many other AS/400 objects.

SEU Syntax Checking

SEU has the capability to check the syntax of source language statements as they are entered to ensure that they meet the requirements of the particular language being used. If a source statement is found to have invalid syntax, SEU notifies you by highlighting the statement and displaying an instructional error message. SEU provides this syntax-checking capability for many AS/400 languages, as well as for some System/36- and System/38-compatible languages that can be used on the AS/400. The following chart lists all of the syntax checkers included as part of the OS/400 operating system, with their associated source type.

AS/400 Syntax Checking Capabilities Within SEU

Description	Source Type
Auto report	RPT
BASIC	BAS
BASIC program	BASP
Bind	BND
C	C
CL	CL
CL program	CLP
COBOL	CBL
COBOL with CICS/400	CICSCBL
COBOL with SQL	SQLCBL
COBOL with SQL and CICS/400	CICSSQLCBL
Command definition	CMD
DFU	DFU
Display file	DSPF
FORTRAN/400	FTN
FORTRAN/400 with SQL	SQLFTN
ICF file	ICFF
ILE C	CLE
ILE C with CICS	CICSC
ILE CL	CLLE
ILE COBOL with CICS or SQL	CICSCBLLE
ILE COBOL with SQL	SQLCBLLE
ILE COBOL	CBLLE
Logical file	LF
Menu	MNU
Menu DDS source	MNUDDS
Physical file	PF
PL/I	PLI
PL/I with SQL	SQLPLI
Printer file	PRTF
Query	QRY
RPG III	RPG
RPG III with SQL	SQLRPG
RPG IV	RPGLE
RPG IV with SQL	SQLRPGLE

System/36 Compatible Source

Description	Source Type
Auto report	RPT36
COBOL	CBL36
RPG	RPG36

System/38 Compatible Source

Description	Source Type
Auto report	RPT38
BASIC	BAS38
BASIC program	BASP38
Bisynch communications	BSCF38
Command definition	CMD38

Description	Source Type
Communication file	CMNF38
CL	CL38
CL program	CLP38
COBOL	CBL38
DFU/38	DFU38
Display file	DSPF38
Logical file	LF38
Mixed file	MXDF38
Physical file	PF38
PL/I	PLI38
Printer file	PRTF38
Query/38	QRY38
RPG	RPG38

Accessing SEU

There are four major ways to access the SEU facility:

- From the PDM Work with Members display, by selecting option 2 or 5
- By entering the STRSEU command on any command line
- From the Programmer's Menu (QPGMMENU)
- From within the AS/400 Screen Design Aid tool

Figure 8.1 shows how you would access SEU using PDM option 2 from the Work with Members Using PDM display.

Figure 8.1 Accessing SEU from PDM

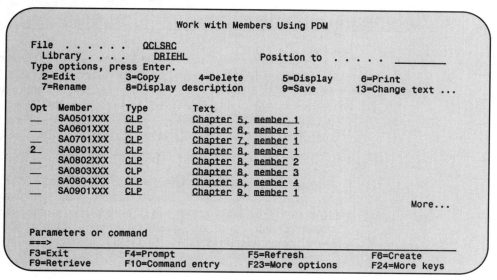

In this example, the source type of the member that will be edited is CLP. The source type of the member being edited determines which syntax checker and prompting facilities SEU will use for this editing session. Because the source type is CLP, SEU will perform all prompts and syntax checking according to rules of AS/400 Control Language programs. Figure 8.2 shows the SEU edit display that results when you enter a 2 next to the member SA0801XXX on the WRKMBRPDM display.

Figure 8.2 The SEU Edit Display

```
 Columns . . . :    1  71              Edit                   DRIEHL/QCLSRC
 SEU==>(D)                                                     SA0801XXX
 FMT **  ...+... 1 ...+... 2 ...+... 3 ...+... 4 ...+... 5 ...+... 6 ...+... 7
 *************** Beginning of data *******************************************
 0001.00 /*  Program name..... SA0801XXX                                   */
 0002.00 /*  Author.......... (Your Name)                                  */
 0003.00 /*  Date completed... (enter the current date)                    */
 0004.00 /*  Program purpose.. CHGVAR and DMPCLPGM exercise                */
 0005.00 /*  Chapter 8, member 1                                           */
 0006.00
 0007.00            PGM
 0008.00
 0009.00 (B)        DCL     &char10 *CHAR 10
 0010.00            DCL     &char24 *CHAR 24
 0011.00            DCL     &dec50  *DEC (5 0)
 0012.00            DCL     &dec72  *DEC (7 2)
 0013.00            DCL     &lgl1   *LGL
 0014.00
 0015.00
 0016.00            CHGVAR    &char10 'My Library'


 F3=Exit   F4=Prompt    F5=Refresh    F9=Retrieve   F10=Cursor
 F16=Repeat find        F17=Repeat change           F24=More keys
```

(A) (B) (C) (D)

Four main sections comprise the SEU edit display. The numbers in the column at (A) are sequence numbers of the records in the source member. You can enter special SEU line commands within the sequence number area by typing over the sequence number. At (B) is the actual typing area for the source statements. It is here that you enter and edit the statements that will constitute the source member. At (C) are the function keys that are valid when you are using SEU; when you press F24 (More keys), the display will show several other valid function keys. At (D) is the SEU command line; unlike the standard AS/400 command line shown on other screens, the SEU command line provides a means to enter special SEU commands, not AS/400 CL commands. These SEU command-line commands are different from those that can be entered in the sequence number area.

The SEU Line Commands

Chapter 9

The SEU sequence number area of the SEU Edit Display shows the SEU line number for each source statement in the member being edited. The sequence number is displayed in the format of 0001.00. The sequence number displayed is input capable, which means you can type data into the area containing the sequence number.

Although SEU does not allow you to change the sequence number of an existing line, you can type special *SEU line commands* over the sequence number that is displayed. The SEU line commands let you manipulate the lines in the source member; they also let you determine what part of the source member is displayed in the typing area. You use the SEU line commands to do things such as moving a source line from one place to another, deleting a source line, and inserting source lines between two existing lines. You can also use the line commands to position the display, so that a specific source line will appear as the first line in the typing area.

Before getting into a full discussion of all the valid SEU line commands, we'll look at a simple example of moving a source line within the member (Figure 9.1).

To move the source line that appears at line 0013.00 in Figure 9.1 to the position immediately following line 0009.00, we place the SEU line command **M** (Move) on line 0013.00, and place the SEU line command **A** (After) on line 0009.00, then press the Enter key. The combination of these two SEU line commands tells SEU to Move line 0013.00 After line 0009.00. The result will be that the statement on line 0013.00 will be moved to the position following line 0009.00, it will be assigned a new sequence number of 0009.01. The sequence number 0013.00 will no longer appear on the display, as shown in Figure 9.2. You also can move lines to appear before a line, by specifying **B** instead of **A**.

Figure 9.1 Using SEU Line Commands

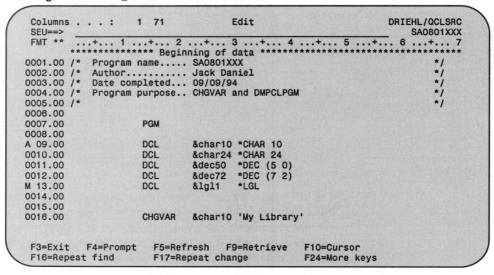

```
  Columns . . . :   1  71              Edit                    DRIEHL/QCLSRC
  SEU==> _____ SA0801XXX
  FMT **  ...+... 1 ...+... 2 ...+... 3 ...+... 4 ...+... 5 ...+... 6 ...+... 7
         *************** Beginning of data ********************************
  0001.00 /*  Program name..... SA0801XXX                                  */
  0002.00 /*  Author.......... Jack Daniel                                 */
  0003.00 /*  Date completed... 09/09/94                                   */
  0004.00 /*  Program purpose.. CHGVAR and DMPCLPGM                        */
  0005.00 /*                                                               */
  0006.00
  0007.00             PGM
  0008.00
  A 09.00             DCL       &char10 *CHAR 10
  0010.00             DCL       &char24 *CHAR 24
  0011.00             DCL       &dec50  *DEC (5 0)
  0012.00             DCL       &dec72  *DEC (7 2)
  M 13.00             DCL       &lgl1   *LGL
  0014.00
  0015.00
  0016.00             CHGVAR    &char10 'My Library'


  F3=Exit    F4=Prompt    F5=Refresh   F9=Retrieve   F10=Cursor
  F16=Repeat find         F17=Repeat change          F24=More keys
```

Figure 9.2 Result of the Move-After Operation

```
  Columns . . . :   1  71              Edit                    DRIEHL/QCLSRC
  SEU==> _____ SA0801XXX
  FMT **  ...+... 1 ...+... 2 ...+... 3 ...+... 4 ...+... 5 ...+... 6 ...+... 7
         *************** Beginning of data ********************************
  0001.00 /*  Program name..... SA0801XXX                                  */
  0002.00 /*  Author.......... Jack Daniel                                 */
  0003.00 /*  Date completed... 09/09/94                                   */
  0004.00 /*  Program purpose.. CHGVAR and DMPCLPGM                        */
  0005.00 /*                                                               */
  0006.00
  0007.00             PGM
  0008.00
  0009.00             DCL       &char10 *CHAR 10
  0009.01             DCL       &lgl1   *LGL
  0010.00             DCL       &char24 *CHAR 24
  0011.00             DCL       &dec50  *DEC (5 0)
  0012.00             DCL       &dec72  *DEC (7 2)
  0014.00
  0015.00
  0016.00             CHGVAR    &char10 'My Library'


  F3=Exit    F4=Prompt    F5=Refresh   F9=Retrieve   F10=Cursor
  F16=Repeat find         F17=Repeat change          F24=More keys
```

In the previous example, we moved one source line to another
position. You can also move several lines together in one operation; this
is called a *block operation*. Consider the example shown in Figure 9.3.

Here we want to move source lines 0009.00 through 0011.00 to the lines after line 0014.00.

We place the block move command **MM** on the first and last line to be moved, and place the target **A** (After) on line 0014.00. When you press the Enter key, SEU will execute the block move.

Figure 9.3 Using Block Operations

```
Columns . . . :    1  71                Edit                    DRIEHL/QCLSRC
SEU==>                                                                SA0801XXX
FMT **   ...+... 1 ...+... 2 ...+... 3 ...+... 4 ...+... 5 ...+... 6 ...+... 7
          ************** Beginning of data ******************************
0001.00 /*  Program name..... SA0801XXX                                      */
0002.00 /*  Author........... (Your Name)                                    */
0003.00 /*  Date completed... (enter the current date)                       */
0004.00 /*  Program purpose.. CHGVAR and DMPCLPGM exercise                   */
0005.00 /*  Chapter 8, member 1                                              */
0006.00
0007.00            PGM
0008.00
MM09.00            DCL      &char10 *CHAR 10
0010.00            DCL      &char24 *CHAR 24
MM11.00            DCL      &dec50  *DEC (5 0)
0012.00            DCL      &dec72  *DEC (7 2)
0013.00            DCL      &lgl1   *LGL
A014.00
0015.00
0016.00            CHGVAR   &char10 'My Library'


 F3=Exit   F4=Prompt    F5=Refresh   F9=Retrieve    F10=Cursor
 F16=Repeat find        F17=Repeat change           F24=More keys
```

As an alternative to the block operation using MM, you could use the SEU line command M*n*, where *n* is the number of lines that you want to move. In this example, we could have specified M3 to move the three lines 0009.00, 0010.00, and 0011.00.

Figure 9.4 displays a summary of all SEU line commands. The remainder of the chapter will explain how and when to use these line commands.

Figure 9.4 The SEU Line Commands

Description of Function   Line Commands

In this figure, 'n' designates a number, 'f' designates a format

Commands affecting the display

Description of Function	Line Commands
Position screen to line number	n, .n, n.n
Position screen relative to top line	+, +n, -, -n
Exclude line(s) from the display	X, XX, Xn
Show excluded line(s)	SF, SFn, SL, SLn
Shift display to a column number	W, Wn

Description of Function	Line Commands

Commands to manipulate lines

After and Before target commands	A, An, B, Bn
Copy line(s)	C, CC, Cn
Copy lines(s) with Repeat	CR, CRn, CCR
Delete line(s)	D, DD, Dn
Duplicate(Repeat) line(s)	RP, RPn, RPP, RPPn
Insert line(s)	I, In
Insert line(s) with Format	IF, IF?, IFn, IFff, IFffn
Insert line(s) with Prompt	IP, IP?, IPff
Move line(s) to target	M, MM, Mn
Overlay line(s) with copied line(s)	O, OO
Shift line(s) right or left	L, Ln, LL, LLn, R, Rn, RR, RRn
Shift line(s) right or left with truncation	LT, LTn, LLT, LLTn, RT, RTn, RRT, RRTn
Print line(s)	LP, LPn, LLP

Commands to assist in line entry

Display column numbers	COLS
Show format line	F, F?
Show prompt display	P, P?, Pff
Identify skeleton line and insert with skeleton	S, IS, Isn
Set column tabs	TABS

Commands Affecting the Display

Position Screen to Line Number (n, .n, n.n)

To position the screen to display a particular line at the top of the typing area, type the line number over an existing sequence number, and press the Enter key. It makes no difference where in the sequence number area this SEU line command is entered. For example, to position the member so that source line 5 appears at the top of the typing area, enter the command 5, as shown in the following illustration.

```
Columns . . . :    1  71          Edit                    DRIEHL/QCLSRC
  SEU==>                                                         CLSOURCE
  FMT **  ...+... 1 ...+... 2 ...+... 3 ...+... 4 ...+... 5 ...+... 6 ...+... 7
       *************** Beginning of data ************************************
0001.00 LINE 111111111111111
0002.00 LINE 222222222222222
0003.00 LINE 333333333333333
5 04.00 LINE 444444444444444
0005.00 LINE 555555555555555
0006.00 LINE 666666666666666
0007.00 LINE 777777777777777
       ***************** End of data ****************************************
```

The resulting display shows the member positioned to line 5.

```
Columns . . . :    1  71          Edit                    DRIEHL/QCLSRC
  SEU==>                                                         CLSOURCE
  FMT **  ...+... 1 ...+... 2 ...+... 3 ...+... 4 ...+... 5 ...+... 6 ...+... 7
0005.00 LINE 555555555555555
0006.00 LINE 666666666666666
0007.00 LINE 777777777777777
       ***************** End of data ****************************************
```

Position Screen Relative to Top Line (+, +n, -, -n)

To move forward or backward in the member, you can use the Page up/down keys; or for more control, you can use relative positioning. To specify relative positioning, overtype a sequence number with a plus sign (+) or a minus sign (-), followed by the number of source lines to be scrolled forward or backward. The commands + and - without a number specifies to change position one line forward or backward. When a number is specified, the screen will move forward or backward that number of lines. For example, if you want to move the member forward two records, you would use the command +2, as shown in the illustration. The command +2 in the example is placed on source line 2.00; however, you can place the +2 in the sequence number area of any line appearing on the display.

```
Columns . . . :   1  71              Edit                 DRIEHL/QCLSRC
SEU==>                                                         CLSOURCE
FMT **   ...+... 1 ...+... 2 ...+... 3 ...+... 4 ...+... 5 ...+... 6 ...+... 7
************** Beginning of data ********************************
0001.00 LINE 111111111111111
+2 2.00 LINE 222222222222222
0003.00 LINE 333333333333333
0004.00 LINE 444444444444444
0005.00 LINE 555555555555555
0006.00 LINE 666666666666666
0007.00 LINE 777777777777777
***************** End of data ********************************************
```

Because the screen originally positioned the member at line number 1.00, the result of the +2 command positions the display at line 3.00.

```
Columns . . . :   1  71              Edit                 DRIEHL/QCLSRC
SEU==>                                                         CLSOURCE
FMT **   ...+... 1 ...+... 2 ...+... 3 ...+... 4 ...+... 5 ...+... 6 ...+... 7
0003.00 LINE 333333333333333
0004.00 LINE 444444444444444
0005.00 LINE 555555555555555
0006.00 LINE 666666666666666
0007.00 LINE 777777777777777
***************** End of data ********************************************
```

To position to an earlier line in the member, the -n command can be used. Here, the -3 command will roll the display backward three records.

```
  Columns . . . :    1  71              Edit                        DRIEHL/QCLSRC
  SEU==> _____              CLSOURCE
  FMT **  ...+... 1 ...+... 2 ...+... 3 ...+... 4 ...+... 5 ...+... 6 ...+... 7
-3 6.00 LINE 666666666666666
0007.00 LINE 777777777777777
        ****************** End of data ****************************************
```

Exclude Line(s) from the display (X, XX, Xn)

When you are working with source members that have many source lines, it is useful to exclude certain lines from the displayed member, allowing you to see lines from different areas of the source on the screen at the same time. Place **X** (Exclude) on any line you want to exclude from the display. This does not delete the line from the source member; it simply causes the excluded line(s) to be temporarily removed from the SEU display.

You can also use the **X** command in block format (**XX**). As shown in the illustration, this command will exclude lines 2.00 through 5.00 from the display.

```
Columns . . . :    1  71              Edit                    DRIEHL/QCLSRC
SEU==>                                                              CLSOURCE
FMT **   ...+... 1 ...+... 2 ...+... 3 ...+... 4 ...+... 5 ...+... 6 ...+... 7
         *************** Beginning of data ********************************************
0001.00 LINE 111111111111111
XX02.00 LINE 222222222222222
0003.00 LINE 333333333333333
0004.00 LINE 444444444444444
XX05.00 LINE 555555555555555
0006.00 LINE 666666666666666
0007.00 LINE 777777777777777
         ***************** End of data ****************************************
```

On the resulting display, the literal '4 data records excluded' is shown to indicate that excluded lines exist at that position. To restore the lines to the display, you can press the F5 (Refresh) key, or use the SF or SL commands discussed next.

```
Columns . . . :    1  71              Edit                    DRIEHL/QCLSRC
SEU==>                                                              CLSOURCE
FMT **   ...+... 1 ...+... 2 ...+... 3 ...+... 4 ...+... 5 ...+... 6 ...+... 7
         *************** Beginning of data ********************************************
0001.00 LINE 111111111111111
- - - - ------------ 4 data records excluded -----------------------------------
0006.00 LINE 666666666666666
0007.00 LINE 777777777777777
         ***************** End of data ****************************************
```

Show Excluded Line(s) (SF, SFn, SL, SLn)

When excluded lines exist on the display, you can use the **SF** (Show first) command to show the first excluded line, or **SL** (Show last) to show the last excluded line. You can also use the **SFn** format of the command to show the first n lines of the excluded group of lines. In the example, the SF2 command is used to show the first two excluded lines.

```
Columns . . . :    1  71            Edit                    DRIEHL/QCLSRC
 SEU==> _____        CLSOURCE
 FMT **  ...+... 1 ...+... 2 ...+... 3 ...+... 4 ...+... 5 ...+.. 6 ...+... 7
         *************** Beginning of data ***********************************
0001.00 LINE 111111111111111
SF2 - - ------------ 4 data records excluded ---------------------------------
0006.00 LINE 666666666666666
0007.00 LINE 777777777777777
         ***************** End of data ***************************************
```

The resulting display shows that the first two excluded records are now restored to the display. Also, the text has changed to '2 data records excluded'.

```
Columns . . . :    1  71            Edit                    DRIEHL/QCLSRC
 SEU==> _____        CLSOURCE
 FMT **  ...+... 1 ...+... 2 ...+... 3 ...+... 4 ...+... 5 ...+... 6 ...+... 7
         *************** Beginning of data ***********************************
0001.00 LINE 111111111111111
0002.00 LINE 222222222222222
0003.00 LINE 333333333333333
- - - - ------------ 2 data records excluded ---------------------------------
0006.00 LINE 666666666666666
0007.00 LINE 777777777777777
         ***************** End of data ***************************************
```

Just as the **SF** command can be used to show the first excluded record(s), the **SL** command is used here to show the last excluded records.

```
Columns . . . :    1  71            Edit                    DRIEHL/QCLSRC
 SEU==> _____        CLSOURCE
 FMT **  ...+... 1 ...+... 2 ...+... 3 ...+... 4 ...+... 5 ...+... 6 ..+... 7
         *************** Beginning of data ***********************************
0001.00 LINE 111111111111111
0002.00 LINE 222222222222222
SL2 - - ------------ 3 data records excluded ---------------------------------
0006.00 LINE 666666666666666
0007.00 LINE 777777777777777
         ***************** End of data ***************************************
```

Shift Display to a Column Number (W, Wn)

At the top left-hand corner of the SEU edit display, the word 'Columns' is followed by two numbers. In the illustration, these numbers are 1 and 71. This means that currently columns 1 through 71 of the records are shown. Most source member types allow you to enter data into columns 72 and higher, usually up to 80. To access those column positions, you can use the **W** (Window) command. When the **W** command is entered without a number, the display will be positioned with column 1 at the far left margin of the typing area. However, using the command **Wn** allows you to specify the column number to be displayed on the left margin. In the illustration, the W5 command is entered, which will cause the member to be displayed at column 5.

```
Columns . . . :    1  71              Edit                    DRIEHL/QCLSRC
SEU==>                                                            CLSOURCE
FMT **  ...+... 1 ...+... 2 ...+... 3 ...+... 4 ...+... 5 ...+... 6 ...+... 7
        *************** Beginning of data ********************************
0001.00 LINE 111111111111111
W5 2.00 LINE 222222222222222
0003.00 LINE 333333333333333
0004.00 LINE 444444444444444
0005.00 LINE 555555555555555
0006.00 LINE 666666666666666
0007.00 LINE 777777777777777
        ***************** End of data **********************************
```

The resulting display shows how the column numbers displayed at the top of the screen now read columns 5 through 75. You will also note that the FMT** line is shifted so that column 5 now appears at the left margin. Simply entering the **W** command without a number will position the display back to column 1.

```
Columns . . . :    5  75              Edit                    DRIEHL/QCLSRC
SEU==>                                                            CLSOURCE
FMT ** +... 1 ...+... 2 ...+... 3 ...+... 4 ...+... 5 ...+... 6 ...+... 7 ...+
        *************** Beginning of data ********************************
0001.00   111111111111111
0002.00   222222222222222
0003.00   333333333333333
0004.00   444444444444444
0005.00   555555555555555
0006.00   666666666666666
0007.00   777777777777777
        ***************** End of data **********************************
```

Commands To Manipulate Lines

The After and Before Target Commands (A, An, B, Bn)

Whenever you use the Move and Copy line commands, you must specify where you want the line moved or copied to. The **A** (After) and **B** (Before) line commands act as the target. **A** means the moved or copied lines will be placed *after* the line; **B** means *before*. In the illustration, line 2.00 will be moved to the line after line 5.00.

```
Columns . . . :    1  71              Edit                    DRIEHL/QCLSRC
   SEU==> _____  CLSOURCE
   FMT **  ...+... 1 ...+... 2 ...+... 3 ...+... 4 ...+... 5 ...+... 6 ...+... 7
          *************** Beginning of data ************************************
0001.00 LINE 111111111111111
M002.00 LINE 222222222222222
0003.00 LINE 333333333333333
0004.00 LINE 444444444444444
A005.00 LINE 555555555555555
0006.00 LINE 666666666666666
0007.00 LINE 777777777777777
          ***************** End of data ****************************************
```

The resulting display shows line 2.00 no longer exists, and line 5.01 has been added. When you exit SEU, you have the option of re-assigning the sequence numbers so that the next time you edit the member, the sequence numbers will be reset to 1.00, 2.00, 3.00, ...

```
Columns . . . :    1  71              Edit                    DRIEHL/QCLSRC
   SEU==> _____  CLSOURCE
   FMT **  ...+... 1 ...+... 2 ...+... 3 ...+... 4 ...+... 5 ...+... 6 ...+... 7
          *************** Beginning of data ************************************
0001.00 LINE 111111111111111
0003.00 LINE 333333333333333
0004.00 LINE 444444444444444
0005.00 LINE 555555555555555
0005.01 LINE 222222222222222
0006.00 LINE 666666666666666
0007.00 LINE 777777777777777
          ***************** End of data ****************************************
```

In addition to specifying **A**, you can specify that a move or copy operation will place the records before a line number. In the following illustration, a copy of line 4.00 will be placed before line 5.00.

```
 Columns . . . :    1  71              Edit                    DRIEHL/QCLSRC
 SEU==>                                                           CLSOURCE
 FMT **   ...+... 1 ...+... 2 ...+... 3 ...+... 4 ...+... 5 ...+... 6 ...+... 7
          ************** Beginning of data **************************************
0001.00 LINE 111111111111111
0003.00 LINE 333333333333333
C004.00 LINE 444444444444444
B005.00 LINE 555555555555555
0005.01 LINE 222222222222222
0006.00 LINE 666666666666666
0007.00 LINE 777777777777777
          ****************** End of data ****************************************
```

The resulting display shows that line 4.01 has been added to the member.

```
 Columns . . . :    1  71              Edit                    DRIEHL/QCLSRC
 SEU==>                                                           CLSOURCE
 FMT **   ...+... 1 ...+... 2 ...+... 3 ...+... 4 ...+... 5 ...+... 6 ...+... 7
          ************** Beginning of data **************************************
0001.00 LINE 111111111111111
0003.00 LINE 333333333333333
0004.00 LINE 444444444444444
0004.01 LINE 444444444444444
0005.00 LINE 555555555555555
0005.01 LINE 222222222222222
0006.00 LINE 666666666666666
0007.00 LINE 777777777777777
          ****************** End of data ****************************************
```

You can specify both the **B** and **A** commands as **Bn** or **An** respectively. In the following example line 1.00 will be copied after line 3.00 three times.

```
 Columns . . . :    1  71              Edit                    DRIEHL/QCLSRC
 SEU==>                                                           CLSOURCE
 FMT **   ...+... 1 ...+... 2 ...+... 3 ...+... 4 ...+... 5 ...+... 6 ...+... 7
          ************** Beginning of data **************************************
C001.00 LINE 111111111111111
0002.00 LINE 222222222222222
A3 3.00 LINE 333333333333333
0004.00 LINE 444444444444444
0005.00 LINE 555555555555555
0006.00 LINE 666666666666666
0007.00 LINE 777777777777777
          ****************** End of data ****************************************
```

The resulting display shows three new lines: 3.01, 3.02, and 3.03. These are the three copies of line 1.00.

```
 Columns . . . :   1  71              Edit                    DRIEHL/QCLSRC
 SEU==>  _____         CLSOURCE
 FMT **   ...+... 1 ...+... 2 ...+... 3 ...+... 4 ...+... 5 ...+... 6 ...+... 7
 *************** Beginning of data *************************************
 0001.00 LINE 111111111111111
 0002.00 LINE 222222222222222
 0003.00 LINE 333333333333333
 0003.01 LINE 111111111111111
 0003.02 LINE 111111111111111
 0003.03 LINE 111111111111111
.0004.00 LINE 444444444444444
 0005.00 LINE 555555555555555
 0006.00 LINE 666666666666666
 0007.00 LINE 777777777777777
 ***************** End of data ****************************************
```

Copy Line(s) (C, CC, Cn)

The copy command works in conjunction with the **A** and **B** target commands. To copy a line of text, place the **C** (Copy) command on the line to be copied, and place one of the target commands on the line to which the line is to be copied. In the following illustration, the **Cn** form of the command is used to copy three lines, lines 4.00, 5.00 and 6.00, to the position after line 1.00.

```
 Columns . . . :    1  71          Edit              DRIEHL/QCLSRC
 SEU==>  _____    CLSOURCE
 FMT **   ...+... 1 ...+... 2 ...+... 3 ...+... 4 ...+... 5 ...+... 6 ...+... 7
         *************** Beginning of data ****************************************
A 01.00 LINE 111111111111111
0002.00 LINE 222222222222222
0003.00 LINE 333333333333333
0003.01 LINE 111111111111111
0003.02 LINE 111111111111111
0003.03 LINE 111111111111111
C3 4.00 LINE 444444444444444
0005.00 LINE 555555555555555
0006.00 LINE 666666666666666
0007.00 LINE 777777777777777
         ****************** End of data ****************************************
```

The resulting screen shows the three copied lines.

```
 Columns . . . :    1  71          Edit              DRIEHL/QCLSRC
 SEU==>  _____    CLSOURCE
 FMT **   ...+... 1 ...+... 2 ...+... 3 ...+... 4 ...+... 5 ...+... 6 ...+... 7
         *************** Beginning of data ****************************************
0001.00 LINE 111111111111111
0001.01 LINE 444444444444444
0001.02 LINE 555555555555555
0001.03 LINE 666666666666666
0002.00 LINE 222222222222222
0003.00 LINE 333333333333333
0003.01 LINE 111111111111111
0003.02 LINE 111111111111111
0003.03 LINE 111111111111111
0004.00 LINE 444444444444444
0005.00 LINE 555555555555555
0006.00 LINE 666666666666666
0007.00 LINE 777777777777777
         ****************** End of data ****************************************
```

You can also use the block form of the copy command (**CC**) to copy a block of records. Here lines 1.00 through 4.00 will be copied after line 6.00.

```
Columns . . . :    1  71              Edit                     DRIEHL/QCLSRC
SEU==> _____            CLSOURCE
FMT **   ...+... 1 ...+... 2 ...+... 3 ...+... 4 ...+... 5 ...+... 6 ...+... 7
         **************** Beginning of data ***************************************
CC 1.00 LINE 111111111111111
0002.00 LINE 222222222222222
0003.00 LINE 333333333333333
CC 4.00 LINE 444444444444444
0005.00 LINE 555555555555555
A 06.00 LINE 666666666666666
0007.00 LINE 777777777777777
         ***************** End of data ***************************************
```

The resulting display shows the four copied lines.

```
Columns . . . :    1  71              Edit                     DRIEHL/QCLSRC
SEU==> _____            CLSOURCE
FMT **   ...+... 1 ...+... 2 ...+... 3 ...+... 4 ...+... 5 ...+... 6 ...+... 7
         **************** Beginning of data ***************************************
0001.00 LINE 111111111111111
0002.00 LINE 222222222222222
0003.00 LINE 333333333333333
0004.00 LINE 444444444444444
0005.00 LINE 555555555555555
0006.00 LINE 666666666666666
0006.01 LINE 111111111111111
0006.02 LINE 222222222222222
0006.03 LINE 333333333333333
0006.04 LINE 444444444444444
0007.00 LINE 777777777777777
         ***************** End of data ***************************************
```

Copy Line with Repeat (CR, CRn, CCR)

The copy with repeat command allows you to specify multiple target commands at different lines. When the copy function is completed, you can make additional copies simply by entering the target commands. The repeat function stays active until F5 (Refresh) is pressed. In the illustration, line 1.00 will be copied after lines 3.00 and 6.00.

```
Columns . . . :   1  71              Edit                    DRIEHL/QCLSRC
SEU==> _____    CLSOURCE
FMT **  ...+... 1 ...+... 2 ...+... 3 ...+... 4 ...+... 5 ...+... 6 ...+... 7
*************** Beginning of data *********************************
CR 1.00 LINE 111111111111111
0002.00 LINE 222222222222222
A003.00 LINE 333333333333333
0004.00 LINE 444444444444444
0005.00 LINE 555555555555555
A006.00 LINE 666666666666666
***************** End of data ***************************************
```

The resulting display shows that the record has been copied to the two positions. The **CR** command is still active and regarded as a Pending command, as shown on the upper right corner of the display. To copy the line again, simply place a target command (**B** or **A**) where you want the line copied to.

```
Columns . . . :   1  71              Edit          Pending . . . . . :   CR
SEU==> _____
FMT **  ...+... 1 ...+... 2 ...+... 3 ...+... 4 ...+... 5 ...+... 6 ...+... 7
*************** Beginning of data *********************************
CR      LINE 111111111111111
0002.00 LINE 222222222222222
0003.00 LINE 333333333333333
0003.01 LINE 111111111111111
0004.00 L"NE 444444444444444
0005.00 LINE 555555555555555
0006.00 LINE 666666666666666
0007.00 LINE 111111111111111
***************** End of data ***************************************
```

You can also use the copy with repeat command as a block command (**CCR**). In this illustration, lines 1.00 and 2.00 will be copied after line 4.00. The repeat capability remains until you press F5 (Refresh).

```
Columns . . . :    1  71              Edit              Pending . . . . . :    CR
SEU==> _____
FMT **   ...+... 1 ...+... 2 ...+... 3 ...+... 4 ...+... 5 ...+... 6 ...+... 7
        *************** Beginning of data *************************************
CCR .00 LINE 111111111111111
CCR .00 LINE 222222222222222
0003.00 LINE 333333333333333
0003.01 LINE 111111111111111
A 04.00 LINE 444444444444444
0005.00 LINE 555555555555555
0006.00 LINE 666666666666666
0007.00 LINE 111111111111111
        ****************** End of data ****************************************
```

Delete Line (D, DD, Dn)

When you must delete source lines, enter the **D** (Delete) command on each line to be deleted. In this example, line 3.00 will be deleted from the member.

```
Columns . . . :   1  71              Edit                   DRIEHL/QCLSRC
SEU==>  _____           CLSOURCE
FMT **   ...+... 1 ...+... 2 ...+... 3 ...+... 4 ...+... 5 ...+... 6 ...+... 7
        *************** Beginning of data ********************************
0001.00 LINE 111111111111111
0002.00 LINE 222222222222222
D 03.00 LINE 333333333333333
0004.00 LINE 444444444444444
0005.00 LINE 555555555555555
0006.00 LINE 666666666666666
0007.00 LINE 777777777777777
        ***************** End of data *************************************
```

You can also specify the delete command in the **Dn** form. In the following illustration, the D3 command will delete three lines: 2.00, 4.00 and 5.00.

```
Columns . . . :   1  71              Edit                   DRIEHL/QCLSRC
SEU==>  _____           CLSOURCE
FMT **   ...+... 1 ...+... 2 ...+... 3 ...+... 4 ...+... 5 ...+... 6 ...+... 7
        *************** Beginning of data ********************************
0001.00 LINE 111111111111111
D3 2.00 LINE 222222222222222
0004.00 LINE 444444444444444
0005.00 LINE 555555555555555
0006.00 LINE 666666666666666
0007.00 LINE 777777777777766
        ***************** End of data *************************************
```

The block form of the delete command is specified as **(DD)**. In this example, lines 6.01 through 7.00 will be deleted.

```
Columns . . . :   1  71              Edit                   DRIEHL/QCLSRC
SEU==>  _____           CLSOURCE
FMT **   ...+... 1 ...+... 2 ...+... 3 ...+... 4 ...+... 5 ...+... 6 ...+... 7
        *************** Beginning of data ********************************
0001.00 LINE 111111111111111
0002.00 LINE 222222222222222
0003.00 LINE 333333333333333
0004.00 LINE 444444444444444
0005.00 LINE 555555555555555
0006.00 LINE 666666666666666
DD06.01 LINE 111111111111111
0006.02 LINE 222222222222222
0006.03 LINE 333333333333333
0006.04 LINE 444444444444444
DD07.00 LINE 777777777777777
        ***************** End of data *************************************
```

Duplicate (Repeat) Line (RP, RPn, RPP, RPPn)

The **RP** (Repeat) command is used to duplicate a line or group of lines. The **RP** command always copies source line(s) to the line(s) immediately following; you do no use any target commands with the **RP** command. In the following example, line 2.00 will be duplicated.

```
Columns . . . :    1  71              Edit                      DRIEHL/QCLSRC
SEU==> _____        CLSOURCE
FMT **   ...+... 1 ...+... 2 ...+... 3 ...+... 4 ...+... 5 ...+... 6 ...+... 7
         *************** Beginning of data *********************************
0001.00 LINE 111111111111111
RP02.00 LINE 222222222222222
0003.00 LINE 333333333333333
0004.00 LINE 444444444444444
0005.00 LINE 555555555555555
0006.00 LINE 666666666666666
0007.00 LINE 777777777777777
         ***************** End of data **************************************
```

The resulting display shows that line 2.00 has been duplicated in line 2.01.

```
Columns . . . :    1  71              Edit                      DRIEHL/QCLSRC
SEU==> _____        CLSOURCE
FMT **   ...+... 1 ...+... 2 ...+... 3 ...+... 4 ...+... 5 ...+... 6 ...+... 7
         *************** Beginning of data *********************************
0001.00 LINE 111111111111111
0002.00 LINE 222222222222222
0002.01 LINE 222222222222222
0003.00 LINE 333333333333333
0004.00 LINE 444444444444444
0005.00 LINE 555555555555555
0006.00 LINE 666666666666666
0007.00 LINE 777777777777777
         ***************** End of data **************************************
```

To duplicate a line multiple times, you can use the **RPn** format of the command. In this example, line 2.00 will be duplicated three times.

```
Columns . . . :    1  71              Edit                      DRIEHL/QCLSRC
SEU==> _____        CLSOURCE
FMT **   ...+... 1 ...+... 2 ...+... 3 ...+... 4 ...+... 5 ...+... 6 ...+... 7
         *************** Beginning of data *********************************
0001.00 LINE 111111111111111
RP3 .00 LINE 222222222222222
0003.00 LINE 333333333333333
0004.00 LINE 444444444444444
0005.00 LINE 555555555555555
0006.00 LINE 666666666666666
0007.00 LINE 777777777777777
         ***************** End of data **************************************
```

To duplicate a block of records, you can use the block form of the repeat command (**RPP**). In this example, lines 2.00 through 4.00 will be duplicated. If you want to duplicate a block of lines multiple times, you can use the command **RPPn**.

```
 Columns . . . :   1  71            Edit                DRIEHL/QCLSRC
 SEU==>  _____  CLSOURCE
 FMT **  ...+... 1 ...+... 2 ...+... 3 ...+... 4 ...+... 5 ...+... 6 ...+... 7
         *************** Beginning of data *************************************
 0001.00 LINE 111111111111111
 RPP  00 LINE 222222222222222
 0003.00 LINE 333333333333333
 RPP .00 LINE 444444444444444
 0005.00 LINE 555555555555555
 0006.00 LINE 666666666666666
 0007.00 LINE 777777777777777
         ***************** End of data ***************************************
```

Insert Line (I, In)

When editing a source member, you often need to add source statements within an existing member. The insert command is used for that purpose. To insert a line between two existing lines, place the **I** (Insert) command on the first of the two lines and press Enter . SEU will insert a new line. After you have entered the new source statement, you can press Enter and an additional new line will be shown, on which you can continue adding another new source member line. SEU will continue to make more empty lines available until you press Enter without previously entering anything into the typing area for the new line. In this example, a new line will be inserted between lines 4.00 and 5.00.

```
Columns . . . :    1  71              Edit              DRIEHL/QCLSRC
SEU==>                                                      CLSOURCE
FMT **   ...+... 1 ...+... 2 ...+... 3 ...+... 4 ...+... 5 ...+... 6 ...+... 7
         *************** Beginning of data ****************************************
0001.00 LINE 111111111111111
0002.00 LINE 222222222222222
0003.00 LINE 333333333333333
I 04.00 LINE 444444444444444
0005.00 LINE 555555555555555
0006.00 LINE 666666666666666
0007.00 LINE 777777777777777
         ***************** End of data ****************************************
```

The resulting display shows the inserted line. No sequence number is assigned for the new line until you finish typing in the source line and press the Enter key.

```
Columns . . . :    1  71              Edit              DRIEHL/QCLSRC
SEU==>                                                      CLSOURCE
FMT **   ...+... 1 ...+... 2 ...+... 3 ...+... 4 ...+... 5 ...+... 6 ...+... 7
         *************** Beginning of data ****************************************
0001.00 LINE 111111111111111
0002.00 LINE 222222222222222
0003.00 LINE 333333333333333
0004.00 LINE 444444444444444
'''''''
0005.00 LINE 555555555555555
0006.00 LINE 666666666666666
0007.00 LINE 777777777777777
         ***************** End of data ****************************************
```

You can use the **In** format of the insert command when you require several new lines. The I5 command in the following example will insert five blank lines after line 4.00.

```
Columns . . . :    1  71              Edit                DRIEHL/QCLSRC
 SEU==> _____ CLSOURCE
 FMT **   ...+... 1 ...+... 2 ...+... 3 ...+... 4 ...+... 5 ...+... 6 ...+... 7
        *************** Beginning of data ************************************
0001.00 LINE 111111111111111
0002.00 LINE 222222222222222
0003.00 LINE 333333333333333
I5 4.00 LINE 444444444444444
0005.00 LINE 555555555555555
0006.00 LINE 666666666666666
0007.00 LINE 777777777777777
        ***************** End of data ****************************************
```

The resulting display shows the inserted lines. Again, sequence numbers will be assigned when you have finished entering the source lines.

```
Columns . . . :    1  71              Edit                DRIEHL/QCLSRC
 SEU==> _____ CLSOURCE
 FMT **   ...+... 1 ...+... 2 ...+... 3 ...+... 4 ...+... 5 ...+... 6 ...+... 7
        *************** Beginning of data ************************************
0001.00 LINE 111111111111111
0002.00 LINE 222222222222222
0003.00 LINE 333333333333333
0004.00 LINE 444444444444444
'''''''
'''''''
'''''''
'''''''
'''''''
0005.00 LINE 555555555555555
0006.00 LINE 666666666666666
0007.00 LINE 777777777777777
        ***************** End of data ****************************************
```

Insert Line with Format (IF, IF?, IFn, IFff, IFffn)

When inserting lines, you can optionally request that a format line also be displayed. Format lines are especially useful with fixed-column source, such as RPG or DDS, which require that information be placed in specific columns in the source; the format line acts as a "ruler" to help you type the information in the proper place. Place the **IF** (Insert with format) command on an existing line, and a new line will be inserted in the member, preceded by a line that displays the format of the record. In this example, a line will be inserted after line 3.00. The line will be preceded by a format line.

```
Columns . . . :    1  71              Edit                    DRIEHL/QCLSRC
  SEU==> _____        CLSOURCE
  FMT **    ...+... 1 ...+... 2 ...+... 3 ...+... 4 ...+... 5 ...+... 6 ...+... 7
           *************** Beginning of data *****************************************
0001.00 LINE 111111111111111
0002.00 LINE 222222222222222
IF03.00 LINE 333333333333333
0004.00 LINE 444444444444444
0005.00 LINE 555555555555555
0006.00 LINE 666666666666666
0007.00 LINE 777777777777777
           ***************** End of data ********************************************
```

The resulting display shows the inserted line following the FMT** line. The format line shown depends upon the source member type. For example, if the member type is CBL, for a COBOL program, a COBOL format line will be displayed.

```
Columns . . . :    1  71              Edit                    DRIEHL/QCLSRC
  SEU==> _____        CLSOURCE
  FMT **    ...+... 1 ...+... 2 ...+... 3 ...+... 4 ...+... 5 ...+... 6 ...+... 7
           *************** Beginning of data *****************************************
0001.00 LINE 111111111111111
0002.00 LINE 222222222222222
0003.00 LINE 333333333333333
  FMT **    ...+... 1 ...+... 2 ...+... 3 ...+... 4 ...+... 5 ...+... 6 ...+... 7
  ''''''''
0004.00 LINE 444444444444444
0005.00 LINE 555555555555555
0006.00 LINE 666666666666666
0007.00 LINE 777777777777777
           ***************** End of data ********************************************
```

Several different styles of format lines are available to help you enter lines. The **IF?** command can be used to insert a line with a format; because ? is specified, SEU will show a prompt display, which allows you to choose the format line style that will be shown.

```
 Columns . . . :    1  71            Edit                    DRIEHL/QCLSRC
 SEU==>                                                          CLSOURCE
 FMT **  ...+... 1 ...+... 2 ...+... 3 ...+... 4 ...+... 5 ...+... 6 ...+... 7
         *************** Beginning of data ********************************
0001.00 LINE 111111111111111
0002.00 LINE 222222222222222
IF73.00 LINE 333333333333333
0004.00 LINE 444444444444444
0005.00 LINE 555555555555555
0006.00 LINE 666666666666666
0007.00 LINE 777777777777777
         ***************** End of data ***********************************
```

The Select Format display results from using the **IF?** command. This display shows all the format styles that you may select within SEU. On this display, the format **F** is chosen. The F-format is the RPG format for file specification lines.

```
                          Select Format

 Type choice, press Enter.

  Format type . . . . . . . . . . .  E       Values listed below

    RPG/400:        H,F,FC,FK,FX,U,E,L,I,IX,J (I cont),JX,DS,SS,SV,C,O,
                    OD,P (O cont),N, * (Comment)
    COBOL:          CB,C*
    REFORMAT/SORT:  RH,RR,RF,RC
    DDS:            LF (Logical file),PF (Physical file),
                    BC (Interactive Communications Feature file),
                    DP (Display and Printer file),
                    A* (Comment)
    MNU:            MS,MMC (MD cont),CC (Comment)
    FORTRAN:        FT, F*
    Other:          NC (No syntax checking),** (Free format)




 F12=Cancel
```

The F-format (RPG F-spec) line is shown at the insertion point in the member.

```
 Columns . . . :    1  71            Edit              DRIEHL/QCLSRC
 SEU==>                                                     CLSOURCE
 FMT **   ...+... 1 ...+... 2 ...+... 3 ...+... 4 ...+... 5 ...+... 6 ...+... 7
          *************** Beginning of data ************************************
 0001.00 LINE 111111111111111
 0002.00 LINE 222222222222222
 0003.00 LINE 333333333333333
 FMT F    .....FFilenameIPEAF....RlenLK1AIOvKlocEDevice+......KExit++Entry+A....U
 ........
 0004.00 LINE 444444444444444
 0005.00 LINE 555555555555555
 0006.00 LINE 666666666666666
 0007.00 LINE 777777777777777
          ***************** End of data ****************************************
```

If you know the format you want to use, you can simply specify IF followed by the format designation. Here, **IFF** is used to insert a line under the RPG F-specification format line.

```
 Columns . . . :    1  71            Edit              DRIEHL/QCLSRC
 SEU==>                                                     CLSOURCE
 FMT **   ...+... 1 ...+... 2 ...+... 3 ...+... 4 ...+... 5 ...+... 6 ...+... 7
          *************** Beginning of data ************************************
 0001.00 LINE 111111111111111
 0002.00 LINE 222222222222222
 IFF3.00 LINE 333333333333333
 0004.00 LINE 444444444444444
 0005.00 LINE 555555555555555
 0006.00 LINE 666666666666666
 0007.00 LINE 777777777777777
          ***************** End of data ****************************************
```

Insert Line with Prompt (IP, IP?, IPff)

As an alternative to presenting a format line on the display, SEU also has an intelligent prompting facility. When inserting lines within a source member, you can request a prompt by using the **IP** (Insert with prompting) command. In the following example, a line will be inserted between line 2.00 and line 3.00, and you will be prompted for the entry that will be inserted.

```
Columns . . . :    1  71              Edit                    DRIEHL/QCLSRC
SEU==>                                                               CLSOURCE
FMT **   ...+... 1 ...+... 2 ...+... 3 ...+... 4 ...+... 5 ...+... 6 ...+... 7
************** Beginning of data ****************************************
0001.00 LINE 111111111111111
IP02.00 LINE 222222222222222
0003.00 LINE 333333333333333
0004.00 LINE 444444444444444
0005.00 LINE 555555555555555
0006.00 LINE 666666666666666
0007.00 LINE 777777777777777
***************** End of data ******************************************
```

The resulting display shows the prompt within the lower portion of the screen. Here the prompt displayed shows columns 1 through 78.

You simply type the source line into the input capable field shown beneath the prompt line.

```
Columns . . . :    1  71              Edit                    DRIEHL/QCLSRC
SEU==>                                                               CLSOURCE
FMT **   ...+... 1 ...+... 2 ...+... 3 ...+... 4 ...+... 5 ...+... 6 ...+... 7
************** Beginning of data ****************************************
0001.00 LINE 111111111111111
0002.00 LINE 222222222222222
'''''''
0003.00 LINE 333333333333333
0004.00 LINE 444444444444444
0005.00 LINE 555555555555555
0006.00 LINE 666666666666666
0007.00 LINE 777777777777777
***************** End of data ******************************************
Prompt type . . .    **       Sequence number . . .  '''''''

Data area
....+... 1 ...+... 2 ...+... 3 ...+... 4 ...+... 5 ...+... 6 ...+... 7 ...+...
```

Just as with the **IF** command, you can request a list of valid prompts by using the **IP?** command, as shown in the following example.

```
Columns . . . :   1  71            Edit              DRIEHL/QCLSRC
SEU==>                                                    CLSOURCE
FMT **   ...+... 1 ...+... 2 ...+... 3 ...+... 4 ...+... 5 ...+... 6 ...+... 7
         *************** Beginning of data ***********************************
0001.00 LINE 111111111111111
0002.00 LINE 222222222222222
IP?3.00 LINE 333333333333333
0004.00 LINE 444444444444444
0005.00 LINE 555555555555555
0006.00 LINE 666666666666666
0007.00 LINE 777777777777777
         ***************** End of data *************************************
```

You can select from any prompt listed on the Select Prompt display Here, the prompt selected is 'I', an RPG I-spec prompt.

```
                        Select Prompt

 Type choice, press Enter.

  Prompt type . . . . . . . . . . .  I      Values listed below

    RPG/400:        H,F,FC,FK,FX,U,E,L,I,IX,J (I cont),JX,DS,SS,SV,C,O,
                    OD,P (O cont),N,* (Comment)
    COBOL:          CB,C*
    REFORMAT/SORT:  RH,RR,RF,RC
    DDS:            LF (Logical file),PF (Physical file),
                    BC (Interactive Communications Feature file),
                    DP (Display and Printer file),
                    A* (Comment)
    MNU:            MS,MH,MD,MC (MD cont),CC (Comment)
    FORTRAN:        FT, F*
    Other:          NC (No syntax checking),** (Free format)
```

The resulting display when an I-prompt is requested shows the prompt in the lower portion of the screen. You use the input capable fields within the prompt to enter your source statement.

```
Columns . . . :   1  71           Edit            DRIEHL/QCLSRC
SEU==> _____   CLSOURCE
FMT **  ...+... 1 ...+... 2 ...+... 3 ...+... 4 ...+... 5 ...+... 6 ...+... 7
        *************** Beginning of daa ********************************
0001.00 LINE 111111111111111
0002.00 LINE 222222222222222
0003.00 LINE 333333333333333
'''''''
0004.00 LINE 444444444444444
0005.00 LINE 555555555555555
0006.00 LINE 666666666666666
Prompt type . . .    I      Sequence number . . .  '''''''

Filename      Sequence      Number     Option    Record ID
_____     _____      ____       __        _____
Record Identification Codes
Position     Not    C/Z/D   Character
1            __      _      __
2            __      _      __
3            __      _      __
```

Move Line to Target (M, MM, Mn)

We covered much of the **M** (Move) command in the introduction to this chapter. But to refresh your memory, here is a simple Move/After command that will move line 2.00 after line 5.00. The **M** command works similarly to the **C** (Copy) command, except that the **M** command moves the line(s) without retaining the original(s).

```
 Columns . . . :    1  71          Edit              DRIEHL/QCLSRC
 SEU==>                                                     CLSOURCE
 FMT **  ...+... 1 ...+... 2 ...+... 3 ...+... 4 ...+... 5 ...+... 6 ...+... 7
 *************** Beginning of data *************************************
0001.00 LINE 111111111111111
M002.00 LINE 222222222222222
0003.00 LINE 333333333333333
0004.00 LINE 444444444444444
A005.00 LINE 555555555555555
0006.00 LINE 666666666666666
0007.00 LINE 777777777777777
 ***************** End of data *************************************
```

Here is the result of the Move/After operation.

```
 Columns . . . :    1  71          Edit              DRIEHL/QCLSRC
 SEU==>                                                     CLSOURCE
 FMT **  ...+... 1 ...+... 2 ...+... 3 ...+... 4 ...+... 5 ...+... 6 ...+... 7
 *************** Beginning of data *************************************
0001.00 LINE 111111111111111
0003.00 LINE 333333333333333
0004.00 LINE 444444444444444
0005.00 LINE 555555555555555
0005.01 LINE 222222222222222
0006.00 LINE 666666666666666
0007.00 LINE 777777777777777
 ***************** End of data *************************************
```

You can also specify block move (**MM**) operations and **Mn** operations.

Overlay Line (O, OO)

You can use the overlay function to overlay a line with another line. This is useful when one line contains a pattern of characters that you want to merge with characters on other lines. You use the overlay command in conjunction with the copy command. In the following example, we use the block form of the overlay command (OO). This will cause the contents of line 0.01 to overlay the contents of line 2.00 through line 5.00. Please note that the overlay characters are the uppercase letter O, not the numeric digit 0 (zero).

```
  Columns . . . :    1  71              Edit                    DRIEHL/QCLSRC
  SEU==>                                                            CLSOURCE
  FMT **   ...+... 1 ...+... 2 ...+... 3 ...+... 4 ...+... 5 ...+... 6 ...+... 7
         *************** Beginning of data ***********************************
  C000.01 /*                                                          */
  0001.00      111111111111111
  0002.00      222222222222222
  0003.00      333333333333333
  0004.00      444444444444444
  0005.00      555555555555555
  0006.00      666666666666666
  0007.00      777777777777777
         ***************** End of data ***************************************
```

The result shows how the lines 2.00 through 5.00 have been overlayed by the content of line 0.01.

```
  Columns . . . :    1  71              Edit                    DRIEHL/QCLSRC
  SEU==>                                                            CLSOURCE
  FMT **   ...+... 1 ...+... 2 ...+... 3 ...+... 4 ...+... 5 ...+... 6 ...+... 7
         *************** Beginning of data ***********************************
  0000.01 /*                                                          */
  0001.00      111111111111111
  0002.00 /*   222222222222222                                        */
  0003.00 /*   333333333333333                                        */
  0004.00 /*   444444444444444                                        */
  0005.00 /*   555555555555555                                        */
  0006.00      666666666666666
  0007.00      777777777777777
         ***************** End of data ***************************************
```

Shift Line Right or Left (L, Ln, LL, LLn, R, Rn, RR, RRn)

Earlier, we presented the **W** command as a way to shift the display right and left. The **L** (Left) and **R** (Right) commands actually shift individual lines or groups of lines left or right in the source member, not just on the display. This is useful for indentation, or for shifting text into the correct column for languages such as RPG and COBOL that require correct columnar placement. In the following example, the text in line 3.00 will be shifted to the right five columns.

```
 Columns . . . :    1  71              Edit                    DRIEHL/QCLSRC
 SEU==>                                                            CLSOURCE
 FMT **    ...+... 1 ...+... 2 ...+... 3 ...+... 4 ...+... 5 ...+... 6 ...+... 7
          *************** Beginning of data ********************************
 0001.00 LINE 111111111111111
 0002.00 LINE 222222222222222
 R5 3.00 LINE 333333333333333
 0004.00 LINE 444444444444444
 0005.00 LINE 555555555555555
 0006.00 LINE 666666666666666
 0007.00 LINE 777777777777777
          **************** End of data ***********************************
```

The resulting display shows that only line 3.00 was affected by the R5 command.

```
 Columns . . . :    1  71              Edit                    DRIEHL/QCLSRC
 SEU==>                                                            CLSOURCE
 FMT **    ...+... 1 ...+... 2 ...+... 3 ...+... 4 ...+... 5 ...+... 6 ...+... 7
          *************** Beginning of data ********************************
 0001.00 LINE 111111111111111
 0002.00 LINE 222222222222222
 0003.00      LINE 333333333333333
 0004.00 LINE 444444444444444
 0005.00 LINE 555555555555555
 0006.00 LINE 666666666666666
 0007.00 LINE 777777777777777
          **************** End of data ***********************************
```

You can use the **L** command to shift contents to the left. Here, the L5 command will shift line 3.00 five positions to the left.

```
  Columns . . . :    1  71           Edit              DRIEHL/QCLSRC
  SEU==>                                                   CLSOURCE
  FMT **  ...+... 1 ...+... 2 ...+... 3 ...+... 4 ...+... 5 ...+... 6 ...+... 7
          *************** Beginning of data *******************************************
  0001.00 LINE 111111111111111
  0002.00 LINE 222222222222222
  L5 3.00      LINE 333333333333333
  0004.00 LINE 444444444444444
  0005.00 LINE 555555555555555
  0006.00 LINE 666666666666666
  0007.00 LINE 777777777777777
          ****************** End of data *******************************************
```

You can also use the **L** and **R** commands in a block form. Here, the contents of line 2.00 through line 6.00 will shift 12 positions to the right.

```
  Columns . . . :    1  71           Edit              DRIEHL/QCLSRC
  SEU==>                                                   CLSOURCE
  FMT **  ...+... 1 ...+... 2 ...+... 3 ...+... 4 ...+... 5 ...+... 6 ...+... 7
          *************** Beginning of data *******************************************
  0001.00 LINE 111111111111111
  RR12 00 LINE 222222222222222
  0003.00 LINE 333333333333333
  0004.00 LINE 444444444444444
  0005.00 LINE 555555555555555
  RR12 00 LINE 666666666666666
  0007.00 LINE 777777777777777
          ****************** End of data *******************************************
```

The resulting display shows that the other lines are not affected.

```
  Columns . . . :    1  71           Edit              DRIEHL/QCLSRC
  SEU==>                                                   CLSOURCE
  FMT **  ...+... 1 ...+... 2 ...+... 3 ...+... 4 ...+... 5 ...+... 6 ...+... 7
          *************** Beginning of data *******************************************
  0001.00 LINE 111111111111111
  0002.00          LINE 222222222222222
  0003.00          LINE 333333333333333
  0004.00          LINE 444444444444444
  0005.00          LINE 555555555555555
  0006.00          LINE 666666666666666
  0007.00 LINE 777777777777777
          ****************** End of data *******************************************
```

If you specify a shift value that will cause positions of the line to be truncated, the lines will not be fully shifted. In this example, specifying a block shift of 60 positions to the right would normally cause some characters of the lines to be lost.

```
 Columns . . . :    1  71              Edit                      DRIEHL/QCLSRC
 SEU==>                                                                 CLSOURCE
 FMT **   ...+... 1 ...+... 2 ...+... 3 ...+... 4 ...+... 5 ...+... 6 ...+... 7
          *************** Beginning of data ************************************
 0001.00 LINE 111111111111111
 RR60 00      LINE 222222222222222
 0003.00      LINE 333333333333333
 0004.00      LINE 444444444444444
 0005.00      LINE 555555555555555
 RR60 00      LINE 666666666666666
 0007.00 LINE 777777777777777
          ***************** End of data ****************************************
```

The result is that the line will be moved only as far to the right as possible without losing any characters. The message at the bottom of the screen indicates the columns marked SHIFT were not moved the full distance requested.

```
 Columns . . . :    1  71              Edit                      DRIEHL/QCLSRC
 SEU==>                                                                 CLSOURCE
 FMT **   ...+... 1 ...+... 2 ...+... 3 ...+... 4 ...+... 5 ...+... 6 ...+... 7
          *************** Beginning of data ************************************
 0001.00 LINE 111111111111111
 SHIFT                                                           LINE 222222
 SHIFT                                                           LINE 333333
 SHIFT                                                           LINE 444444
 SHIFT                                                           LINE 555555
 SHIFT                                                           LINE 666666
 0007.00 LINE 777777777777777
          ***************** End of data ****************************************




 F3=Exit   F4=Prompt   F5=Refresh   F9=Retrieve   F10=Cursor
 F16=Repeat find       F17=Repeat change          F24=More keys
 SHIFT displayed for lines not completely shifted.
```

Shift Line Right or Left with Truncation (LT, LTn, LLT, LLTn, RT, RTn, RRT, RRTn

The **LT** and **RT** commands work just like the **L** and **R** commands, with the exception that truncation will occur if the lines are shifted outside the column positions of the source line. See the discussion of the **L** and **R** commands.

Print Line (LP, LPn, LLP)

You can use the **LP** (Line print) command to print a line or group of lines from a source member. There may be times that you do not want to print an entire source member, but perhaps only a complex subroutine. The **LP** command gives you that capability. In the following example, the LP5 command will cause five lines starting at line 2.00 to be printed.

```
Columns . . . :    1  71              Edit                   DRIEHL/QCLSRC
SEU==> _____       CLSOURCE
FMT **   ...+... 1 ...+... 2 ...+... 3 ...+... 4 ...+... 5 ...+... 6 ...+... 7
         *************** Beginning of daa ********************************
0001.00 LINE 111111111111111
LP5 .00 LINE 222222222222222
0003.00 LINE 333333333333333
0004.00 LINE 444444444444444
0005.00 LINE 555555555555555
0006.00 LINE 666666666666666
0007.00 LINE 777777777777777
         **************** End of data ***********************************
```

You can also use the block form of the LP command (LPP) as shown here. This will cause lines 2.00 through 5.00 to be printed.

```
Columns . . . :    1  71              Edit                   DRIEHL/QCLSRC
SEU==> _____       CLSOURCE
FMT **   ...+... 1 ...+... 2 ...+... 3 ...+... 4 ...+... 5 ...+... 6 ...+... 7
         *************** Beginning of daa ********************************
0001.00 LINE 111111111111111
LPP2.00 LINE 222222222222222
0003.00 LINE 333333333333333
0004.00 LINE 444444444444444
LPP5.00 LINE 555555555555555
0006.00 LINE 666666666666666
0007.00 LINE 777777777777777
         **************** End of data ***********************************
```

Commands To Assist in Line Entry

Display Column Numbers (COLS)

When you enter the **COLS** line command, a horizontal line containing column numbers is inserted at that line.

```
Columns . . . :   1  71              Edit                    DRIEHL/QCLSRC
SEU==>                                                             CLSOURCE
FMT **   ...+... 1 ...+... 2 ...+... 3 ...+... 4 ...+... 5 ...+... 6 ...+... 7
         *************** Beginning of data ***********************************
0001.00 LINE 111111111111111
COLS 00 LINE 222222222222222
0003.00 LINE 333333333333333
0004.00 LINE 444444444444444
0005.00 LINE 555555555555555
0006.00 LINE 666666666666666
0007.00 LINE 777777777777777
         **************** End of data ****************************************
```

The resulting display shows the FMT** line. To remove the FMT** line from the display, press F5 (Refresh).

```
Columns . . . :   1  71              Edit                    DRIEHL/QCLSRC
SEU==>                                                             CLSOURCE
FMT **   ...+... 1 ...+... 2 ...+... 3 ...+... 4 ...+... 5 ...+... 6 ...+... 7
         *************** Beginning of data ***********************************
0001.00 LINE 111111111111111
FMT **   ...+. 1 ...+... 2 ...+... 3 ...+... 4 ...+... 5 ...+... 6 ...+... 7
0002.00 LINE 222222222222222
0003.00 LINE 333333333333333
0004.00 LINE 444444444444444
0005.00 LINE 555555555555555
0006.00 LINE 666666666666666
0007.00 LINE 777777777777777
         **************** End of data ****************************************
```

Show Format Line (F, F?)

When you are editing the source members written in certain languages, it is helpful to see a format line displayed on the screen. For example, the RPG language has several different formats that are used: C-specs use one format, F-specs use another, and so on. Columnar languages such as RPG are easier to edit when a language format line is displayed.

Here, the **F** (Show format) command is used to display a format line; the format line displayed is the F format line, the RPG F-Spec format.

```
 Columns . . . :    1  71              Edit              DRIEHL/QCLSRC
 SEU==>                                                        CLSOURCE
 FMT **   ...+... 1 ...+... 2 ...+... 3 ...+... 4 ...+... 5 ...+... 6 ...+... 7
         *************** Beginning of data ********************************
0001.00 LINE 111111111111111
0002.00 LINE 222222222222222
FF03.00 LINE 333333333333333
0004.00 LINE 444444444444444
0005.00 LINE 555555555555555
0006.00 LINE 666666666666666
0007.00 LINE 777777777777777
         ***************** End of data ***********************************
```

The resulting display includes the RPG F-spec format line at the position where the **FF** command was entered. To remove the format line from the display, press F5 (Refresh).

```
 Columns . . . :    1  71              Edit              DRIEHL/QCLSRC
 SEU==>                                                        CLSOURCE
 FMT **   ...+... 1 ...+... 2 ...+... 3 ...+... 4 ...+... 5 ...+... 6 ...+... 7
         *************** Beginning of data ********************************
0001.00 LINE 111111111111111
0002.00 LINE 222222222222222
FMT F    .....FFilenameIPEAF....RlenLK1AIOvKlocEDevice+......KExit++Entry+A....U
0003.00 LINE 333333333333333
0004.00 LINE 444444444444444
0005.00 LINE 555555555555555
0006.00 LINE 666666666666666
0007.00 LINE 777777777777777
         ***************** End of data ***********************************
```

Show Prompt Display (P, P?, Pff)

The **P** (Show prompt) command is used to show a prompt display for the current line. In this COBOL example, COBOL area A and area B are seen in the FMT line at the top of the display. SEU determines the format line based upon the source type. Here, the source type is CBL. The **P** command is used here to display line 2.00 within a COBOL prompt.

```
Columns . . . :    1  71            Edit              DRIEHL/QCLSRC
SEU==>                                                      CLSOURCE
FMT CB .......-A+++B++++++++++++++++++++++++++++++++++++++++++++++++++++++
        *************** Beginning of data ********************************
0001.00       01  DATA-AREA.
P002.00           05  FILLER  PIC X(05)    VALUE 'MYLIB'.
0003.00           05  FILLER  PIC X(25)    VALUE SPACES.
0004.00
0005.00
        ***************** End of data ****************************************
```

The resulting display shows the COBOL prompt, ready for input. Again, SEU determines the prompt to use from the source type and the content of the line selected.

```
Columns . . . :    1  71            Edit              DRIEHL/QCBLSRC
SEU==>                                                      CBLSOURCE
FMT CB .......-A+++B++++++++++++++++++++++++++++++++++++++++++++++++++++++
        *************** Beginning of data ********************************
0001.00       01  DATA-AREA.
0002.00           05  FILLER  PIC X(05)    VALUE 'MYLIB'.
0003.00           05  FILLER  PIC X(25)    VALUE SPACES.
0004.00
0005.00
        ***************** End of data ****************************************


Prompt type . . .  CB     Sequence number . . .  0002.00

Continuation
_____
Area-A        Area-B
              05 FILLER PIC X(05)    VALUE 'MYLIB'.
_____
```

Identify Skeleton Line and Insert with Skeleton (S, IS, ISn)

A skeleton line is a template or model line for other lines that you want to insert into the member. In this example, placing an **S** (Skeleton) command on line 2.00 identifies this line as the skeleton line.

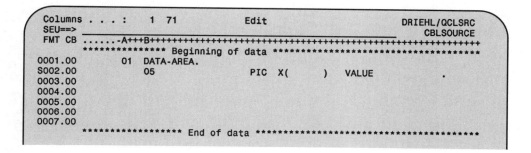

```
Columns . . . :   1  71           Edit                    DRIEHL/QCLSRC
SEU==>                                                          CBLSOURCE
FMT CB ......-A+++B++++++++++++++++++++++++++++++++++++++++++++++++++++++++++
************** Beginning of data ********************************
0001.00      01  DATA-AREA.
S002.00          05              PIC  X(      )   VALUE               .
0003.00
0004.00
0005.00
0006.00
0007.00
**************** End of data ********************************
```

Once you have selected the skeleton line, you can use it when inserting new lines. The following example shows an **IS** (Insert with skeleton) command on line 3.00, to insert a line using the skeleton as a model.

```
Columns . . . :   1  71           Edit                    DRIEHL/QCLSRC
SEU==>                                                          CBLSOURCE
FMT CB ......-A+++B++++++++++++++++++++++++++++++++++++++++++++++++++++++++++
************** Beginning of data ********************************
0001.00      01  DATA-AREA.
0002.00          05              PIC  X(      )   VALUE               .
IS03.00
0004.00
0005.00
0006.00
0007.00
**************** End of data ********************************
```

The resulting display shows that the **IS** command has caused SEU to display the skeleton line in insert line mode. This is the same as normal insert mode except that all inserted lines are first presented with the skeleton characters instead of with the normal blank lines.

```
 Columns . . . :    1  71            Edit                    DRIEHL/QCBLSRC
 SEU==> _____  CBLSOURCE
 FMT CB .......-A+++B+++++++++++++++++++++++++++++++++++++++++++++++++++++++++++
        *************** Beginning of data **********************************
 0001.00        01  DATA-AREA.
 0002.00            05                   PIC  X(     )    VALUE            .
 0003.00
 ........           05                   PIC  X(     )    VALUE            .
 0004.00
 0005.00
 0006.00
 0007.00
        ***************** End of data ***************************************
```

Set Column Tabs (TABS)

You can set column tabs to assist in line entry using the **TABS** command. The tabs feature in SEU is not used very often because it is quite slow and cumbersome. When you use tabs in SEU, you don't use the tab key; instead, you use the Enter key to move from tab stop to tab stop. This makes the **TABS** command a very slow function that generates a lot of extra work for the workstation controller.

To use the tab function, you first type the command **TABS** and press the Enter key. Then, in that same source line, you place any non-blank character where you want the tab stops to be placed, as shown in the example. Here, hyphens are used to designate the tab stops.

```
Columns . . . :   1  71              Edit                    DRIEHL/QCLSRC
SEU==>                                                            CLSOURCE
FMT **    ...+... 1 ...+... 2 ...+... 3 ...+... 4 ...+... 5 ...+... 6 ...+... 7
************** Beginning of data ****************************************
0001.00 LINE 111111111111111
0002.00 LINE 222222222222222
0003.00 LINE 333333333333333
TABS    -              -          -              -
0004.00 LINE 444444444444444
0005.00 LINE 555555555555555
0006.00 LINE 666666666666666
0007.00 LINE 777777777777777
***************** End of data ******************************************
```

The **TABS** function requires that your SEU session is configured to use tabs. You can accomplish this with the SEU **SET** command as shown here. Now your tab stops can be used, by pressing the Enter key.

```
Columns . . . :   1  71              Edit                    DRIEHL/QCLSRC
SEU==> set tabs on                                                CLSOURCE
FMT **    ...+... 1 ...+... 2 ...+... 3 ...+... 4 ...+... 5 ...+... 6 ...+... 7
************** Beginning of data ****************************************
0001.00 LINE 111111111111111
0002.00 LINE 222222222222222
0003.00 LINE 333333333333333
TABS    -              -          -              -
0004.00 LINE 444444444444444
0005.00 LINE 555555555555555
0006.00 LINE 666666666666666
0007.00 LINE 777777777777777
***************** End of data ******************************************
```

SEU Function Keys

Chapter 10

When SEU presents its edit display, there are several valid function keys. While not all the function keys are shown on a single display, all the valid keys are always available. Pressing F24 (More keys) will display the other available function keys.

The set of function keys available from within SEU can be broken down into three categories:

1) Screen Control

2) System Services

3) SEU Services

Screen Control Function Keys

This set of function keys allows you to manipulate the SEU display. Figure 10.1 shows the screen control function keys, and a description of the processing each key performs.

Figure 10.1 Screen Control Function Keys

Function Key	Processing Performed
F5=Refresh	Refresh the screen; used for undoing changes and resetting attributes on the screen.
F6=Move the split line	When working in split-screen mode, this function key repositions the split line.
F10=Cursor	Moves the cursor from the typing area to the SEU command line, and vice versa.
F19=Left	Move the leftmost portion of the source member into the typing area. This is used when the source member text cannot be fully contained in the 71-position typing area.
F20=Right	Move the rightmost portion of the source member into the typing area.

System Services Function Keys

This set of function keys provides access to standard AS/400 system features. The system services function keys, and a description their functions, are listed in Figure 10.2.

Figure 10.2 System Services Function Keys

Function Key	Processing Performed
F1=Help	Invokes the AS/400 Help facility.
F3=Exit	Exits from SEU.
F9=Retrieve	Retrieves the last SEU command entered on the SEU command line.
F21=System command	Displays an AS/400 command line for entry of CL commands.
F24=More keys	Displays the additional function keys that are allowed.

SEU Services Function Keys

This set of function keys provides access to special SEU functions such as find/change services and browse/copy services, and lets you change your SEU default values. Figure 10.3 lists the SEU services function keys and their functions.

Figure 10.3 SEU Services Function Keys

Function Key	Processing Performed
F4=Prompt	Invokes the SEU prompt facility.
F11=Previous record	When you are using the SEU prompter, presents a prompt for the previous record in the member.
F13=Change session defaults	Allows you to view and change your SEU session defaults.
F14=Find/Change options	Allows you to find information in the source member, and optionally to change one or all occurrences of the information.
F15=Browse/Copy options	Allows you to browse other source members or printed reports, and optionally to copy information from them into the source member being edited.
F16=Repeat find	Repeats the last Find operation performed using the Find/Change options.
F17=Repeat change	Repeats the last Change operation that was performed using the Find/Change options.

Find/Change Options

Chapter 11

The SEU Find/Change options locate source member lines that match specific search criteria, and optionally allow you to change the contents of the source member lines that were found.

When you are dealing with a large source member, it is helpful to be able to find where in the member a particular set of characters is used. For instance, you may want to locate the position in a CL program where the variable name &error is used. To find lines containing that variable, you can use the Find portion of the Find/Change options. In many other editors, this feature is called the Search function.

You can also use the Find/Change options to locate each occurrence of a set of characters in the member, and to change the characters (Search and Replace function). For example, you may want to find all occurrences of the variable name &program, and change each occurrence of the variable to have a new name, &pgm. You would use the Change portion of the Find/Change options.

You can also use the Find/Change options to locate the records in the member that were modified on a certain date or since a certain date. Finally, you can use the Find/Change options to locate any syntax errors contained in the source member.

When you press F14=Find/Change options from the SEU work display, SEU presents a screen like the one in Figure 11.1.

Figure 11.1 Find/Change Options Display

```
                       Find/Change Options

Type choices, press Enter.

   Find  . . . . . . . . . . . . .     _____
   Change  . . . . . . . . . . . .     _____
   From column number  . . . . . .   1           1-80
   To column number  . . . . . . .   80          1-80 or blank
   Occurrences to process  . . . .   1           1=Next, 2=All
                                                 3=Previous
   Records to search . . . . . . .   1           1=All, 2=Excluded
                                                 3=Non-excluded
   Kind of match . . . . . . . . .   2           1=Same case
                                                 2=Ignore case
   Allow data shift  . . . . . . .   Y           Y=Yes, N=No

   Search for date . . . . . . . .   94/11/19    YY/MM/DD or YYMMDD
      Compare . . . . . . . . . . .   _          1=Less than
                                                 2=Equal to
                                                 3=Greater than


   F3=Exit    F5=Refresh     F12=Cancel    F13=Change session defaults
   F15=Browse/Copy options   F16=Find      F17=Change
```

On this display, you specify the criteria that will be used to find the record(s). Optionally, you can specify what change is to be made to the records that match the Find criteria and how the change is to be processed.

First, in the Find prompt, you specify the character string you want to find. This is called the search string. If you want to find syntax errors in the member, you can enter the special value *ERR. In the Change prompt, you optionally specify a string of characters that will be used as replacement characters.

The From column and To column prompts specify which columns of the source member should be searched for the search string.

The Occurrences to process prompt allows you to specify whether you want to process the next occurrence where the search string is found in the member, the previous occurrence, or all occurrences in the member.

The Records to search prompt indicates whether or not excluded records are to be included in the find operation. Excluded records are those that have been excluded from the display with the X line command. The Kind of match prompt allows you to specify whether or not the search is case sensitive. For instance, if the search string is specified as &program and if the value &PROGRAM is to be considered an occurrence of the string, you must specify that you want to ignore the case of the string.

The Allow data shift prompt determines whether or not the data on a line can be shifted when the search string is not the same length as the change string. For example, if you are looking for the string &program, which is eight characters long, and you are replacing it with the value &pgm, which is only four characters long, you will have four additional blanks after the replacement is performed. The value in Allow data shift determines whether or not you want to shift the remaining characters on the line, thus removing the four new blanks.

The last prompts on the display are Search for date and Compare. These prompts allow you to find the records in a source member that were modified since a certain date. If you specify a value for the Compare prompt, the Search for date operation will be executed. You specify the date to search for in YYMMDD format; you can compare for a value of greater than, less than, or equal to.

When all the prompts are set correctly to perform your Find/Change operation, you press F16 (Find) or F17 (Change) to process your request.

While these prompts provide a necessary function for new SEU users, most experienced AS/400 programmers do not use the Find/Change options display. Instead, they perform the Find/Change operations directly from the SEU work display by typing the SEU Find or Change command on the SEU command line. For more information about this approach, see Chapter 15, which deals with SEU command-line operations.

Browse/Copy Options
and Split-Screen Mode

Chapter 12

The SEU Browse/Copy options allow you to view information from other sources without leaving your current editing session. You can also copy information from other sources into the source member you are currently editing. The Browse/Copy options have two primary purposes: to copy source lines into the member being edited from another member, and to view program compile listings while you are editing the member that was compiled.

To let you view information from another source while you continue editing the current member, SEU provides a split-screen display. Figure 12.1 illustrates the split-screen display used when you are editing member SA0801XXX and viewing (i.e., browsing) member SA0701XXX.

Figure 12.1 Split-Screen Operations

```
 Columns . . . :   1  71              Edit                    CLTEXT/QCLSRC
 SEU==>                                                              SA0801XXX
 FMT **   ...+... 1 ...+... 2 ...+... 3 ...+... 4 ...+... 5 ...+... 6 ...+... 7
0008.00
0009.00              DCL      &text10 *CHAR 10
0010.00              DCL      &char24 *CHAR 24
0011.00              DCL      &dec50  *DEC (5 0)
0012.00              DCL      &dec72  *DEC (7 2)
A 13.00              DCL      &lgl1   *LGL
0014.00
 Columns . . . :   1  71             Browse                   CLTEXT/QCLSRC
 SEU==>                                                              SA0701XXX
0012.00              DCL      &customer   *DEC   (7 0)  VALUE(55345)
0013.00              DCL      &taxrate    *DEC   (5 4)  VALUE(7.1625)
C 14.00              DCL      &errorflag  *LGL
0015.00
0016.00
0017.00              SNDPGMMSG  MSG('I'm done now')
0018.00


 F3=Exit    F5=Refresh    F9=Retrieve    F10=Cursor    F12=Cancel
 F16=Repeat find          F17=Repeat change            F24=More keys
```

In Figure 12.1, you can see that you can copy (the line command C) from the source member you are viewing into the source member being edited (the line command A). This is by far the most heavily used function of the Browse/Copy services: copying source lines from an existing member into a member being edited.

When in split-screen mode, you cannot change the contents of the source member being viewed; you can only change the contents of the member currently being edited. You can, however, copy any lines from the member being viewed into the member being edited.

To access the Browse/Copy options of SEU, press the function key F15=Browse/Copy Options from the SEU work display. SEU then presents the display shown in Figure 12.2.

Figure 12.2 Browse/Copy Options

```
                        Browse/Copy Options

Type choices, press Enter.

   Selection . . . . . . . . . . .    1              1=Member
                                                     2=Spool file
                                                     3=Output queue
   Copy all records  . . . . . . .    N              Y=Yes, N=No
   Browse/copy member  . . . . . .    SAO801XXX      Name, F4 for list
      File  . . . . . . . . . . .  Ⓐ QCLSRC         Name, F4 for list
         Library . . . . . . . . .    CLTEXT         Name, *CURLIB, *LIBL

   Browse/copy spool file  . . . .    SAO801XXX      Name, F4 for list
      Job . . . . . . . . . . . .     SAO801XXX      Name
         User  . . . . . . . . . . Ⓑ STUDENT1       Name, F4 for list
         Job number  . . . . . . .     *LAST         Number, *LAST
      Spool number  . . . . . . . .    *LAST         Number, *LAST, *ONLY

   Display output queue  . . . .  Ⓒ QPRINT          Name, *ALL
      Library . . . . . . . . . . .    *LIBL         Name, *CURLIB, *LIBL


F3=Exit        F4=Prompt       F5=Refresh       F12=Cancel
F13=Change session defaults    F14=Find/Change options
```

The Selection prompt allows you to select whether you want to view (1) a source member, (2) a spooled output file, or (3) an output queue. Depending on your answer to this prompt, certain other prompts on the display will be evaluated. For example, if the Selection prompt value is 1, the prompts shown at (A) are evaluated to determine what member you want to view; the other prompts at (B) and (C) on the display are ignored. If the Selection prompt contains the value 2, SEU evaluates the prompts at (B) to determine what spooled file you want to view; it ignores the prompts at (A) and (C).

If the Selection prompt contains the value 3, the prompts at (C) are evaluated to determine what output queue you want to view, and the prompts at (A) and (B) are ignored.

Several prompts on the display allow you to press the F4=Prompt key to present a list of possible choices. This is handy when you don't know the exact name of a member or a spooled file that you wish to view.

When you select option 1 or 2 from this display, the result will be a split-screen display, as in Figure 12.1. When you select option 3 to display an output queue, no split screen is provided; you simply go to the DSPOUTQ display.

At (A) in Figure 12.2, you are prompted for Copy all records. Here, if you specify the value Y, the copy does not occur immediately, but rather a split-screen display will be presented. When SEU presents this split screen, a CC (block copy) line command will appear in the first and last line of the member you are viewing. You then enter an A (after) or B (before) line command in the member you are editing to tell SEU where to copy the records to.

Saving Your Work

Chapter 13

When you have completed editing a source member, you can press the F3 (Exit) key to exit from the current editing session. When you do this, you are presented with the SEU Exit display as shown in Figure 13.1. Here, you tell SEU what to do with the editing work you have just performed.

Figure 13.1 The SEU Exit Display

```
                               Exit

Type choices, press Enter.

    Change/create member  . . . . . . .    Y           Y=Yes, N=No
       Member  . . . . . . . . . . . .     MYPROGRAM1  Name, F4 for list
       File  . . . . . . . . . . . . .     QCLSRC      Name, F4 for list
          Library . . . . . . . . . . .      DRIEHL    Name
       Text  . . . . . . . . . . . . .     Test Pgm Number 1
       Resequence member . . . . . . . .    Y           Y=Yes, N=No
          Start . . . . . . . . . . . .     0001.00     0000.01-9999.99
          Increment . . . . . . . . . .     01.00       00.01-99.99

    Print member  . . . . . . . . . . .    N           Y=Yes, N=No

    Return to editing . . . . . . . . .    N           Y=Yes, N=No




F3=Exit    F4=Prompt    F5=Refresh    F12=Cancel
```

The first prompt — Change/create member — tells SEU what to do with the member that you just edited. If you want to save the changes you just made, enter a Y in this prompt, and on the next set of prompts specify where you want to save the source member. If you specify the value N, the work performed in your editing session will be lost.

When editing a member with SEU, you are not actually editing the member itself; you are editing a working copy that SEU has temporarily created for you. If you do not save your work by selecting Y for the Create/change member prompt, the actual source member will not be changed to reflect your editing changes.

For the Member, File, and Library prompts, you specify where SEU should store the member. The Text prompt lets you associate some descriptive text with the source member you are saving; if you are not saving the member, the Text prompt is ignored. The Resequence member prompts allow you to tell SEU to assign new sequence numbers to the source member lines. This prompt is only in effect if you are saving the member.

The Print member prompt directs SEU to print the contents of the member to a spooled output file (i.e., a report).

The Return to editing prompt allows you to return to the editing session. If syntax errors have been detected by SEU and not resolved in your editing session, SEU will place the value Y into this prompt; otherwise, the prompt will default to N (Do not return to the editing session).

SEU Session Defaults

Chapter 14

When you use SEU, you can customize certain attributes of the SEU edit session for your own personal preferences. To customize SEU, press F13=Change session defaults from the SEU work display; the screen in Figure 14.1 will appear. Any changes made at this screen will be saved and will be in effect for your current editing session; most will be in effect for subsequent editing sessions as well.

The following discussion explains each attribute available on the screen.

Figure 14.1 Change Session Defaults, Pages 1 and 2

```
                        Change Session Defaults

Type choices, press Enter.

    Amount to roll . . . . . . . . . .   H          H=Half, F=Full
                                                    C=Cursor, D=Data
                                                    1-999
    Uppercase input only . . . . . . .   N          Y=Yes, N=No
    Tabs on  . . . . . . . . . . . . .   Y          Y=Yes, N=No
    Increment of insert record . . . .   0.01       0.01-999.99
    Full screen mode . . . . . . . . .   N          Y=Yes, N=No

    Source type  . . . . . . . . . . .   CLP
    Syntax checking:
      When added/modified  . . . . . .   Y          Y=Yes, N=No
      From sequence number . . . . . .   _____    0000.00-9999.99
      To sequence number . . . . . . .   _____    0000.00-9999.99

    Set records to date  . . . . . . .   __/__/__   YY/MM/DD or YYMMDD
                                                                 More...
```

```
                                                   P=Previous
    Default to uppercase input
      for this source type . . . . . .   N          Y=Yes, N=No

















                                                            Bottom
  F3=Exit      F5=Refresh   F12=Cancel
  F14=Find/Change options   F15=Browse/Copy options
```

Amount to roll

This attribute determines how SEU will process the PageUp/PageDown
keys. F (Full) specifies that the editing screen will roll a full screen when
you press Page Up/Down; H (Half) indicates a half-screen roll. C(CSR)
rolls the screen so that the line where the cursor is currently positioned
will be at the top of the screen when you press Page Down (or at the

bottom of the screen when you press Page Up). D (Data) rolls the screen so that the last line of one screen will be the first line of the next screen. You can also specify an exact number of lines to roll in the range 1-999.

Uppercase input only

This attribute determines whether or not you can enter lowercase characters into the source member. To enable lowercase entry, specify N. To disable lowercase entry, specify Y. The default setting of this attribute is determined by the source type and the SEU session attribute, 'Default to uppercase input only for this source type', which we will discuss in a moment.

Tabs on

This session characteristic is used to determine whether or not you can use TAB stops in the editing session. To enable Tab stops, specify Y; to disable tab stops, specify N. You must use this attribute in conjunction with the TABS line command discussed under SEU line commands.

Increment of insert record

This attribute specifies the increment value that is used when records are inserted during an SEU editing session. That is, if you insert a record into a source member, this attribute will be used to determine the sequence number of that source line, in relationship to the line just before it. The default value is .01, but can be any number in the range .01-999.99.

Full-screen mode

This attribute determines whether or not SEU edit displays will be presented in full-screen mode. Full-screen mode, also known as expert mode, presents more source member lines on a single SEU display, but does not display the F-keys and other useful information. To enable full-screen mode, specify Y; for normal mode, specify N.

Source type

This value decides which syntax checker, prompts, and format lines will be available within the current SEU editing session. The default value depends upon the source member type. It is useful to change this value when you are working on members that include the source statements from various languages, as may be the case with program documentation.

Syntax checking when added/modified

This attribute determines whether syntax checking is to be performed when records are added to the source member or modified during the SEU editing session. To enable syntax checking, specify Y; to disable the checking, type N.

Syntax checking; From and To sequence number

You can use this entry to check the syntax of source lines when they are not being added or modified. Enter the From- and To- sequence numbers as they appear in the source member. Syntax checking for those lines will occur immediately.

Set records to date

This entry sets the changed date of all records in the member to the date you specify.

Resequence member default

This attribute determines the default value for the resequence member prompt on the SEU Exit/Save display. To set the default value to resequence the member, type Y; for no resequencing, specify N. To set the default according to the option setting used for the previous SEU editing session, specify P.

Default to uppercase input only for this source type

This value sets your session defaults when you are editing source members of different types. When you are editing a member of a certain member type, you may access this display and set the value that you want to routinely use for that source type. For instance, if you routinely enter lowercase characters in your CL source members, you will want to set this attribute to N when you are editing a CL or CLP member. If you always want to use uppercase characters for a member type, start an editing session for that member type and then set this attribute to Y.

The SEU Command Line

Chapter 15

Most functions that you can perform from the Find/Change Options display, the Change Session Defaults display, and the Exit display, you also can perform directly from the SEU command line. In addition, there are some SEU functions that you can only enter on the SEU command line. The SEU command line appears at the top of the SEU work display, and it is used to enter the SEU commands and their parameters shown in Figure 15.1. *You cannot enter CL commands into this command line.*

Figure 15.1 Summary of SEU Commands

SEU Command	Command Parameters
BOTTOM (B, BOT)	
CANCEL (CAN)	
CHANGE (C)	find-string (Required)
	change-string (Required)
	direction (Optional)
	excluded-records-option (Optional)
	starting-column ending-column (Optional)
FILE	library-name/file name (Optional)
	member name (Optional)
FIND (F)	character-string (Required)
	direction (Optional)
	excluded-records-option (Optional)
	starting-column ending-column (Optional)
HIDE (H)	character-string (Required)
	starting-column ending-column (Optional)
	directional-option (Optional)
SAVE	library-name/file name (Optional)
	member name (Optional)
SET CAPS	ON/OFF (Required)
SET EXPERT	ON/OFF (Required)
SET MATCH	ON/OFF (Required)

SEU Command	Command Parameters
SET ROLL	HALF/FULL/CSR/DATA/nnn (Required)
SET SHIFT	ON/OFF (Required)
SET TABS	ON/OFF (Required)
TOP (T)	

The commands allowed from the SEU command line are not the same commands that you enter over a sequence number. The following example uses the SEU FIND command. The command, FIND CHGVAR, will find the first occurrence of the character string CHGVAR in the source member and display that line on the current work display. The FIND command used here invokes the same procedure as that used from the Find/Change options display.

```
 Columns . . . :    1  71              Edit              DRIEHL/QCLSRC
 SEU==> FIND CHGVAR                                         SA0801XXX
 FMT **  ...+... 1 ...+... 2 ...+... 3 ...+... 4 ...+... 5 ...+... 6 ...+... 7
        *************** Beginning of data ************************************
0001.00 /*  Program name..... SA0801XXX                              */
0002.00
0003.00          PGM
0004.00
0005.00          DCL      &char10 *CHAR 10
0060.00          DCL      &char24 *CHAR 24
0007.00          DCL      &dec50  *DEC (5 0)
0008.00          DCL      &dec72  *DEC (7 2)
0009.00          DCL      &lgl1   *LGL
0010.00
0011.00
0012.00          CHGVAR   &char10 'My Library'
```

The next example shows how you can enter the SEU CHANGE command on the SEU command line.

```
 Columns . . . :    1  71              Edit              DRIEHL/QCLSRC
 SEU==> CHANGE &char10 &text10 ALL                          SA0801XXX
 FMT **  ...+... 1 ...+... 2 ...+... 3 ...+... 4 ...+... 5 ...+... 6 ...+... 7
        *************** Beginning of data ************************************
0001.00 /*  Program name..... SA0801XXX                              */
0002.00
0003.00          PGM
0004.00
0005.00          DCL      &char10 *CHAR 10
0006.00          DCL      &char24 *CHAR 24
0007.00          DCL      &dec50  *DEC (5 0)
0008.00          DCL      &dec72  *DEC (7 2)
0009.00          DCL      &lgl1   *LGL
0010.00
0011.00
0012.00          CHGVAR   &char10 'My Library'
```

The result of executing the previous CHANGE command would appear as follows:

```
 Columns . . . :    1  71              Edit                    DRIEHL/QCLSRC
 SEU==>                                                              SA0801XXX
 FMT **  ...+... 1 ...+... 2 ...+... 3 ...+... 4 ...+... 5 ...+... 6 ...+... 7
        *************** Beginning of data ********************************
 0001.00 /*  Program name..... SA0801XXX                                  */
 0002.00
 0003.00          PGM
 0004.00
 CHANGED          DCL       &text10 *CHAR 10
 0006.00          DCL       &char24 *CHAR 24
 0007.00          DCL       &dec50  *DEC (5 0)
 0008.00          DCL       &dec72  *DEC (7 2)
 0009.00          DCL       &lgl1   *LGL
 0010.00
 0011.00
 CHANGED          CHGVAR    &text10 'My Library'




 F13=Change session defaults    F14=Find/Change options
 F15=Browse/Copy options        F24=More keys
 String &char10 changed 2 times.
```

HIDE Command

You can use the Hide (H) command to temporarily remove certain records from the SEU display. It is similar to the exclude (X) line command, but is more powerful. For instance, using the Hide command, you can exclude all records containing a certain character string in certain columns. To display the hidden records, simply press F5 (Refresh).

Required Parameters	**Description**
character-string	Any string of characters and should be enclosed in apostrophes.
Optional Parameters	
starting-column ending-column	This parameter allows you to specify the starting and ending column positions within each record that must contain the character string for the record to be hidden. If this parameter is not specified, the default is to search all columns.

Optional Parameters	Description
directional-option	This parameter allows you to specify the direction of the hide operation. The allowable values are TOP or T, BOTTOM or B, and ALL or A. If no value is specified, the default value is ALL.

Examples:

HIDE 'I' 6	This command will hide all records containing an 'I' in column 6. This could be used to hide all RPG I-Specs.
HIDE '*' 7 TOP	This command will hide the records containing an asterisk in column 7 that are located between the cursor position and the first record of the member. This would hide all COBOL, RPG, and DDS comments on previous screens.
H 'PIC(' ALL	This command will hide all the records containing the characters PIC(in the source member. This could be useful for hiding all COBOL data items that contain the COBOL PICTURE clause.

FIND Command

The FIND (F) command processes the SEU FIND options without the need to go to the FIND/CHANGE Options display.

Parameters	Description
character-string	Any string of characters and should be enclosed in apostrophes. You can specify the value *ERR to locate syntax errors, or the value * to specify that you want to use the same character string that was specified the last time you used the Find or Change command

Optional Parameters	
direction	Specifies which occurrences of the string to find. The allowable values are NEXT or N, PREV or P, FIRST or F, LAST or L, and ALL or A. If not specified, the default is NEXT or N.
excluded-records-option	Specifies whether or not excluded records are to be

Optional Parameters	Description
	searched for the string. The allowable values are X and NX. If X is specified, excluded records will be searched for the string; if NX is specified, only non-excluded records are searched for the string. The default is to search all records.
starting-column ending-column	This optional parameter specifies a starting and ending column within the member that is to be searched for the character string. The default is to search all column positions.

Examples:

F *ERR	This command will locate the next syntax error.
F 'STREET' ALL	This command will find all occurrences of the string STREET.
F 'DAVE' P NX	This command will find the previous occurrence of the string DAVE in any non-excluded records.

CHANGE Command

You use the CHANGE (C) command to change occurrences of a character string to another character string.

Required Parameters	Description
find-string change-string	Any character string that you want to change to a new value. The change-string is the string that is to replace found occurrences of the find-string. Both the find-string and the change-string should be enclosed in apostrophes, and they must be separated by a blank.

Optional Parameters

direction

excluded-records-option

starting-column ending-column

All the optional parameters have the same allowable values and defaults as the FIND command; refer to the FIND command for more information on these.

Examples:

C 'STATE' 'LOCAL'	This command will change the next occurrence of STATE to the value LOCAL.
C 'STATE' 'LOCAL' A 20 60	This command will change all occurrences of the string STATE to the value LOCAL when the string STATE is found in columns 20 through 60.

SET MATCH Command

You use this command in conjunction with the FIND and CHANGE commands. The SET MATCH command determines whether or not the FIND and CHANGE commands will be case sensitive. To ignore case, use the command SET MATCH OFF. To consider case, use the command SET MATCH ON. The default setting if the SET MATCH command is not used is SET MATCH OFF.

SET SHIFT Command

This command functions with the FIND and CHANGE commands. SET SHIFT determines whether or not the CHANGE command will adjust data left or right within the source line when the find-string and change-string are of different lengths. To cause data to be shifted, use the command SET SHIFT ON. To ensure data is not shifted, use the command SET SHIFT OFF. The default setting for the SHIFT attribute is determined by the source type of the member. For instance, for RPG, the default is SET SHIFT OFF, so that data is not shifted into the wrong columns.

Do not confuse SET SHIFT with SET CAPS, described next.

SET CAPS Command

You use this command to specify whether or not you want to allow lowercase characters in the source member. To enable lowercase entry, use the command SET CAPS OFF. To disable lowercase entry, use SET CAPS ON. The default setting of this attribute is determined by the source type and your SEU session defaults.

SET TABS Command

This command specifies whether or not TAB stops can be used in the editing session. To enable Tab stops, use the command SET TABS ON. To disable tab stops, use SET TABS OFF. You must use this command in conjunction with the TABS line command discussed under SEU line commands.

SET EXPERT Command

This command specifies whether or not SEU edit displays will be presented in full-screen mode. Full-screen mode, also known as expert mode, presents more source member lines on a single SEU display, but does not display the F-keys and other useful information. To enable expert mode, use the command SET EXPERT ON. To disable expert mode, use SET EXPERT OFF. The default value is determined by your SEU session defaults.

SET ROLL Command

You use the command SET ROLL to set the screen paging (Amount to roll) attribute of the editing session. The command can be entered as SET ROLL HALF, SET ROLL FULL, SET ROLL CSR, SET ROLL DATA, or SET ROLL nnn, where *nnn* is the number of lines to roll. SET ROLL FULL specifies that the editing screen will roll a full screen when you press Page Up/Down. SET ROLL HALF specifies a half-screen roll. SET ROLL CSR rolls the screen so that the line where the cursor is currently positioned will be at the top of the screen when you press Page Down (or at the bottom of the screen when you press Page Up). SET ROLL DATA rolls the screen so that the last line of one screen will be the first line of the next screen.

TOP/BOTTOM Commands

You use the SEU command TOP to position the SEU display to the first line of the source member. You can alternately enter the TOP command simply as T.

You use the SEU command BOTTOM to position the SEU display to show the last line of the source member. You can alternately enter the BOTTOM command simply as BOT or B.

SAVE/FILE Commands

You use the SAVE command to save the changes you have made to the current source member. The SAVE command performs the same function as saving your work from the SEU Exit display, but it does not end the editing session.

To save the member, simply type the SAVE command on the SEU command line. If you want to save the current source member to a different source member, you can specify the SAVE command followed by a library-name/file-name member-name. If you are saving the member to a different member of the same source file, you can simply use the SAVE command followed by the member-name.

The FILE command is similar to the SAVE command except the FILE command ends the current editing session. To end the current editing session and save your work, you would simply enter the FILE command; SEU would bypass its Exit display. As with the SAVE command, you can use the FILE command to save your work in a different member, either in the same source file or a different source file.

CANCEL Command

You use the CANCEL command to exit from SEU; this command also tells SEU not to save your work. You also can use the CANCEL command on the bottom portion of a split-screen display to remove the split screen. You can alternately enter the CANCEL command as CAN.

Section 3

Screen Design Aid (SDA)

Introduction to Display Files and SDA

Chapter 16

On the AS/400 a special type of file, called a *display file*, is used by interactive programs to send formatted screens of data to a workstation, and then to receive input from the workstation user. You can think of the display file as the medium through which your program communicates with the user. For example, your program, using a display file, can send a screen asking the user to enter a customer number and then present a list of orders on file for that customer.

Just as AS/400 programs are created from source code, such as RPG or COBOL, display files are created from AS/400 Data Description Specification (DDS) source code. The DDS language is a terse columnar language that can be difficult to code and understand, especially where you are defining complex display files. While it is possible to create complex display files by manually entering the DDS source code, most programmers prefer to use Screen Design Aid (SDA).

SDA is a tool designed to eliminate the tedious task of entering DDS source code for display files by providing an easy-to-use, interactive environment for designing, creating, and testing your display file screens. When you have designed a screen using SDA, SDA creates the DDS source code for you. You then use that source code to create the display file.

You can also use SDA to create standard AS/400 menus. In most cases, the menus you create using SDA are indistinguishable from the AS/400 menus IBM supplies as part of the operating system. Like SEU and PDM, SDA is part of the IBM licensed program product called Application Development Toolset/400.

Accessing Screen Design Aid

There are two main methods of beginning a Screen Design Aid session. First, when creating a new display file, you typically will use the Start Screen Design Aid (STRSDA) command. When you enter the STRSDA command, the SDA main menu (as shown in Figure 16.1) is presented. From this screen, select option 1 when you want to design display screens, option 2 when you want to create AS/400 style menus, and option 3 when you want to test a display file.

Figure 16.1 The SDA Main Menu

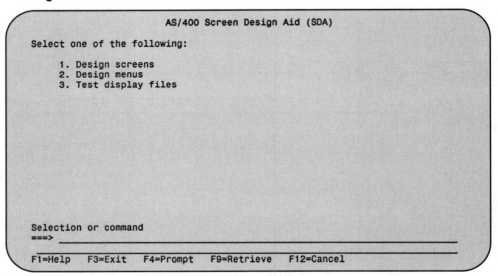

Second, if you are modifying a display file that already exists, you will most likely want to use option 17 from the PDM Work with Members display.

Figure 16.2 shows how you can start SDA by using option 17 from within PDM.

Figure 16.2 Accessing SDA Using PDM Option 17

```
                         Work with Members Using PDM

 File  . . . . . .     QDDSSRC__
   Library . . . .     DRIEHL               Position to  . . . . . _____

 Type options, press Enter.
   14=Compile           15=Create module      16=Run procedure
   17=Change using SDA  19=Change using RLU   25=Find string ...

 Opt  Member     Type      Text
  17  MYDSPF     DSPF      My Display file_____
  __  MYDSPF2    DSPF      My Display file_2_____
  __  MYDSPF3    DSPF      My Display file_3_____
  __  MYDSPF4    DSPF      My Display file_4_____
  __  MYDSPF5    DSPF      My Display file_5_____
  __  MYDSPF6    DSPF      My Display file_6_____

                                                              Bottom
 Parameters or command
 ===>  _____

 F3=Exit          F4=Prompt          F5=Refresh         F6=Create
 F9=Retrieve       F10=Command entry  F23=More options   F24=More keys
```

Working with Display Records

Chapter 17

When you start SDA, the first screen you are presented with is the Work with Display Records screen. This is the main SDA display for working with display file record formats. Using the options listed, you can add a new record format to the display file, copy one format to another, delete a format, and rename a format. You can also edit the comments for a display record and select record-level keywords for a record. Using option 12, you can design the actual image of the record format. When designing the image of the record format, you specify what fields and constants will be displayed on the screen, as well as how the data will be displayed.

In Figure 17.1, we use option 1 to add a record format to the display file. The record format name is specified as SCREEN1.

Figure 17.1 The Work with Display Records Screen

```
                      Work with Display Records

  File  . . . . . . :   QDDSSRC          Member . . . . . . :   MYDSPF
    Library . . . . :     DRIEHL         Source type  . . . :   DSPF

  Type options, press Enter.
    1=Add                2=Edit comments        3=Copy        4=Delete
    7=Rename             8=Select keywords     12=Design image

  Opt  Order    Record      Type     Related Subfile   Date       DDS Error
   1            SCREEN1

    (No records in file)




                                                                    Bottom
  F3=Exit                  F12=Cancel        F14=File-level keywords
  F15=File-level comments  F17=Subset        F24=More keys
```

Understanding Record Formats

A display file can contain one or more record formats. For example, you can design a screen Heading record format that displays the time and date, and the name of the application. You could also have a Trailer record format, which could contain function key information for the screen. You could then design a Body record format that contains the major data to be displayed on the screen.

As an example of the concept of multiple-record formats, examine the IBM-supplied screen Work with Members Using PDM shown below in Figure 17.2. In this screen, we can consider the area marked H the header format, B the main body format, and T the trailer format. Having the screen broken up into the individual formats makes it easy to change the appearance of one part of the screen without rewriting the screen's entire contents. For example, when you press F24 from the PDM display, only the function keys in the trailer format of the screen need to be changed, not the entire display. Defining multiple-record formats can give your program more flexibility and control than if the entire screen was made up of only one record format.

Figure 17.2 Example of Multiple-Record Formats Combining To Create a Full Display Screen

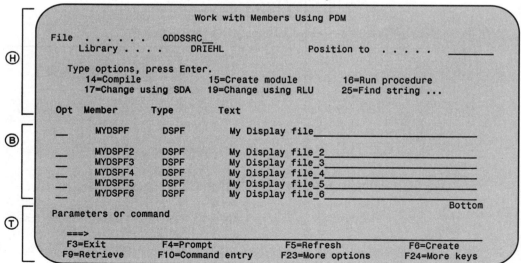

Adding a New Record Format

When you are adding the record format SCREEN1 as shown in Figure 17.1, SDA needs to know what type of record format you are adding. The Add New Record screen in Figure 17.3 demonstrates how you can identify the type of record format. The default value is RECORD, which is simply a standard display file record type. Other options include USRDFN, SFL, SFLMSG, WINDOW, WDWSFL, PULDWN, and PDNSFL. The USRDFN type is a user-defined record format. You use the SFL type for adding a subfile record format. SFLMSG specifies a message subfile format, Window specifies a window format. WDWSFL specifies a window containing a subfile. PULDWN specifies a pull-down menu format, and PDNSFL specifies a pull-down subfile format.

Figure 17.3 Adding a New Record Format

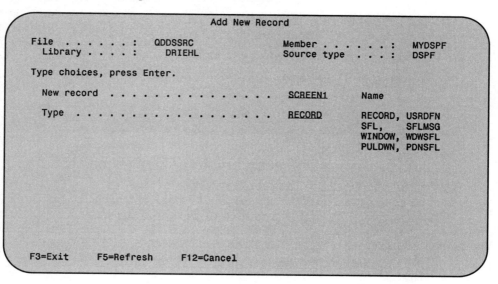

Specifying Record-Level Keywords

Keywords are special DDS reserved words that effect the display, either in the way it appears or the way in which it is processed by your program or internally by the system. The various DDS keywords must be specified at one of three levels: The file level, the record level, or the field level. For example, one of the DDS keywords is DSPATR. When you want a particular field or constant to be displayed with a high-intensity display attribute, you specify DSPATR(HI) at the field level. While the DSPATR keyword can be used at the field level, it may not be specified at the record level or at the file level. Display attributes for fields are assigned by DDS keywords occurring only at the field level.

SDA assists you in entering the DDS keywords at the proper level by providing separate functions for entering keywords for each level. For example, file level keywords can be entered only from the Work with Display Records screen shown in Figure 17.4 after pressing the F14 key. record-level keywords are only accessible by entering option 8 next to the record format. Field-level keywords can be entered only from the SDA Work Display, or the Work with Fields display, which are discussed later.

Figure 17.4 The Work with Display Records Screen

```
                          Work with Display Records

 File  . . . . . . :    QDDSSRC            Member . . . . . . :   MYDSPF
   Library . . . . :    DRIEHL             Source type  . . . :   DSPF

 Type options, press Enter.
   1=Add               2=Edit comments        3=Copy        4=Delete
   7=Rename            8=Select keywords      12=Design image

 Opt  Order   Record        Type      Related Subfile   Date        DDS Error
 8_    10     SCREEN1       RECORD                       09/26/94
 _     20     FKEYS         RECORD                       09/26/94




                                                            Bottom
 F3=Exit                    F12=Cancel       F14=File-level keywords
 F15=File-level comments    F17=Subset       F24=More keys
```

Figure 17.4 shows an example of placing option 8 next to the record format SCREEN1. The resulting display in shown in Figure 17.5. This is the Select Record Keywords screen. SDA breaks the Record-Level keywords down into several categories, as shown in Figure 17.5. Here you see that you can select to access and manipulate General keywords, Indicator keywords, and so on. To specify that you want to work with the keywords that fall into a particular category, place the letter Y next to the category as shown in the figure. For instance, if you want to enter record-level keywords that pertain to Application Help displays, you simply place the letter Y next to that category. In the figure, we select to enter General keywords for the SCREEN1 record format.

Figure 17.5 Selecting Record-Level Keywords

```
                          Select Record Keywords

     Record . . . :    SCREEN1

     Type choices, press Enter.

                                           Y=Yes
         General keywords  . . . . . . . . Y
         Indicator keywords  . . . . . . . _
         Application help  . . . . . . . . _
         Help keywords . . . . . . . . . . _
         Output keywords . . . . . . . . . _
         Input keywords  . . . . . . . . . _
         Overlay keywords  . . . . . . . . _

         Print keywords  . . . . . . . . . _
         ALTNAME keyword . . . . . . . . . _

         TEXT keyword  . . . . . . . . . . _____




     F3=Exit    F12=Cancel
```

The resulting screen in Figure 17.6 shows the screen on which general keywords may be entered for the SCREEN1 record format. Here you simply select which DDS keywords should appear at the record level, and press Enter.

As shown in the display in Figure 17.6, a description of the keyword is presented, followed by the DDS keyword name. Input fields are then provided to specify whether or not you want to use the keyword. For some fields a value or field name can be entered, as can be seen in the case of the RTNCSRLOC keyword.

In this example, we select the keyword CHGINPDFT by placing a Y next to the keyword. The CHGINPDFT keyword will now be in effect for the SCREEN1 record format.

Our attempt here is not to explain all of the DDS keywords, but rather to explain the workings of SDA. However, we will discuss some of the keywords for illustrative purposes in the following chapters.

Figure 17.6 Selecting General Keywords

```
                       Select General Keywords

   Record . . . :   SCREEN1

   Type choices, press Enter.
                                                    Keyword    Y=Yes
      If this record is not on display, write it
         to the display before issuing read . . . . . . .  INZRCD      _
      Keep record on display
         when closing the file  . . . . . . . . . . . .   KEEP        _
      Assume record is on display
         when file is opened  . . . . . . . . . . . . .   ASSUME      _
      Allow rolling of lines . . . . . . . . . . . . .    ALWROL
      Retain CLEAR HELP HOME and ROLL keys . . . . . . .  RETKEY      _
      Retain command function (CFnn and CAnn) keys . . .  RETCMDKEY
      Change input defaults  . . . . . . . . . . . . .    CHGINPDFT   Y
         Select parameters  . . . . . . . . . . . . . .
      Return cursor location . . . . . . . . . . . . .    RTNCSRLOC   _
         Cursor-record  . . . . . . . . . . . . . . . . .             _____  Name
         Cursor-field . . . . . . . . . . . . . . . . . .             _____  Name
         Cursor-position  . . . . . . . . . . . . . . . .             _____  Name


   F3=Exit   F12=Cancel
```

While we selected only to enter General Keywords, we could have entered keywords for any category appearing on the Select Record Keywords display. By placing a Y next to each category of keyword to be entered, SDA presents the keyword entry display for each category.

Specifying File-Level Keywords

Chapter 18

You have now seen how record-level keywords can be entered for a
selected record format. Now we need to look at how file-level keywords
can be entered. To enter file-level keywords, you press the F14 key from
the Work with Display Records screen shown in Figure 17.4. The
resulting Select File Keywords screen is shown here in Figure 18.1. As
in the case of record-level keywords, you select file-level keywords by
category.

Figure 18.1 Selecting File-Level Keywords

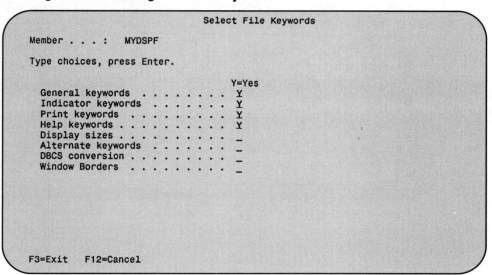

```
                              Select File Keywords

     Member . . . :    MYDSPF

     Type choices, press Enter.

                                          Y=Yes
         General keywords . . . . . . . .   Y
         Indicator keywords . . . . . . .   Y
         Print keywords . . . . . . . . .   Y
         Help keywords . . . . . . . . . .  Y
         Display sizes . . . . . . . . . .  _
         Alternate keywords . . . . . . .   _
         DBCS conversion . . . . . . . . .  _
         Window Borders . . . . . . . . .   _




     F3=Exit    F12=Cancel
```

Four categories of file-level keywords have been selected in the figure. When you press the Enter key, SDA will present a selection screen for each of these categories.

The first category of file-level keywords selected is General Keywords. As shown in the display in Figure 18.2, a description of the keyword is presented, followed by the DDS keyword name. Input fields are then provided to specify whether or not you want to use the keyword, and if so, what conditioning indicators (if any) must be true before the keyword is activated. As you can see, some keywords allow conditioning indicators; others, such as the INDARA and ERRSFL keyword, do not. By placing the letter Y next to a keyword, you cause the keyword to be included in the DDS for the display file. Other keywords, such as the REF keyword shown in the figure, have no area in which to specify Y, and no area for conditioning indicators. Instead, in the case of the REF keyword, SDA prompts you for the name of the file that will be used as the reference file. If a file name is not supplied, the REF keyword will not appear within the DDS. In this example, we specify that a reference file named CUSTFILE will be used.

Figure 18.2 Selecting General Keywords

```
                        Select General Keywords

 Member . . . :    MYDSPF

 Type choices, press Enter.                    Keyword    Y=Yes   Indicators/+
   Invite devices for later read . . . . . .   INVITE      _      __ __ __
   Allow graphics  . . . . . . . . . . . .     ALWGPH      _      __ __ __
   Sound alarm on messages . . . . . . . .     MSGALARM    _      __ __ __
   Separate indicators area  . . . . . . .     INDARA      _
   Manage display in S/36 mode . . . . . .     USRDSPMGT   _
   Allow blanks  . . . . . . . . . . . .       CHECK(AB)   _
   Move cursor right-left, top-bottom  . . .    CHECK(RLTB) _
   Move cursor right to left . . . . . . .      CHECK(RL)   _
   Right to left processing  . . . . . . .      DSPRL       _
   Change input defaults . . . . . . . . .      CHGINPDFT   _
     Select parameters . . . . . . . . . .
   Write error messages to subfile . . . .      ERRSFL      Y
   Reference database file . . . . . . . .      REF         CUSTFILE     Name
     Library . . . . . . . . . . . . . .                    *LIBL        Name
     Record  . . . . . . . . . . . . . .                    CUSTREC      Name
   Record to pass unformatted data . . . . .    PASSRCD     _____      Name


 F3=Exit    F12=Cancel
```

The next category of file-level keywords selected is Indicator Keywords. Here, you specify what indicator-type keywords will appear at the file level. In Figure 18.3, the CA03 keyword is specified with no conditioning indicators. The response indicator sent back to the program when a user presses the F3 key will be indicator 03. Next, the HELP keyword is included to enable the Help key whenever any record format within the display file is written to the screen. Again, there are no conditioning indicators specified, and in this case, no response indicator. When a user of this display file presses the Help key, control will not return to the application program. Instead, the Help key will be handled by the system. If text is entered next to the keywords, it appears within a program compile listing as comments.

Figure 18.3 Selecting Indicator Keywords

```
                         Define Indicator Keywords

    Member . . . :   MYDSPF

    Type keywords and parameters, press Enter.
      Conditioned keywords:       CFnn CAnn CLEAR PAGEDOWN/ROLLUP PAGEUP/ROLLDOWN
                                  HOME HELP HLPRTN
      Unconditioned keywords:     INDTXT VLDCMDKEY

    Keyword   Indicators/+   Resp   Text
    CA03      __ __ __ _      03    F3=Exit_____
    HELP      __ __ __ - __         _____
    _____    __ __ __ - __         _____
    _____    __ __ __ - __         _____
    _____    __ __ __ - __         _____
    _____    __ __ __ - __         _____
    _____    __ __ __ - __         _____
    _____    __ __ __ - __         _____

                                                              Bottom

    F3=Exit    F12=Cancel
```

The file-level Print keywords in Figure 18.4 allow you to specify whether or not the Print key will be enabled when the display file is used by your program. You can also specify how the Print key will be handled.

Figure 18.4 Selecting Print Keywords

```
                          Define Print Keywords

  Member . . . :   MYDSPF

  Type choices, press Enter.
                                        Keyword
     Enable keyword . . . . . . . . .   PRINT    Y           Y=Yes
        Indicators . . . . . . . . . .           __ __ __

     Program handles print:
        Response indicator . . . . . .           _           01-99
        Text . . . . . . . . . . . . .           _____

     System handles print:
        Print file . . . . . . . . . .           _____     Name, *PGM
           Library  . . . . . . . . . .           _____     Name,
                                                                *LIBL, *CURLIB
     Leave print file open until
        display file is closed . . . .  OPENPRT   _           Y=Yes


  F3=Exit    F12=Cancel
```

The file-level Help keywords display shown in Figure 18.5 allows you to specify whether or not a Help record or Help document will be used for the display file. Alternately, you may press F9 to specify the name of a Help panel group.

Figure 18.5 Selecting Help Keywords

```
                          Select Help Keywords
Member . . . . :   MYDSPF

Type choices, press Enter.
                                  Keyword
   Help text in record . . . .    HLPRCD   _              Y=Yes
   -- OR --
   Help text in document . . .    HLPDOC   _              Y=Yes
      Indicators . . . . . . . .             __  __  __
      Record or document . . . .                          Name
      File . . . . . . . . . . .                          Name
         Library  . . . . . . . .                         Name, *LIBL, *CURLIB
      HLPDOC label . . . . . . .                          Name
      HLPDOC folder  . . . . . .
                                             _____




F3=Exit    F9=Select HLPPNLGRP keyword
F12=Cancel
```

When you are dealing with the file-level keywords, four other categories of keywords may be specified. These are Display size keywords, Alternate keywords, DBCS conversion keywords, and Window border keywords. To specify these keywords, simply enter a Y next to the corresponding category on the Select File Keywords display shown in Figure 18.1.

The SDA Work Display

Chapter 19

To design the actual image of a display record, you place option 12 next to the record format name on the Work with Display Records screen, as shown in Figure 19.1.

Figure 19.1 Select the Design Image Option

```
                          Work with Display Records
   File  . . . . . . :     QDDSSRC              Member . . . . . . :    MYDSPF
      Library . . . . :     DRIEHL              Source type  . . . :    DSPF

   Type options, press Enter.
     1=Add                 2=Edit comments       3=Copy        4=Delete
     7=Rename              8=Select keywords    12=Design image

   Opt   Order   Record          Type      Related Subfile   Date       DDS Error

    12     10    SCREEN1         RECORD                       09/26/94
    __     20    FKEYS           RECORD                       09/26/94




                                                                     Bottom
   F3=Exit                    F12=Cancel       F14=File-level keywords
   F15=File-level comments    F17=Subset       F24=More keys
```

When you select the Design image option for a new display record, you are presented with the SDA Work Display, which is simply a blank screen on which you will design the screen. Figure 19.2 shows the display as it is originally presented. As you can see, it can be a somewhat bewildering display for new SDA users. Pressing the F1 or Help key from the display provides a very good description of the functions and features that you can use within the SDA Work Display.

Figure 19.2 The Work Display for the New Record Format SCREEN1

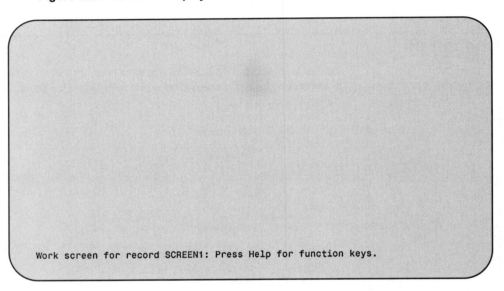

```
Work screen for record SCREEN1: Press Help for function keys.
```

Adding Constants on the Work Display

When designing screens, you will normally start by defining headings and other descriptive text as screen constants. In Figure 19.3 you can see that the company name (Acme Accounting Service) is included, as well as several other constants (e.g., Customer Number: and Name:). When constants are entered on the work display, they should be enclosed in apostrophes. For instance, if the constant 'Acme Accounting Service' is not enclosed in apostrophes, SDA will treat it as three separate constants: 'Acme', 'Accounting' and 'Service'. The apostrophes are needed whenever blanks appear within a constant. When you press the Enter key, the constant will be created and the apostrophes will be removed. In addition to the normal constants that are shown enclosed in apostrophes, there are four special constants included on the display. These are *DATE, *TIME, *SYSNAME, and *USER. These special constants are entered without apostrophes and are used to tell SDA to include the DDS keywords DATE, TIME, SYSNAME, and USER within the display record, at the position specified. Whenever your application program sends this record format to a workstation screen, these special constants will be replaced by the current date, time, system name, and workstation user ID.

Figure 19.3 Adding Constants to the Work Display

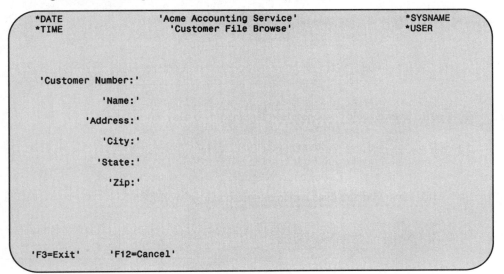

When you press the Enter key, the resulting display in Figure 19.4 shows the constants in place on the screen. The *TIME, *DATE, *SYSNAME, and *USER constants show the format in which they will be displayed when the display record is used within your application.

Figure 19.4 The Resulting Display after Constants Are Added

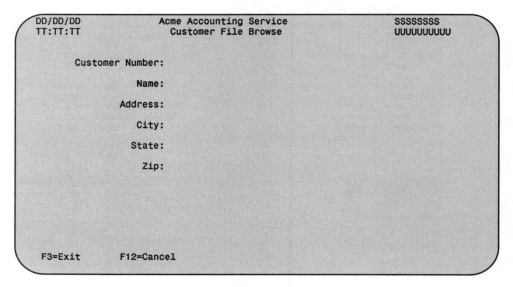

Adding Data Fields

In addition to constants, most interactive applications require that screens contain changeable data fields. These fields can be filled in either by the workstation user, or by your application program. Figure 19.5 shows how you can add data fields to the display.

Figure 19.5 Adding Data Fields

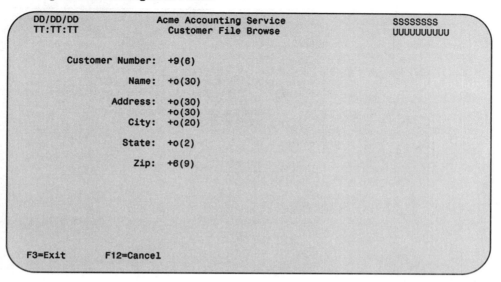

```
DD/DD/DD                    Acme Accounting Service          SSSSSSSS
TT:TT:TT                    Customer File Browse             UUUUUUUUUU


      Customer Number:   +9(6)

               Name:   +o(30)

            Address:   +o(30)
                       +o(30)
               City:   +o(20)

              State:   +o(2)

                Zip:   +6(9)




   F3=Exit        F12=Cancel
```

The + sign is used to tell SDA that you are adding a data field. After the + sign you use certain characters to inform SDA about the data type and length of the field. You also specify whether the field will be used by the workstation operator to input data, whether the field will be output only, or whether both input and output are allowed for the field. For instance, in Figure 19.5 the constant 'Customer Number:' is followed by the SDA command +9(6). The character 9 identifies the field type, and the (6) specifies the length of the data field. The command tells SDA to add a field at that position, and that the field will be a 6-digit numeric field that can be used for both user input and program output.

After the 'Name:' constant, the command +o(30) is specified. The o character specifies the field type, and the (30) specifies the length of the field. This tells SDA to add a 30-byte character field that will be used for output purposes only (i.e., the user will not be able to enter data into this field).

After you press the Enter key on the previous display, SDA executes the commands that have been entered. Figure 19.6 shows the resulting display. You will notice that all the commands have been replaced with data fields. You can see that the command +9(6) has been transformed into a field consisting of the characters 999999-. SDA positions the new field one position to the right of where the + sign was entered. The second data field has been converted into a string of 30 O characters (the letter O, not zero).

Figure 19.6 Resulting Display with Data Fields Added

```
DD/DD/DD                 Acme Accounting Service              SSSSSSSS
TT:TT:TT                   Customer File Browse               UUUUUUUUUU


       Customer Number:    999999-

                  Name:    OOOOOOOOOOOOOOOOOOOOOOOOOOOOOOO

               Address:    OOOOOOOOOOOOOOOOOOOOOOOOOOOOOOO
                           OOOOOOOOOOOOOOOOOOOOOOOOOOOOOOO
                  City:    OOOOOOOOOOOOOOOOOOOO

                 State:    OO

                   Zip:    666666666




   F3=Exit       F12=Cancel
```

As you have seen, when you are adding fields to the work display, the + sign is followed by the designation of the field to be added. Figure 19.7 lists the field types that can be added and the SDA character used to represent the data type.

Figure 19.7 Field Types and Their SDA Representation

Data Type and Usage	SDA Character
Character Input only field	I or i
Character Output only field	O or o (The letter O, not zero)
Character both Input/Output field	B or b
Numeric Input only field	3
Numeric Output only field	6
Numeric Both Input/Output field	9
Message constant field	M

Let's look at a few examples of commands that define data fields (Figure 19.8). Notice in these examples that parentheses can be used; however, they are not required. You can also see how decimal positions can be defined within numeric fields.

Figure 19.8 Examples of Adding Data Fields

Command	Field
+B(2)	A 2-position character field, both input- and output-capable
+BB	Another way to define a +B(2) field. The parentheses are not required.
+6(4)	A 4-position numeric field, output only
+6666	Another way to define a +6(4) field. The parentheses are not required.
+OOOOOO	A 6-position character field, output only
+9(5,2)	A 7-position numeric field with two digits to the right of the decimal point. The field can be used for both input and output operations.

Once you add a field to the work display, you might determine that you need to change the field's data type or I/O usage. When this occurs, you can simply overtype the first position of the field with the new data type or usage. For example, if a field is displayed on the work display as OOOOO and you determine that the field should be an input-only field, simply overtype the first O with the letter I, and press Enter. The field will then display IIIII; an input-only field.

When new fields are added to the display, SDA assigns the field name. The first field defined will be assigned the name FLD001. Other field names will be assigned sequentially in the order in which they were added (i.e., FLD002, FLD003, and so on). These assigned names are certainly not very intuitive; you will most surely want to change them. To change the name or length of a field you have added to the screen, you can place a ? (question mark) character in the *attribute position* of the field. The attribute position for a field is always the first character before the field's starting position. If a field starts in position 6 of a line, the attribute position would be position 5 of the same line. Figure 19.9 shows an example of placing a ? in the attribute position of the data field that will be used to present the customer number.

Figure 19.9 The Attribute Position

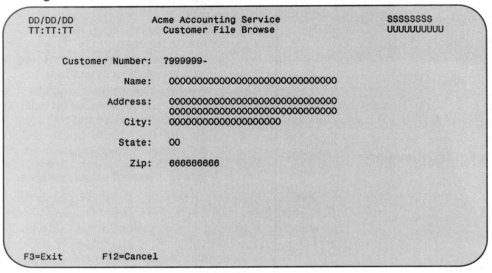

```
DD/DD/DD                 Acme Accounting Service            SSSSSSSS
TT:TT:TT                   Customer File Browse             UUUUUUUUUU


       Customer Number:   ?999999-

                  Name:   OOOOOOOOOOOOOOOOOOOOOOOOOOOOOOO

               Address:   OOOOOOOOOOOOOOOOOOOOOOOOOOOOOOO
                          OOOOOOOOOOOOOOOOOOOOOOOOOOOOOOO
                  City:   OOOOOOOOOOOOOOOOOOOO

                 State:   OO

                   Zip:   666666666




 F3=Exit      F12=Cancel
```

After you place the ? in the attribute position of the data field and press the Enter key, the following display is shown (Figure 19.10).

Figure 19.10 Changing the Name of a Data Field

```
DD/DD/DD                 Acme Accounting Service            SSSSSSSS
TT:TT:TT                   Customer File Browse             UUUUUUUUUU


       Customer Number:   999999-

                  Name:   OOOOOOOOOOOOOOOOOOOOOOOOOOOOOOO

               Address:   OOOOOOOOOOOOOOOOOOOOOOOOOOOOOOO
                          OOOOOOOOOOOOOOOOOOOOOOOOOOOOOOO
                  City:   OOOOOOOOOOOOOOOOOOOO

                 State:   OO

                   Zip:   666666666




 F3=Exit      F12=Cancel
 FLD001     Length: 00006 TEXT: _____
```

At the bottom of the display, the field name, length, and text are displayed. The field name shown here is FLD001. To change the field name, simply overtype the characters FLD001 with the name you want to assign to the field — for example, CUSTNO — and press the Enter key. The field's name is changed to CUSTNO.

For ease of use, the F18 key will move the cursor between the attribute positions of the fields on the screen. Using F18 is similar to using a TAB function. The F19 key provides the back-TAB function between field attribute positions.

Manipulating Fields and Constants on the Work Display

You have already seen that the SDA command + is used to add a new data field to the display, and that the command ? can be used to change the name of a field. Several other commands can be used on the SDA Work Display. Figure 19.11 provides a summary of those commands. Most of these commands must be entered in the attribute position of the field or constant that is to be affected.

Figure 19.11 Summary of SDA Field Manipulation Commands

Command	Function
+	Add a data field
d or D	Delete a field
ac	Center the field within the current line
-	Copy or Move field to target
=	Target position of Move
==	Target position of Copy
*	Go to the Field Level Keywords display for this field
<	Move the field left one position
<<<	Move the field left three positions. (The number of <s determines how many positions to move to the left.)
>	Move the field one position to the right. Place the > character in the first position following the field to be moved.
>>>	Move the field right three positions. (The number of >s determines how many positions to move to the right.)

To move a single field, place the character - in the attribute position of the field, and place the character = in the position to which the field should be moved. An example is shown in Figure 19.12, where the constant 'Customer File Browse' will be moved down one line on the display.

Also shown in the example is how you could move the constant 'F12=Cancel' several positions to the right. You can see that the > character is used. When > is used, you position the first > after the last position in the field instead of in the attribute position for the field.

Figure 19.12 Moving Fields

```
DD/DD/DD              Acme Accounting Service              SSSSSSSS
TT:TT:TT              -Customer File Browse                UUUUUUUUUU
                        =

    Customer Number:   999999-

             Name:    OOOOOOOOOOOOOOOOOOOOOOOOOOOOOO

          Address:    OOOOOOOOOOOOOOOOOOOOOOOOOOOOOO
                      OOOOOOOOOOOOOOOOOOOOOOOOOOOOOO
             City:    OOOOOOOOOOOOOOOOOOOO

            State:    OO

              Zip:    666666666




 F3=Exit        F12=Cancel>>>>>>>>>>
```

You can also move several fields as a block using the character - at the beginning and ending of the block of fields to be moved. The beginning and ending - characters indicate a rectangular area that is to be moved. You place the character = at the uppermost left position of where you want to move the block of fields.

When you need to make a copy of a field, place the character - in the attribute position of the field, and place the characters == at the position to which the field is to be copied. The new field will be assigned the next sequential name (e.g., FLD012). Figure 19.13 shows an example of copying the city field to a position below the zip code field.

As with the Move fields operation, you can also copy several fields as a block using the character - at the beginning and ending of the block of fields to be copied. You place the characters == at the position to which the block will be copied. You can create many new fields using a block copy. Each new field will be assigned a name (e.g., FLD021).

Figure 19.13 Copying a Single Field

```
DD/DD/DD              Acme Accounting Service              SSSSSSS
TT:TT:TT              Customer File Browse                 UUUUUUUUUU


    Customer Number:   999999-

               Name:   OOOOOOOOOOOOOOOOOOOOOOOOOOOOOOO

            Address:   OOOOOOOOOOOOOOOOOOOOOOOOOOOOOOO
                       OOOOOOOOOOOOOOOOOOOOOOOOOOOOOOO
               City:   -OOOOOOOOOOOOOOOOOOOO

              State:   OO

                Zip:   666666666




                        ==

F3=Exit        F12=Cancel
```

Placing Database Reference Fields on the Work Display

Instead of creating and naming new fields as they are added to the display, you can place fields on the display that are defined in a database file. From the SDA Work Display you can press the F10 key and select the database file from which the definition of the screen fields should be derived.

On the resulting display, you enter the name of one or more database files from which the screen field definitions and names are to be derived. In Figure 19.14 we selected a file named CUSTFILE. We also specified that we wanted to use option 1 (Display database field list). This presents a list of all fields within the file, as shown in Figure 19.15. In Figure 19.14 we could have alternately selected option 2, 3, or 4. These options are used, respectively, to select all the fields from the file for input only, output only, or both input and output.

Figure 19.14 Selecting Database File References

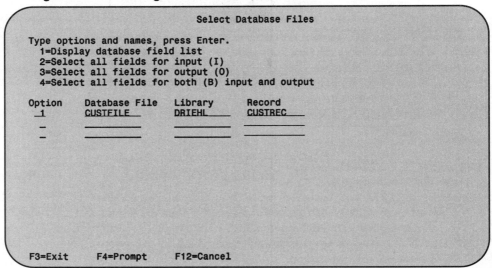

Figure 19.15 Selecting Fields

```
                        Select Database Fields

Record . . . :   CUSTREC

Type information, press Enter.
  Number of fields to roll . . . . . . . . . . . . . . . . .        8
  Name of field to search for . . . . . . . . . . . . . . .

Type options, press Enter.
  1=Display extended field description
  2=Select for input (I), 3=Select for output (O),4=Select for both (B)

Option  Field      Length   Type    Column Heading
   3    CUSTNO      6,0      S       Customer Number
   3    CUSTNM      30       A       Customer Name
   3    CUSTAD      30       A       Customer Address
   3    CUSTCT      20       A       Customer City
   3    CUSTST      2        A       Customer State
   3    CUSTZP      9,0      S       Customer Zip Code

                                                            Bottom
F3=Exit    F12=Cancel
```

Once you have selected the database fields to use on your display, you are returned to the SDA Work Display (Figure 19.16). The names of the selected fields are shown at the bottom of display, but they have not yet been added to the display. SDA is waiting for you to tell it where to place the selected fields.

Figure 19.16 Displaying the List of Selected Fields

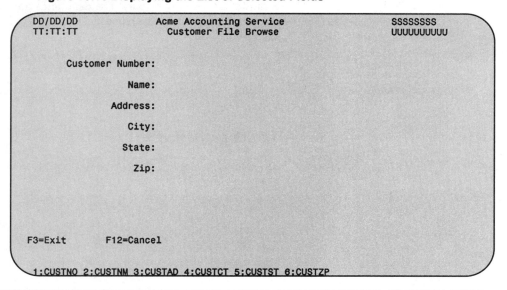

```
DD/DD/DD              Acme Accounting Service              SSSSSSSS
TT:TT:TT                Customer File Browse               UUUUUUUUUU


      Customer Number:

              Name:

           Address:

              City:

             State:

               Zip:




F3=Exit        F12=Cancel

 1:CUSTNO  2:CUSTNM  3:CUSTAD  4:CUSTCT  5:CUSTST  6:CUSTZP
```

To place the fields on the display, you use the command &n, where *n* is the number of the field as listed at the bottom of the display. For instance, in Figure 19.17 you can see &1, &2, &3, and so on. SDA will place field #1 from the bottom of the display at the location of the &1 specification, field #2 at the &2 specification, and so on.

Figure 19.17 Placing Reference Fields on the Display

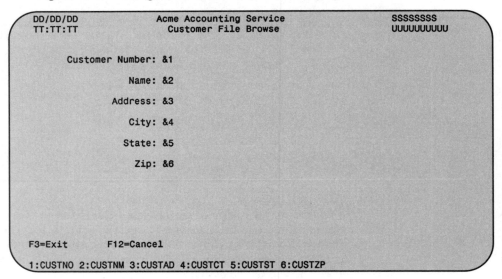

```
DD/DD/DD              Acme Accounting Service              SSSSSSSS
TT:TT:TT                Customer File Browse               UUUUUUUUUU


     Customer Number: &1

               Name: &2

            Address: &3

               City: &4

              State: &5

                Zip: &6




F3=Exit        F12=Cancel
1:CUSTNO 2:CUSTNM 3:CUSTAD 4:CUSTCT 5:CUSTST 6:CUSTZP
```

When you press the Enter key, SDA performs the field substitutions. Figure 19.18 shows the resulting display. The data fields now appearing on the display have been assigned the names CUSTNO, CUSTNM, CUSTAD, and so on.

Figure 19.18 Reference Fields Added

```
DD/DD/DD              Acme Accounting Service           SSSSSSSS
TT:TT:TT               Customer File Browse             UUUUUUUUUU


     Customer Number:   666666

               Name:    OOOOOOOOOOOOOOOOOOOOOOOOOOOOOO

            Address:    OOOOOOOOOOOOOOOOOOOOOOOOOOOOOO
                        OOOOOOOOOOOOOOOOOOOOOOOOOOOOOO
               City:    OOOOOOOOOOOOOOOOOOO

              State:    OO

                Zip:    666666666




 F3=Exit       F12=Cancel
```

When you are placing fields on the display from a database file, the SDA command is &n, where *n* is the field number from the list at the bottom of the display. SDA also provides a few variations of the &n command that you may find useful (Figure 19.19).

Figure 19.19 Commands To Place Reference Fields on the Display

SDA Command	Function
&n	Place the field on the display
&nL	Place the field on the display with column heading at left
&nR	Place the field on the display with column heading at right
&nC	Place the field on the display with column heading above
&nP	Place the column heading for this field on the display, but not the field itself

Changing the Display Attributes of Fields on the Work Display

The commands listed in the preceding figures are used to manipulate fields. The SDA commands presented in Figure 19.20 are provided so that you can control the physical appearance of fields on the display. For example, fields can blink, or be shown in reverse image, or be underlined. You manipulate the appearance of a field by manipulating the display attribute of the field. The SDA commands presented here must be entered into the attribute position of the field to which they apply.

Figure 19.20 Commands To Specify Display Attributes

Command	Function
B or b	Blink field
S or s	Column separators
H or h	High Intensity (bold)
R or r	Reverse image
U or u	Underline
N or n	Non-display (e.g., for passwords)

Display attributes are cumulative; you can add several display attributes to the same field. So you could have a blinking, reverse-image, underlined field. If you decide that you want to remove one of the display attributes from a field, you use the minus sign followed by the attribute you want to remove. For example, to remove the H (High intensity) display attribute from a field, enter the command -h or -H in the attribute position of the field. If you decide you want to remove all the display attributes from a field, you can use the command -a or -A.

Display attributes behave differently on color displays and monochrome displays. For example, the (B) blink attribute on a monochrome display causes the field to blink; however, on a color display, the field is simply displayed in the color red. If you want the field to blink on a color display, you must specify both the B (blink) attribute and the H (High intensity) attribute. Figure 19.21 summarizes the effect of display attributes when they appear on a color display.

Figure 19.21 Effect of Display Attributes on a Color Display

Display Attribute	Color and Effect
(none)	Green
R	Green, Reverse image
U	Green, Underline
U + R	Green, Reverse image, Underline
B	Red
B + R	Red, Reverse image
B + U	Red, Underline
B + U + R	Red, Reverse image, Underline
B + H	Red, Blinking
B + R + H	Red, Reverse image, Blinking
B + H + U	Red, Blinking, Underline
H	White

Display Attribute	Color and Effect
H + R	White, Reverse image
H + U	White, Underlined
S	Turquoise, Column separators
S + R	Turquoise, Column separators, Reverse image
S + U	Turquoise, Column separators, Underline
S + R + U	Turquoise, Column separators, Reverse image, Underline
S + B	Pink
S + B + R	Pink, Reverse image
S + B + U	Pink, Underline
S + B + U + R	Pink, Underline, Reverse image
S + H	Yellow, Column separators
S + H + R	Yellow, Column separators, Reverse image
S + H + U	Yellow, Column separators, Underline
S + H + B	Blue
S + H + B + R	Blue, Reverse image
S + H + B + U	Blue, Underline

Specifying Color Attributes for Fields

In addition to specifying the preceding display attributes for fields and constants, you can also directly specify the color of a field or constant. The commands used to specify color (see Figure 19.22) are similar to those that define display attributes. Again, the command must be entered into the attribute position of the affected field.

Figure 19.22 Commands To Specify Field Color

Command	Field Color
CB or cb	Blue
CR or cr	Red
CW or cw	White
CT or ct	Turquoise (cyan)
CY or cy	Yellow
CG or cg	Green
CP or cp	Pink (magenta)

Since these commands consist of two characters, you simply enter the letter C into the attribute position of a field, followed by the first letter of the color (e.g., B for blue). Similar to display attributes, colors can be cumulative, and you can add several color attributes to a field. If you decide to remove a color, use the command -C followed by the first letter of the color. For example, to remove the blue color from a field, use the command -CB or -cb in the attribute position for the field. To remove all colors from a field, use the command -CA or -ca in the field's attribute position. When the color attributes are specified, and the display record is used on a monochrome display, the color attributes are ignored.

Work Display Function Keys

Because the SDA Work Display requires the use of the full screen, there is no room to display the allowable function keys. Pressing the F1 key provides a very good series of help screens that can serve as an on-line reference not only to SDA function keys, but also to many other features of SDA. Figure 19.23 presents a table of the function keys that can be used within the SDA Work Display.

Figure 19.23 Work Display Function Keys

F Key	Function
F1	Help
F3	Exit
F4	Go to the Work with Fields screen
F6	Go to the Condition Work Display screen
F9	Go to the Select Additional Records screen
F10	Go to the Select Database Fields screen
F11	Switch between field lists at the bottom of the display
F12	Return to the Work with Records screen
F13	Go to the Change SDA Defaults screen
F14	Display ruler at cursor position. This key acts as a toggle switch, first displaying the ruler, then removing it.
F15	Show prompt for SFLPAG and SFLLIN. This key is only valid when working with a subfile format.
F17	Print the current work display
F18	Tab forward to the next field's attribute position.
F19	Tab backward to the prior field's attribute position.
F20	Shows screen constants in reverse image. This key is a toggle switch, first displaying constants in reverse image, then normal.
F21	Remove additional records from the display. This key is a toggle switch, first removing any additional records from the display, then showing them. F9 will have been used first to select additional records.
F22	Present an OS/400 command line window, allowing you to enter CL commands from within an SDA work session.

Specifying Field-Level Keywords

Chapter 20

Just as DDS keywords may be specified at the file and record level, they may also be specified at the field level. Field-level keywords are used to specify such things as validity-checking rules, editing rules — and yes, display attributes and colors. You might not have realized it, but when you used the SDA commands to modify a field's display attribute or color, you were assigning field-level keywords to the field.

The screen shown in Figure 20.1 is the Select Field Keywords display. It is from here that you specify all the keywords you want to have in effect for an individual field. You can access this display by placing an asterisk (*) in the attribute position of any field displayed on the SDA Work Display. Again, the field-level keywords are broken down into several categories, such as Display attributes, Colors, and so on. Place the letter Y next to any category of keyword that you want to view or modify.

Figure 20.1 Selecting Field Keywords

```
                        Select Field Keywords

Field . . . . . :   CUSNAM                 Usage . . :  B
Length  . . . . :   30                      Row . . . :  5 Column . . . :  27

Type choices, press Enter.
                                     Y=Yes    For Field Type
    Display attributes  . . . . . . .   Y     All except Hidden
    Colors  . . . . . . . . . . . .     Y     All except Hidden
    Keying options  . . . . . . . . .   _     Hidden, Input or Both
    Validity check  . . . . . . . . .   _     Input or Both, not float
    Input keywords  . . . . . . . . .   _     Input or Both
    General keywords  . . . . . . . .   _     All types

    Database reference  . . . . . . .   _     Hidden, Input, Output, Both
    Error messages  . . . . . . . . .   _     Input, Output, Both
    Message ID (MSGID)  . . . . . . .   _     Output or Both


    TEXT keyword  . . . . . . . . .           _____


 F3=Exit    F12=Cancel
```

In this example, we placed Y next to the categories Display attributes and Colors. The resulting Select Display Attributes screen is shown in Figure 20.2. Here, you can see that we selected display attributes BL and PC if indicator 89 is on. This generates the DDS keyword DSPATR(BL PC) conditioned by indicator 89.

Figure 20.2 Selecting Display Attributes

```
                        Select Display Attributes

Field . . . . . :   CUSNAM                 Usage . . :  B
Length  . . . . :   30                      Row . . . :  5    Column . . . :  27

Type choices, press Enter.
                                         Keyword   Y=Yes   Indicators/+
    Field conditioning  . . . . . . . . . . .                       __ __ __
    Program-to-system field . . . . . . . .    _____             __ __ __
    Display attributes:                      DSPATR
      High intensity . . . . . . . . . . .     HI       _          __ __ __
      Reverse image  . . . . . . . . . . .     RI       _          __ __ __
      Column separators  . . . . . . . . .     CS       _          __ __ __
      Blink  . . . . . . . . . . . . . .       BL       Y          _89 __ __
      Nondisplay . . . . . . . . . . . . .     ND       _          __ __ __
      Underline  . . . . . . . . . . . . .     UL       _          __ __ __
      Position cursor  . . . . . . . . . .     PC       Y          _89 __ __
      Set modified data tag  . . . . . . .     MDT      _          __ __ __
      Protect field  . . . . . . . . . . .     PR       _          __ __ __
      Operator ID magnetic card  . . . . .     OID      _          __ __ __
      Select by light pen  . . . . . . . .     SP       _

 F3=Exit    F12=Cancel
```

After pressing Enter from this display, you are presented with the next display, to select the color keywords. SDA evaluates the Color keyword conditions in the order specified. You specify the order from 1 to 7. The reason for this is that a field cannot be displayed in two colors at the same time.

In the example shown in Figure 20.3, if indicator 55 and 56 are both ON, the field will be White. However, if indicator 55 is ON but 56 is OFF, the field will be Red.

Figure 20.3 Selecting Color Keywords

```
                            Select Colors

   Field . . . . . :   CUSNAM           Usage . . :  B
   Length . . . . :   30                Row . . . :  5     Column . . . :  27

   Type choices, press Enter.

                                        Keyword   Order    Indicators/+
                                                  (1-7)
      Colors:                           COLOR
         Blue . . . . . . . . . . . . .    BLU      _       __  __  __
         Green  . . . . . . . . . . . .    GRN      _       __  __  __
         Pink . . . . . . . . . . . . .    PNK      _       __  __  __
         Red  . . . . . . . . . . . . .    RED      2       55  __  __
         Turquoise  . . . . . . . . . .    TRQ      _       __  __  __
         White  . . . . . . . . . . . .    WHT      1       55  56  __
         Yellow . . . . . . . . . . . .    YLW      _       __  __  __




   F3=Exit   F12=Cancel
```

Pressing the F4 key from the SDA Work Display will present you with the Work with Fields display as shown in Figure 20.4. This display presents a list of screen fields and constants, and allows you to manipulate them individually. Using option 1, you can select the keywords for a particular field, and using option 4, you can delete fields. On this display, you can also add special fields. These are Hidden fields, Message fields, and Program-to-System fields. When you enter the name of the special field in the appropriate location, SDA prompts you for the field size and data type, then adds it to the field list.

Fields are assigned a sort order based upon which field was defined first. When you examine the DDS source code for a display file, you will see the fields in that order. Normally, you would rather see the fields in the DDS source code sorted by the row and column that the field appears in. You can accomplish that using the F6 key from this display. The fields will then be sorted by row and column not only in the DDS source, but also in the Work with Fields display.

Figure 20.4 The Work with Fields Screen

```
                        Work with Fields

 Record . . . :   SCREEN1

 Type information, press Enter.
   Number of fields to roll . . . . . . . . . . . . . . . .        6

 Type options, change values, press Enter.
   1=Select keywords    4=Delete field

 Option   Order   Field      Type Use   Length  Row/Col  Ref Condition Overlap
            70    Customer N   C           16    05 008
            80    CUSNAM            B       30    05 027
            90    Name:        C            5    07 019
           100    FLD002            O       30    07 027
           110    Address:     C            8    09 016
           120    FLD003            O       30    09 027
                                                                      More...
 Add      _____   HIDEME        H    ____         Hidden
 Add      _____   _____     M    ____         Message
 Add      _____   _____     P    ____         Program-to-system


 F3=Exit    F6=Sort by row/column    F12=Cancel
```

Using SDA To Define Subfiles

Chapter 21

Subfiles are used to display multiple data items that have similar or identical characteristics. For example, a subfile can be used to display a list of customer numbers, a list of customer names, or a list of products on order. SDA makes it easy to create very functional subfile formats. A subfile actually consists of two record formats: a subfile record format and a subfile control record format. The subfile record format contains the repeating list of data items that will appear on the display; the subfile control format contains information that controls the subfile, and optionally contains headings for the subfile fields. To create a subfile in SDA, you can use option 1 to add a record format, as shown in Figure 21.1. Here, we give the format the name SFL, but you can use any name.

Figure 21.1 Adding a New Record

```
                        Work with Display Records

File . . . . . . . :    QDDSSRC              Member . . . . . . :   MYDSPF
   Library . . . . :    DRIEHL               Source type  . . . :   DSPF

Type options, press Enter.
  1=Add                 2=Edit comments       3=Copy          4=Delete
  7=Rename              8=Select keywords    12=Design image

Opt  Order   Record       Type      Related Subfile   Date        DDS  Error
 1_          SFL
 __    10    SCREEN1      RECORD                        10/15/94
 __    20    FKEYS        RECORD                        09/26/94
```

When the Add New Record display is shown, you select the record type. In Figure 21.2 we choose the record type SFL. When we press the Enter key, the prompt for the name of the subfile control record is shown. Here we give the subfile control record the name SFLCTL. SDA will create both the subfile record and the subfile control record.

Figure 21.2 Specifying a Subfile Record Type

```
                           Add New Record
  File  . . . . . . :   QDDSSRC         Member . . . . . . :   MYDSPF
    Library . . . . :     DRIEHL        Source type  . . . :   DSPF

  Type choices, press Enter.

    New record  . . . . . . . . . . . . . .   SFL        Name

    Type  . . . . . . . . . . . . . . . . .   SFL        RECORD, USRDFN
                                                         SFL,    SFLMSG
                                                         WINDOW, WDWSFL
                                                         PULDWN, PDNSFL

    Subfile control record  . . . . . . . .   SFLCTL     Name
```

When a subfile record type is selected, SDA walks you through what seems an endless series of keyword entry screens. On the first screen, shown in Figure 21.3, we specify that the SFLNXTCHG keyword should be in effect if indicator 88 is ON.

Figure 21.3 Selecting General Keywords for a Subfile Record

```
                       Select General Keywords
    Subfile record . . . . . . . :    SFL

    Type choices, press Enter.

                                          Keyword    Y=Yes  Indicators/+
      Return this record
        on read next changed . . . . . . . . .   SFLNXTCHG    Y      _88 __ __
      Write this record to the job log . . . . .  LOGOUT       _      __ __ __
      Write this record to the job log . . . . .  LOGINP       _
      Keep records on display
        when closing the file  . . . . . . . .   KEEP         _

      Allow blanks . . . . . . . . . . . . . .   CHECK(AB)    _
      Move cursor right to left  . . . . . . . .  CHECK(RL)    _

      Change input defaults  . . . . . . . . .   CHGINPDFT    _
        Select parameters  . . . . . . . . . . .               _



    F3=Exit    F12=Cancel
```

We next must specify subfile control record keywords, as shown in Figure 21.4. On the Subfile control record format, we specify that the SFLDSP keyword will be in effect when indicator 55 is ON. The SFLDSPCTL keyword will be in effect when indicator 56 is on. Also, the SFLEND keyword will be in effect when indicator 77 is on. The value 'More...' will be displayed when more subfile records exist than will fit on the current display. The value 'Bottom' will appear when no more subfile records exist.

Figure 21.4 Selecting General Keywords for a Subfile Control Record

```
                        Define General Keywords

Subfile control record . . . . . . . . . :   SFLCTL

Type choices, press Enter.                 Keyword
  Related subfile record . . . . . . .     SFLCTL      SFL        Name
  Subfile cursor relative record . . .     SFLCSRRRN  _____   Name
  Subfile mode . . . . . . . . . . . .     SFLMODE    _____   Name


                                                      Y=Yes        Indicators/+
  Display subfile records  . . . . . .     SFLDSP       Y           _55 __ __
  Display control record . . . . . . .     SFLDSPCTL    Y           _56 __ __
  Initialize subfile fields  . . . . .     SFLINZ       _           __ __ __
  Delete subfile area  . . . . . . . .     SFLDLT       _           __ __ __
  Clear subfile records  . . . . . . .     SFLCLR       _           __ __ __
  Indicate more records  . . . . . . .     SFLEND       Y           _77 __ __
    SFLEND parameter  . . . . . . . . .    *MORE        Y
  Record not active  . . . . . . . . .     SFLRNA       _

                                                                     More...
F3=Exit    F12=Cancel
```

The next display shown in Figure 21.5 asks for the number of records that can fit in the subfile; here we specify 12 records. We also specify that 11 subfile records can appear on any one page.

Figure 21.5 Specifying SFLSIZ and SFLPAG Keywords

```
                        Define Display Layout

Subfile control record . . . . . . . . . :   SFLCTL

Type values, press Enter.

                                           Keyword  Number
  Records in subfile . . . . . . . . . .   SFLSIZ    _12
  Records per display  . . . . . . . . .   SFLPAG    _11
  Spaces between records . . . . . . . .   SFLLIN    ____
```

A myriad of other screens are presented, but the ones we have included are the most commonly used.

Once the subfile record and subfile control record have been defined, it is time to define what they look like on the SDA Work Display. Figure 21.6 shows that by placing option 12 next to the SFLCTL record format, you access the SDA Work Display for the subfile control record format.

Figure 21.6 Select Design Image Option 12

```
                         Work with Display Records

  File . . . . . . :    QDDSSRC              Member . . . . . . :   MYDSPF
    Library . . . . :    DRIEHL               Source type  . . . :   DSPF

  Type options, press Enter.
    1=Add               2=Edit comments       3=Copy           4=Delete
    7=Rename            8=Select keywords     12=Design image

  Opt  Order   Record       Type      Related Subfile   Date        DDS Error

  __      10   SCREEN1      RECORD                       10/15/94
  __      20   FKEYS        RECORD                       09/26/94
  __      30   SFL          SFL                          10/15/94
  12      40   SFLCTL       SFLCTL    SFL                10/15/94




                                                                   Bottom
  F3=Exit                    F12=Cancel       F14=File-level keywords
  F15=File-level comments    F17=Subset       F24=More keys
```

When you are defining the screen layout of a subfile control record, you typically enter field headings and any other related fields. In the example, we define two constants as headings (Figure 21.7).

Figure 21.7 The SDA Work Display for a Subfile Control Record

Once the subfile control record has described where the headings are located, it's time to add the subfile fields. These are the repeating data items. To do this we place option 12 next to the SFL record format (Figure 21.8).

Figure 21.8 Selecting Design Image Option 12

```
                          Work with Display Records

File . . . . . . :    QDDSSRC              Member . . . . . . :    MYDSPF
   Library . . . . :     DRIEHL              Source type  . . . :    DSPF

Type options, press Enter.
  1=Add              2=Edit comments         3=Copy        4=Delete
  7=Rename           8=Select keywords      12=Design image

Opt  Order    Record          Type        Related Subfile   Date         DDS Error
__    __10    SCREEN1         RECORD                         10/15/94
__    __20    FKEYS           RECORD                         09/26/94
12    __30    SFL             SFL                            10/15/94
__    __40    SFLCTL          SFLCTL      SFL                10/15/94
```

When you are defining subfile records, SDA automatically displays the subfile control record.. This makes it much easier to line up the subfile fields in the correct row and column. If SDA did not do this, you would need to remember the row and column where the headings were defined to properly line up your data with the headings. In the example shown in Figure 21.9, we are adding two subfile fields. One is 20 characters long, the other 30 characters long. They are both output-only fields.

Figure 21.9 The SDA Work Display for Subfile Records

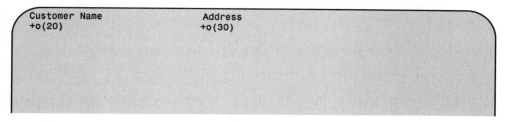

When you press the Enter key, SDA creates the repeating group of fields. The number of times the fields are repeated depends upon the value you entered earlier for the SFLPAG keyword. Here, we have the data items repeated 11 times: SFLPAG(11). If you decide you would like to change the number of subfile records displayed on a page, you can press the F15 key, which displays the prompt shown at the bottom of the display in Figure 21.10. This lets you change the SFLPAG and SFLLIN keywords but (sadly) does not let you change the SFLSIZ keyword. Typically, when you create a subfile, you specify the SFLSIZ value to be one greater than the SFLPAG value. This allows great subfile flexibility. So if you increase the SFLPAG value (Number of records on a page), you should go back and change the SFLSIZ value as well. However, you must change that keyword from the Work with Records display; you cannot do it from here.

Figure 21.10 The Resulting Subfile Records

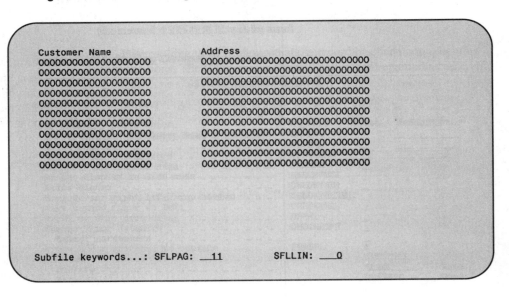

When you are dealing with subfiles, or with any multiple-format display, it is very handy to be able to display other record formats while you are working on one. For example, when we were defining subfile records on the work display, SDA automatically displayed the subfile control record. But, in this example, we also have a format for the function keys that will be displayed at the bottom of the screen. Pressing the F9 key from the SDA Work Display will let you select other records that should be displayed. Figure 21.11 shows the display. Here, we select the FKEYS format as an additional record to display. The SFLCTL record format is already selected. The result is that three record formats will be displayed on the SDA Work Display at once: the SFLCTL format; the FKEYS format; and the format we are currently working on, the SFL format.

Figure 21.11 Selecting Additional Records for Display

```
                 Select Additional Records for Display

File  . . . . . . :   QDDSSRC              Member . . . . . . :   MYDSPF
   Library . . . . :   DRIEHL              Source type  . . . :   DSPF

Type options, press Enter.
  1,2,3=Select for display as additional record

Option   Record        Type     Status
  1      SFLCTL__
  2      _____
  3
  _      SCREEN1       RECORD
  2      FKEYS         RECORD
         SFL           SFL      In use
  _      SFLCTL        SFLCTL   Selected




                                                                  Bottom

 F3=Exit     F5=Refresh     F12=Cancel
 Records currently selected: SFLCTL  .
```

In Figure 21.12 you can see the resulting display, with all three record formats shown. We can now do any work needed to tune the SFL format. The other formats, SFLCTL and FKEYS, are simply displayed here; they cannot be modified while we are working with the SFL format. Only one format can be active for change in an SDA Work Display session. If you determine that you need to change the headings or the function keys, you must return to the Work with Display Records screen and select the record format to be changed.

Figure 21.12 Multiple Records Displayed at Once

```
Customer Name               Address
OOOOOOOOOOOOOOOOOOOO        OOOOOOOOOOOOOOOOOOOOOOOOOOOOOO
OOOOOOOOOOOOOOOOOOOO        OOOOOOOOOOOOOOOOOOOOOOOOOOOOOO
OOOOOOOOOOOOOOOOOOOO        OOOOOOOOOOOOOOOOOOOOOOOOOOOOOO
OOOOOOOOOOOOOOOOOOOO        OOOOOOOOOOOOOOOOOOOOOOOOOOOOOO
OOOOOOOOOOOOOOOOOOOO        OOOOOOOOOOOOOOOOOOOOOOOOOOOOOO
OOOOOOOOOOOOOOOOOOOO        OOOOOOOOOOOOOOOOOOOOOOOOOOOOOO
OOOOOOOOOOOOOOOOOOOO        OOOOOOOOOOOOOOOOOOOOOOOOOOOOOO
OOOOOOOOOOOOOOOOOOOO        OOOOOOOOOOOOOOOOOOOOOOOOOOOOOO
OOOOOOOOOOOOOOOOOOOO        OOOOOOOOOOOOOOOOOOOOOOOOOOOOOO
OOOOOOOOOOOOOOOOOOOO        OOOOOOOOOOOOOOOOOOOOOOOOOOOOOO
OOOOOOOOOOOOOOOOOOOO        OOOOOOOOOOOOOOOOOOOOOOOOOOOOOO
OOOOOOOOOOOOOOOOOOOO        OOOOOOOOOOOOOOOOOOOOOOOOOOOOOO
OOOOOOOOOOOOOOOOOOOO        OOOOOOOOOOOOOOOOOOOOOOOOOOOOOO
OOOOOOOOOOOOOOOOOOOO        OOOOOOOOOOOOOOOOOOOOOOOOOOOOOO
OOOOOOOOOOOOOOOOOOOO        OOOOOOOOOOOOOOOOOOOOOOOOOOOOOO



    F3=Exit        F6=Print Customer      F6=Display Messages
    F12=Cancel

Additional record(s) selected: SFLCTL FKEYS
```

Working with Windows

Chapter 22

Window formats are used extensively by IBM within the OS/400 operating system. For instance, all OS/400 Help text is presented in a window, the QUSCMDLN API presents a command line in a window, and several other IBM-supplied functions display windows. SDA allows you to easily create window display formats, and to control such things as window sizing, placement, and border characteristics. To create a window record format, you create a new record, as shown in Figure 22.1. Here, we name the format WINDOW, but you can choose any name you wish.

Figure 22.1 Adding a New Record Format

```
                        Work with Display Records

File  . . . . . . :    QDDSSRC            Member . . . . . . :    DANTEST
   Library . . . . :      DRIEHL          Source type  . . . :    DSPF

Type options, press Enter.
  1=Add              2=Edit comments      3=Copy          4=Delete
  7=Rename           8=Select keywords    12=Design image

Opt  Order    Record         Type     Related Subfile  Date         DDS Error
1             WINDOW

  (No records in file)
```

We must mention one caveat to using the WINDOW keywords here. Using the WINDOW formats within display files can have a negative impact on your interactive response time. This is especially true if you have remote sites communicating to your AS/400 at low speeds like 9600 or 19.2 bps. You should experiment with these keywords before deciding to build production applications with them. If your response time is good, they are a very valuable tool. However, if the response time is poor, you should consider an alternative method. The book *Powertools for the AS/400, Volume I* from Duke Press provides several samples of how to implement windows without using the WINDOW keywords.

When the Add New Record screen is shown, you enter the type WINDOW, as shown in Figure 22.2.

Figure 22.2 Specifying the WINDOW Record Type

```
                           Add New Record

File . . . . . . :    QDDSSRC          Member . . . . . . :    DANTEST
   Library . . . . :     DRIEHL         Source type  . . . :    DSPF

Type choices, press Enter.

   New record . . . . . . . . . . . . . . .    WINDOW      Name

   Type  . . . . . . . . . . . . . . . . . .    WINDOW      RECORD, USRDFN
                                                            SFL,    SFLMSG
                                                            WINDOW, WDWSFL
                                                            PULDWN, PDNSFL
```

SDA then walks you through a series of displays where you specify the keywords for the window format. In Figure 22.3, we specify that we want to select the parameters for the DDS keywords WINDOW and WDWBORDER.

Figure 22.3 Selecting General Keywords for Windows

```
                          Select General Keywords
Window record . . . . . . . . . . . .  . . . :   WINDOW

Type choices, press Enter.

                                               Keyword    Y=Yes  Indicators/+

   Window parameters  . . . . . . . . . . .    WINDOW       Y
      Select parameters . . . . . . . . . .                 Y
   Window borders . . . . . . . . . . . . .    WDWBORDER    Y
      Select parameters . . . . . . . . . .                 Y
   Remove windows . . . . . . . . . . . .      RMVWDW       _    __  __  __
   User Restore Display . . . . . . . . . .    USRRSTDSP    _    __  __  __
```

When you have finished entering the keywords for the WINDOW and WDWBORDER keywords, the window is basically complete. Selecting option 12 from the Work with Display Records screen in Figure 22.4 lets you see the window you have created.

Figure 22.4 Selecting Design Image Option 12

```
                        Work with Display Records

File  . . . . . . :    QDDSSRC              Member . . . . . . :   DANTEST
  Library . . . . :      IWSDEV             Source type  . . . :   DSPF

Type options, press Enter.
  1=Add                2=Edit comments        3=Copy         4=Delete
  7=Rename             8=Select keywords     12=Design image

Opt  Order    Record        Type      Related Subfile   Date       DDS Error
 12     10    WINDOW        WINDOW                       10/30/94
```

The resulting window display is shown in Figure 22.5. From this SDA Work Display you can enter fields or constants in the window, as shown in the figure.

Figure 22.5 The Resulting Window on the SDA Work Display

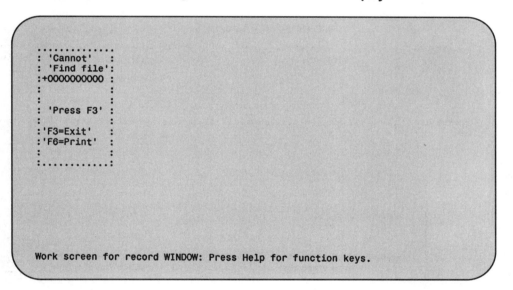

```
. . . . . . . . . . . . .
: 'Cannot'   :
: 'Find file':
:+0000000000 :
:            :
:            :
: 'Press F3' :
:            :
:'F3=Exit'   :
:'F6=Print'  :
:            :
:. . . . . . . . . . . .:



Work screen for record WINDOW: Press Help for function keys.
```

Creating a Subfile in a Window

Chapter 23

While it is quite simple to create a window format, SDA makes it really easy to create a subfile within a window. Once SDA knows you are creating a subfile in a window, it steps you completely through the creation process. We start by adding a new record called SFL, as shown in Figure 23.1.

Figure 23.1 Adding a New Record Format

```
                         Work with Display Records

 File . . . . . . :    QDDSSRC           Member . . . . . . :    MYDSPF
    Library . . . . :     DRIEHL           Source type  . . . :    DSPF

 Type options, press Enter.
   1=Add                2=Edit comments      3=Copy          4=Delete
   7=Rename             8=Select keywords   12=Design image

 Opt  Order   Record        Type      Related Subfile  Date       DDS Error
 1_           SFL____
 __    10     SCREEN1       RECORD                      10/15/94
 __    20     FKEYS         RECORD                      09/26/94
```

On the Add New Record display shown in Figure 23.2, we specify that the type of record is WDWSFL. This tells SDA you are creating a subfile within a window.

Figure 23.2 Specifying the WDWSFL Type

```
                              Add New Record
  File  . . . . . . :   QDDSSRC            Member . . . . . . :   MYDSPF
    Library . . . . :   DRIEHL             Source type  . . . :   DSPF

  Type choices, press Enter.

    New record . . . . . . . . . . . . . .    SFL        Name

    Type . . . . . . . . . . . . . . . . .    WDWSFL     RECORD, USRDFN
                                                         SFL,    SFLMSG
                                                         WINDOW, WDWSFL
                                                         PULDWN, PDNSFL
```

SDA then prompts you for the name of the subfile control record, as shown in Figure 23.3. Here we enter the name SFLCTL (you can use any name).

Figure 23.3 Specifying the Name of the Subfile Control Record

```
                              Add New Record
  File  . . . . . . :   QDDSSRC            Member . . . . . . :   MYDSPF
    Library . . . . :   DRIEHL             Source type  . . . :   DSPF

  Type choices, press Enter.

    New record . . . . . . . . . . . . . .    SFL        Name

    Type . . . . . . . . . . . . . . . . .    WDWSFL     RECORD, USRDFN
                                                         SFL,    SFLMSG
                                                         WINDOW, WDWSFL
                                                         PULDWN, PDNSFL

    Subfile control record . . . . . . . .    SFLCTL     Name
```

SDA then walks you though the screens required to make a subfile in a window. The screen in Figure 23.4 lets you enter the window size and coordinates on the screen. Here, we define a window that is 10 rows by 10 columns, starting at Row 10 Column 10. We also specify that we *do* want a message line included within the window.

Figure 23.4 Selecting the Window Parameters

```
                      Define Window Parameters

   Record . . . :    SFLCTL
   Keyword  . . :    WINDOW

   Referenced window . . . . . . . . . . . .     _____      Name
   -OR-
   Window definition
     Default start positioning . . . . . .     _             Y=Yes
     -OR-
     Start line
       Program-to-system field . . . . . .     _____      Name
       -OR-
       Actual line . . . . . . . . . . . .     10            1-25
     Start position
       Program-to-system field . . . . . .     _____      Name
       -OR-
       Actual position . . . . . . . . . .     10            1-128
     Window lines . . . . . . . . . . . . .     10            1-25
     Window position . . . . . . . . . . .     10            1-128
     Message line . . . . . . . . . . . . .     Y             Y=Yes


  F3=Exit    F12=Cancel
```

After we go through a few more screens to select the subfile keywords and subfile control record keywords, we are ready to design the image. First, we will select to design the subfile format, as shown in Figure 23.5.

Figure 23.5 Selecting Design Image Option 12

```
                      Work with Display Records

  File  . . . . . . :   QDDSSRC           Member . . . . . . :   MYDSPF
    Library . . . . :     DRIEHL          Source type  . . . :   DSPF

  Type options, press Enter.
    1=Add              2=Edit comments       3=Copy        4=Delete
    7=Rename           8=Select keywords    12=Design image

  Opt  Order   Record      Type      Related Subfile  Date        DDS Error

  __    10     SCREEN1     RECORD                      10/15/94
  __    20     FKEYS       RECORD                      09/26/94
  12    30     SFL         SFL                         10/15/94
  __    40     SFLCTL      WINDOW    SFL               10/15/94
```

The 10x10 window is shown on the work display. Now we simply define the subfile fields we want displayed within the window. In Figure 23.6 we create a field that is eight characters long and is an output-only field.

Figure 23.6 Defining the Subfile Fields

The resulting display in Figure 23.7 shows the subfile field expanded to its SFLPAG value, which we set at eight records per subfile page.

Figure 23.7 The Resulting Subfile Records

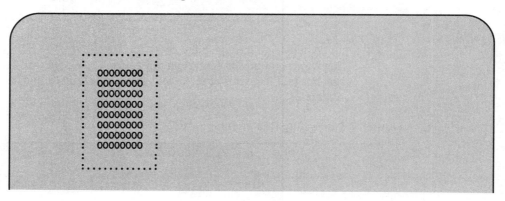

We now want to create a heading for the subfile inside the window. For this purpose we will use the design image option 12 for the subfile control record (Figure 23.8).

Figure 23.8 Selecting Design Image Option 12

```
                    Work with Display Records

File . . . . . . :   QDDSSRC              Member . . . . . . :   MYDSPF
   Library . . . . :   DRIEHL             Source type . . . :   DSPF

Type options, press Enter.
   1=Add              2=Edit comments          3=Copy          4=Delete
   7=Rename           8=Select keywords        12=Design image

Opt  Order   Record        Type      Related Subfile   Date        DDS Error
__    __10   SCREEN1       RECORD                       10/15/94
__    __20   FKEYS         RECORD                       09/26/94
__    __30   SFL           SFL                          10/15/94
12    __40   SFLCTL        WINDOW    SFL                10/15/94


                                                                   Bottom
F3=Exit                         F12=Cancel      F14=File-level keywords
F15=File-level comments         F17=Subset      F24=More keys
```

In Figure 23.9 we enter the constant value 'Customer' as the heading for the subfile. You will notice that SDA also displays the subfile format when the Subfile control record is being designed. Note also that we save the last line of the window for the message line.

Figure 23.9 Adding the Subfile Control Record Heading Text

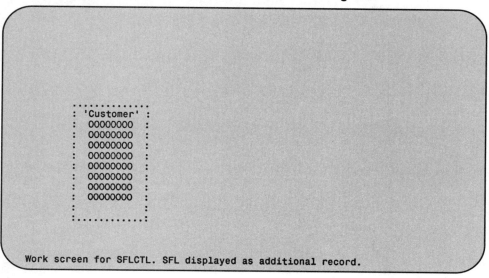

```
              ..............
              : 'Customer' :
              :  00000000  :
              :  00000000  :
              :  00000000  :
              :  00000000  :
              :  00000000  :
              :  00000000  :
              :  00000000  :
              :  00000000  :
              :            :
              :............:

Work screen for SFLCTL. SFL displayed as additional record.
```

The subfile in a window is now complete and ready to use in your applications, as demonstrated in Figure 23.10.

Figure 23.10 The Completed Subfile Within a Window

Creating Menus

Chapter 24

In addition to helping you design display files, SDA can be used to create AS/400-style menus. The menu creation process is very straightforward and quite simple. You can create a fully functional AS/400-style menu in a few minutes using SDA.

After entering the command STRSDA, you are presented with the SDA menu shown in Figure 24.1. To create a menu, select option 2.

Figure 24.1 The SDA Main Menu

```
                        AS/400 Screen Design Aid (SDA)

   Select one of the following:

        1. Design screens
        2. Design menus
        3. Test display files















   Selection or command
   ===> 2_____

   F1=Help    F3=Exit    F4=Prompt    F9=Retrieve    F12=Cancel
```

You are then prompted for the name of the source file where you want to store the menu's source code, and for the name of the menu, as shown in Figure 24.2. Here, we specified the source file as QDDSSRC, but you might want to create a different source file for menu source code. QMENUSRC or QMNUSRC would be a good choice. We assign the menu name MYMENU in the Menu prompt. This will be the name of the menu when it is created.

Figure 24.2 Specifying Source File and Menu Name

```
                              Design Menus
 Type choices, press Enter.

    Source file . . . . . . . .    qddssrc      Name, F4 for list

       Library . . . . . . . .     driehl       Name, *LIBL, *CURLIB

    Menu  . . . . . . . . . .      mymenu       Name, F4 for list
```

You are then presented with the display shown in Figure 24.3. Here, you specify whether you want to work with the menu itself, or with the Help screens that will be used for the menu. In this example, we will first work with the menu then come back and work with the Help screens later.

Figure 24.3 Selecting To Work with Menu Image and Commands

```
                         Specify Menu Functions
 File  . . . . . . :    QDDSSRC              Menu . . . . . . . :   MYMENU
    Library . . . . :       DRIEHL

 Type choices, press Enter.

    Work with menu image and commands  . . . . . .   Y   Y=Yes, N=No

    Work with menu help  . . . . . . . . . . . . .   N   Y=Yes, N=No
```

Because we selected to work with the menu first, we are presented with the SDA menu design screen shown in Figure 24.4. This screen presents a menu template that you modify. The menu name and title are displayed at the top of the screen, and option numbers are also supplied.

Figure 24.4 The SDA Menu Design Work Display

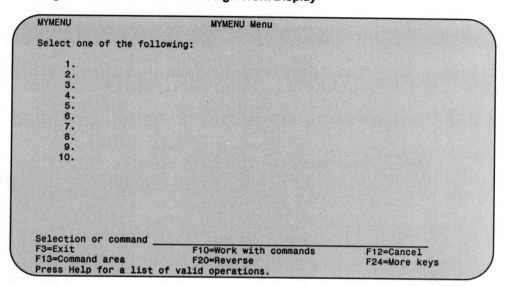

```
MYMENU                          MYMENU Menu
Select one of the following:

      1.
      2.
      3.
      4.
      5.
      6.
      7.
      8.
      9.
     10.




Selection or command
F3=Exit                 F10=Work with commands      F12=Cancel
F13=Command area        F20=Reverse                 F24=More keys
Press Help for a list of valid operations.
```

When the menu template is displayed, you simply enter the constants that you want to appear on the display, as shown in Figure 24.5. You enter constants in exactly the same way you do on the regular SDA Work Display. As you can see, the special constants of *DATE, *TIME, and *USER can be used on the menu. All of the constants included in the menu template can be moved, changed, or deleted. You simply use the same commands you used on the SDA Work Display. You can see here that we deleted option numbers 8-10 and added a constant for option number 90.

Figure 24.5 Adding and Removing Constants on the Menu

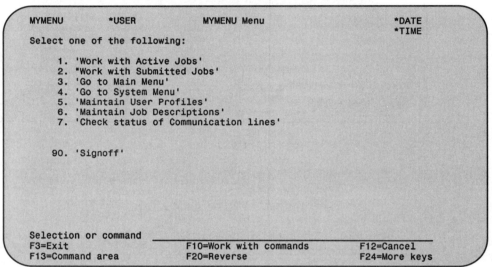

```
MYMENU          *USER              MYMENU Menu                        *DATE
                                                                      *TIME
Select one of the following:

     1. 'Work with Active Jobs'
     2. 'Work with Submitted Jobs'
     3. 'Go to Main Menu'
     4. 'Go to System Menu'
     5. 'Maintain User Profiles'
     6. 'Maintain Job Descriptions'
     7. 'Check status of Communication lines'


    90. 'Signoff'




Selection or command _____
F3=Exit                   F10=Work with commands        F12=Cancel
F13=Command area          F20=Reverse                   F24=More keys
```

You cannot add input or output data fields to the display as you can on the normal SDA Work Display, but you can make the menu somewhat dynamic by placing message constants on the display. In Figure 24.6, we specify +MMMM to tell SDA we want to display a 4-position constant that is stored in a message file. To support multilingual menus, the constants that appear next to the option numbers can also be entered as message constants instead of the hard-coded constants that we have supplied in this example.

Figure 24.6 Adding Message Constants to the Menu

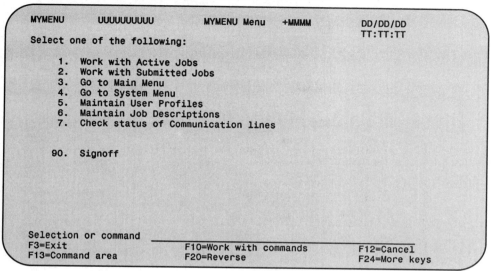

```
MYMENU        UUUUUUUUUU         MYMENU Menu    +MMMM       DD/DD/DD
                                                           TT:TT:TT
Select one of the following:

     1.   Work with Active Jobs
     2.   Work with Submitted Jobs
     3.   Go to Main Menu
     4.   Go to System Menu
     5.   Maintain User Profiles
     6.   Maintain Job Descriptions
     7.   Check status of Communication lines


    90.   Signoff




Selection or command  _____
F3=Exit                    F10=Work with commands        F12=Cancel
F13=Command area           F20=Reverse                   F24=More keys
```

When you enter a message constant, as in +MMMM, SDA prompts
you for the name of the message file and for the message ID that
contains the text to be displayed on the menu (see Figure 24.7). Then
when the menu is displayed, the text for the message constant will be
derived from the text of the specified message.

Figure 24.7 Defining a Message Constant for the Menu

```
                        Define Message Constant

Length . . . . :   4
Row . . . . . . :   1
Column . . . . :   48

Type choices, press Enter.

  Message file . . . . . . . . . .    SYSMSGF      Name, F4 for list

     Library  . . . . . . . . . . .    *LIBL       Name, *LIBL, *CURLIB

  Message identifier . . . . . . .    USR2105      Message ID, *LIST
```

In the example shown in Figure 24.8, the text contained in the message ID is the word TEST. This lets us know that the menu is currently running in a test environment rather than in the production environment. *Note: A test and production version of the message file SYSMSGF must exist in order to accomplish this.* This is one use of message constants, but you can use them in your menus for whatever purpose you choose.

Figure 24.8 The Resulting Display with Message Constant

```
 MYMENU        UUUUUUUUUU         MYMENU Menu              TEST     DD/DD/DD
                                                                    TT:TT:TT
 Select one of the following:

       1.  Work with Active Jobs
       2.  Work with Submitted Jobs
       3.  Go to Main Menu
       4.  Go to System Menu
       5.  Maintain User Profiles
       6.  Maintain Job Descriptions
       7.  Check status of Communication lines


      90.  Signoff




 Selection or command                         Position to . . . . . . . _
 Option . . . .   01   WRKACTJOB_____
                                                                More...
```

Once you have completed the design of the menu screen, you need to tell SDA what action should be taken when a user of the menu chooses one of the option numbers that appear on the menu. There are two ways to assign commands to the menu options. First, when you press the F13 key from the menu design display, SDA displays the command information related to your menu options. For example, in the preceding figure, you can see that we are assigning the WRKACTJOB command to option 01. You can use the PageUp/Down keys to assign commands for each menu option in this way.

Second, as an alternative to assigning commands to option numbers one at a time, you can press the F10 key, which allows you to assign all the commands needed for your menu options. As shown in Figure 24.9, you simply enter the appropriate CL command next to the option number that is to perform that function.

Figure 24.9 Assigning Commands to Menu Options

```
                            Define Menu Commands
Menu . . . . . . :   MYMENU            Position to menu option . . . . . __

Type commands, press Enter.

Option    Command
  01      WRKACTJOB
                                                                              _
  02      WRKSBMJOB
                                                                              _
  03      GO MAIN
                                                                              _
  04      GO SYSTEM
                                                                              _
  05      CALL USERAUT
                                                                              _
  06      CALL JOBDMAINT
                                                                              _
  07      CALL COMMLINES
                                                                              _

                                                                        More...
F3=Exit        F11=Defined only options    F12=Cancel        F24=More keys
```

After you have associated all the menu options on the display with a command, you are done with the main portion of the menu. The only part left is to create Help text for the menu.

To create help text for the menu, you place a Y next to the Work with menu help option on the screen shown in Figure 24.10.

Figure 24.10 Working with Menu Help Text

```
                            Specify Menu Functions
File . . . . . . :   QDDSSRC            Menu . . . . . . . :   MYMENU
  Library . . . . :    DRIEHL

Type choices, press Enter.

  Work with menu image and commands  . . . . . .   N    Y=Yes, N=No

  Work with menu help  . . . . . . . . . . . . .   Y    Y=Yes, N=No
```

You are then presented with the display shown in Figure 24.11. Here, you tell SDA how you want to build your Help text. You can either build one Help screen for the entire menu, or you can build separate Help screens for each menu option or group of options. In Figure 24.11, we specify that we want to create a new Help record.

Figure 24.11 Working with Menu Help Records

```
                        Work with Menu Help Records

File . . . . . . :    QDDSSRC            Menu . . . . . . . :    MYMENU
  Library . . . . :    DRIEHL

Type options (and Range), press Enter.
  1=Create         3=Copy           4=Delete            12=Update

Opt   Range    Text
1     __ - __

  (No menu help records in member)
```

The resulting display in Figure 24.12 lets you specify what menu options you are creating Help text for at this time. You can either create Help text for a single option, a range of options, or for the entire menu. Here we specify that we are creating Help text only for menu option 01.

Figure 24.12 Creating a Help Menu Record

```
                        Create Menu Help Record

File . . . . . . :    QDDSSRC            Menu . . . . . . . :    MYMENU
  Library . . . . :    DRIEHL

Type choices, press Enter.

  Create help for option . . . . . . . . . . . . . . .    01    01-99

  -OR-

  Create help for option range (range xx-yy)
    From menu option . . . . . . . . . . . . . . . . .    __    00-99
    To menu option . . . . . . . . . . . . . . . . . .    __    01-99

  -OR-

  Create general help (range 00-00) . . . . . . . . .    N     Y=Yes, N=No




F3=Exit    F5=Refresh    F9=Display image    F12=Cancel
```

You are then presented with another SDA design-type screen, as shown in Figure 24.13. Here, we include Help text that will be shown if the user of the menu presses the Help key while the cursor is positioned on the line containing option 01. When you have finished defining the Help screen for option 01, you should continue with Help text for option 02, 03, and so on. Each menu option should have its own Help text.

One inconsistency between IBM-supplied menus and SDA-created menus is in the area of the Help text provided. IBM's menus use UIM panel groups to show Help text, whereas SDA only allows you to associate a Help screen with a menu option.

Figure 24.13 Designing the Help Record

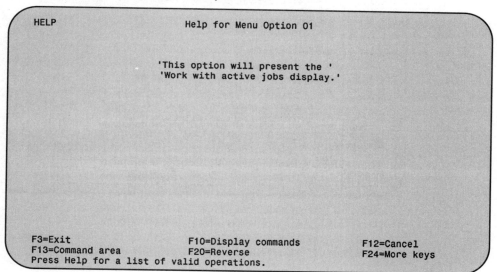

```
HELP                         Help for Menu Option 01



                        'This option will present the '
                        'Work with active jobs display.'
















 F3=Exit                      F10=Display commands         F12=Cancel
 F13=Command area             F20=Reverse                  F24=More keys
 Press Help for a list of valid operations.
```

When you have completed your menu design, SDA will save your work and create the menu for you. You can then access the menu using the GO command. By entering GO MYMENU, the menu in Figure 24.14 is displayed. When you select a menu option, the command that you associated with the option will be executed. You can see that the AS/400 command line and standard function keys have been provided for you. You now have a fully functional AS/400-style menu.

Figure 24.14 The Completed Menu MYMENU

```
MYMENU      DRIEHL              MYMENU Menu      TEST      10/23/94
                                                           11:30:19
 Select one of the following:

       1.  Work with Active Jobs
       2.  Work with Submitted Jobs
       3.  Go to Main Menu
       4.  Go to System Menu
       5.  Maintain User Profiles
       6.  Maintain Job Descriptions
       7.  Check status of Communication lines


      90.  Signoff




 Selection or command
 ===> _____

 F3=Exit   F4=Prompt   F9=Retrieve   F12=Cancel
 F13=Information Assistant  F16=System main menu
```

Testing Display Files

Chapter 25

You use option 3 of the SDA main menu (Figure 25.1) to test display files after you have successfully created them. You test display files for several reasons, such as ensuring that indicators are defined correctly, that record formats are positioned correctly, that input and output buffers contain data in the correct order, and so on.

Figure 25.1 The SDA Main Menu

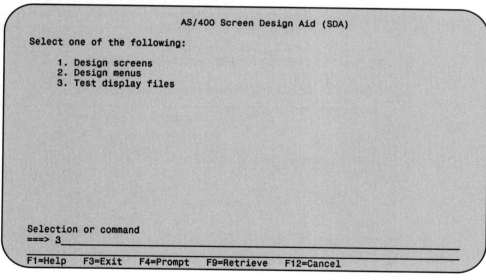

```
                          AS/400 Screen Design Aid (SDA)
  Select one of the following:

       1. Design screens
       2. Design menus
       3. Test display files










  Selection or command
  ===> 3
  F1=Help    F3=Exit    F4=Prompt    F9=Retrieve    F12=Cancel
```

When you select option 3, you are presented with the screen shown in Figure 25.2. Here, you specify the name of the display file to be tested and the record formats that should be included in the test. You can either enter the names of the record formats or press the F4 key, which will display a list of record formats from which you can choose. For this example, assume that we have pressed the F4 key to retrieve a list of record formats.

Figure 25.2 Selecting the Display File that Is To Be Tested

```
                          Test Display File

Type choices, press Enter.

    Display file . . . . . . . . . . . .    MYDSPF      Name, F4 for list
       Library  . . . . . . . . . . . . .   DRIEHL      Name, *LIBL ...

    Record to be tested  . . . . . . . .                Name, F4 for list

    Additional records to display  . . . .              Name, F4 for list
```

From the list of record formats shown in Figure 25.3, you can select the record format to be tested, along with any record formats that you want to appear on the display at the same time. Here, we select record format SCREEN1 as the format to be tested, and we select the format FKEYS as an additional format to display.

Figure 25.3 Selecting Record Formats To Be Tested

```
                         Select Records for Test

Display file . . . . . :  MYDSPF          Library . . . :   DRIEHL

Type information, press Enter.
   Number of records to roll . . . . . . . . . . . . . .   10

Type options, press Enter.
   1=Select for test   2,3,4=Display additional records

Option   Record      Type      Related Subfile
   1     SCREEN1     RECORD
   2     FKEYS       RECORD
```

To begin the test, SDA prompts you for the output fields that appear within the record format you are testing. The output field names appear, as well as the format of the output field, as shown in Figure 25.4.

Figure 25.4 Initial Display of Screen Output Data

```
                          Set Test Output Data

  Record . . . :   SCREEN1

  Type indicators and output field values, press Enter.

  Field          Value
  CUSTNO         999999:
  CUSTNM         OOOOOOOOOOOOOOOOOOOOOOOOOOOOOOOO:
  CUSTAD         OOOOOOOOOOOOOOOOOOOOOOOOOOOOOOOO:
  CUSTCT         OOOOOOOOOOOOOOOOOOOO:
  CUSTST         OO:
  CUSTZP         666666666:
```

To set values for the output fields, you simply overtype the field's
format, as in Figure 25.5.

Figure 25.5 Assigning Initial Values to Output Fields

```
                          Set Test Output Data

  Record . . . :   SCREEN1

  Type indicators and output field values, press Enter.

  Field          Value
  CUSTNO         123456:
  CUSTNM         Pundits Painting Co.        :
  CUSTAD         5562 Main Street            :
  CUSTCT         Seattle            :
  CUSTST         WA:
  CUSTZP         986251111 :
```

The SDA test function then displays the output display for the record
formats you selected. You can see in Figure 25.6 that all special
constants such as *DATE and *TIME have been replaced by actual
values, and that the output fields contain the data we entered on the
previous display.

Figure 25.6 The Test Display

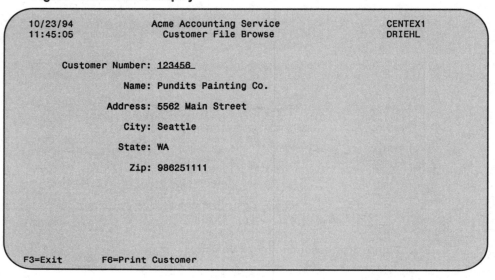

```
10/23/94                Acme Accounting Service              CENTEX1
11:45:05                 Customer File Browse                DRIEHL


        Customer Number: 123456_

                   Name: Pundits Painting Co.

                Address: 5562 Main Street

                   City: Seattle

                  State: WA

                    Zip: 986251111




F3=Exit        F6=Print Customer
```

For this display, you can now enter data into the input-capable fields,
and press a function key if you want. This will let you test your display
records to ensure that they will work properly with your program.

In Figure 25.7 you can see that the CUSTNO field contains the value

Figure 25.7 Displaying the Input Data

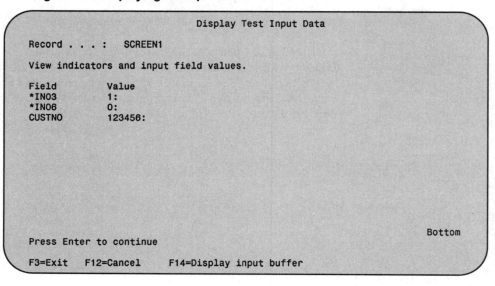

```
                        Display Test Input Data

    Record . . . :   SCREEN1

    View indicators and input field values.

    Field          Value
    *IN03          1:
    *IN06          0:
    CUSTNO         123456:








                                                            Bottom
    Press Enter to continue

    F3=Exit    F12=Cancel      F14=Display input buffer
```

123456. That is the value that appeared on the display screen for the customer number field in Figure 25.6. You can also see that indicator 03 has a value of 1. This means that the F3 key was pressed when the previous screen was displayed. If F6 had been pressed, indicator 06 would have had a value of 1.

To display the input buffer for the display file record, you can press the F14 key. This results in the display shown in Figure 25.8. Here you can see the input area as your program would see it. The two indicators *IN03 and *IN06 are shown in positions 1 and 2; positions 3-8 contain the data for the CUSTNO field.

Figure 25.8 Displaying the Input Buffer

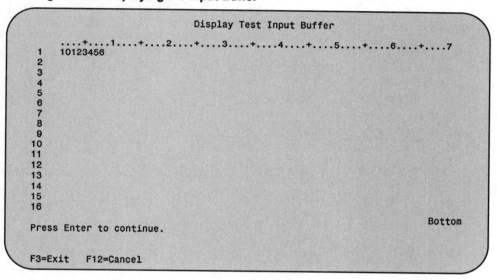

When you have completed your testing, press F3 to exit the test.

Section 4

Report Layout Utility (RLU)

Introduction to
Printer Files and RLU

Chapter 26

On the AS/400, programs use a special type of file called a *printer file* to create reports. IBM supplies many generic printer file descriptions within OS/400, such as QPRINT, which may be used when a program internally describes its printed output, as is the case when you are using RPG O-specs. However, a customized printer file definition can include information about the report format (headings, detail lines, total lines, etc.), as well as the character size and form type that will be used when the report is generated. You can use these customized printer files when the report is not defined internally within the program, but instead is externally described.

Customized printer files are created from AS/400 Data Description Specification (DDS) source code. DDS can be especially difficult to code and understand when you are trying to line up report columns and headings correctly. In the past, you might have worked with printer spacing charts to correctly determine the columns in which data was to appear. Report Layout Utility (RLU) is a tool designed to eliminate the task of entering DDS source code for printer files by providing you with an easy-to-use, interactive environment in which you can design and prototype your report layouts. When you have designed a report using RLU, the utility then creates the DDS source code for you. That source code is then used to create the printer file. RLU provides many productivity gains over the old printer spacing charts.

Operationally, RLU is an OS/400 hybrid application that combines the operations of the Source Entry Utility (SEU) with the operations of the Screen Design Aid (SDA). The result is a good tool, but not a great tool, which can explain why some third-party vendors make a good living providing RLU replacements that use the SDA model, instead of combining the SEU and SDA models, as IBM does.

Accessing RLU

There are two main ways to begin an RLU session. First, when you create a new printer file, you typically will use the Start Report Layout Utility (STRRLU) command and press F4 to prompt for the command parameters (Figure 26.1). The default value for the SRCFILE and SRCMBR parameters of the STRRLU command is *PRV. If you do not override the default value with the actual source file and member name you want to use, you will be placed into an RLU session for the report you last worked on.

Figure 26.1 Prompt for STRRLU Command

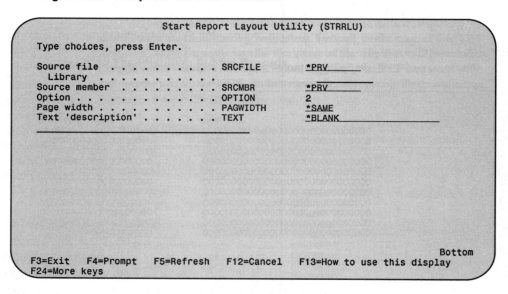

```
                    Start Report Layout Utility (STRRLU)

 Type choices, press Enter.

 Source file  . . . . . . . . . .   SRCFILE       *PRV
   Library  . . . . . . . . . .
 Source member  . . . . . . . . .   SRCMBR        *PRV
 Option . . . . . . . . . . . .     OPTION        2
 Page width . . . . . . . . . .     PAGWIDTH      *SAME
 Text 'description'  . . . . . .    TEXT          *BLANK
 _____




                                                               Bottom
 F3=Exit    F4=Prompt    F5=Refresh    F12=Cancel    F13=How to use this display
 F24=More keys
```

If you do not want to work with the printer file you worked with in your previous RLU session, enter the source file name, perhaps QDDSSRC, and the library in which the source file resided. In the SRCMBR parameter, enter the name of the source member that contains, or will contain, the updated printer file DDS when you have finished designing the report with RLU.

The Option parameter value can contain either the option number 2, as shown here, or it can contain the value 6. Option 2 is used to create a new printer file, or to modify an existing one. Option 6 is used to print a prototype report using the printer file DDS as a basis for the prototype. Figure 26.2 shows a RLU prototype report for a sample printer file.

Figure 26.2 The RLU Report Prototype Report

```
          RLU REPORT PROTOTYPE
5738PW1 V2R3MO  931105                          S9999999 12/14/94 16:21:51

Source file . . . . . . . . . . . . . . . . . :   QDDSSRC
   Library . . . . . . . . . . . . . . . . . . :     DRIEHL
Source member . . . . . . . . . . . . . . . . :   CUSTPRT1
Spooled output queue . . . . . . . . . . . . :   SCPRO1
   Library . . . . . . . . . . . . . . . . . . :     QUSRSYS
Print device . . . . . . . . . . . . . . . . :   PRT01
Number of copies . . . . . . . . . . . . . . :   1
Forms type . . . . . . . . . . . . . . . . . :   *STD
Lines per inch . . . . . . . . . . . . . . . :   6
Characters per inch . . . . . . . . . . . . :   10
User profile . . . . . . . . . . . . . . . . :   DRIEHL
Indicators conditioned on . . . . . . . . . :


     12/14/94            Acme Accounting Services
     16:21:54            Customer Master Listing




     Cust#              Customer Name              Contact Name
     999999   XXXXXXXXXXXXXXXXXXXXXXXXXXXXXX   XXXXXXXXXXXXXXXXXXXX
     999999   XXXXXXXXXXXXXXXXXXXXXXXXXXXXXX   XXXXXXXXXXXXXXXXXXXX
     999999   XXXXXXXXXXXXXXXXXXXXXXXXXXXXXX   XXXXXXXXXXXXXXXXXXXX
     999999   XXXXXXXXXXXXXXXXXXXXXXXXXXXXXX   XXXXXXXXXXXXXXXXXXXX
     999999   XXXXXXXXXXXXXXXXXXXXXXXXXXXXXX   XXXXXXXXXXXXXXXXXXXX
     999999   XXXXXXXXXXXXXXXXXXXXXXXXXXXXXX   XXXXXXXXXXXXXXXXXXXX
 * * * *  E N D   O F   R E P O R T   P R O T O T Y P E  * * * *
```

The STRRLU PAGEWIDTH parameter specifies the width of the report you are designing. You can specify that a report be from 1 through 378 columns wide. When you are modifying an existing printer file, the default value *SAME means that the width of the report does not change from its current value. If you are creating a new printer file, the value *SAME means that you will be creating a report that is 132 columns wide.

The TEXT parameter is used to assign descriptive text to the DDS source member. You should always assign descriptive text to every source member and every object.

When you are modifying an existing printer file, it's probably easiest to start RLU through PDM, using option 19 from the Work with Members Using PDM display. Figure 26.3 shows how you can start RLU using PDM option 19.

Figure 26.3 Accessing RLU Through PDM

```
                       Work with Members Using PDM

     File  . . . . . .    QDDSSRC___
        Library . . . .      DRIEHL____       Position to . . . . .  _____

     Type options, press Enter.
        14=Compile         15=Create module      16=Run procedure
        17=Change using SDA  19=Change using RLU   25=Find string ...

     Opt   Member    Type       Text
      _    CUSTFILE  PF         My Customer file
      19   CUSTPRT1  PRTF       Customer Master listing
      _    MYDSPF    DSPF       My Display file
      _    MYMENU    MNUDDS
      _    MYMENUQQ  MNUCMD



                                                                    Bottom
     Parameters or command
     ===>
     F3=Exit          F4=Prompt          F5=Refresh        F6=Create
     F9=Retrieve      F10=Command entry  F23=More options  F24=More keys
```

The RLU Work Display

When you start RLU, the first screen you are presented with is the RLU Design Report display. Figure 26.4 shows the Design Report display containing a partially completed report layout. As you can see, this display is very similar to the SEU edit display. As in SEU, the top of the display contains a command line, the left side of the display is the sequence number area, the majority of the screen is the editing area, and function keys are listed at the bottom of the screen.

Figure 26.4 The RLU Design Report Display

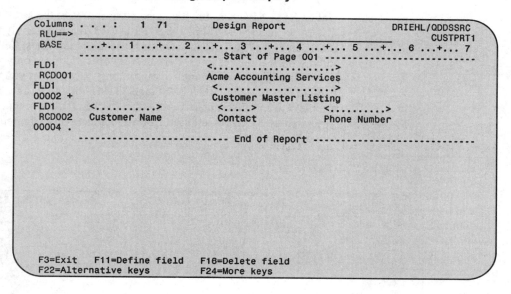

```
Columns . . . :   1  71        Design Report              DRIEHL/QDDSSRC
  RLU==>                                                            CUSTPRT1
  BASE     ...+... 1 ...+... 2 ...+... 3 ...+... 4 ...+... 5 ...+... 6 ...+... 7
         ------------------------ Start of Page 001 -----------------------
FLD1                           <.....................>
  RCD001                       Acme Accounting Services
FLD1                           <.....................>
00002 +                        Customer Master Listing
FLD1     <...........>         <.....>              <..........>
  RCD002  Customer Name        Contact              Phone Number
00004 .
         ------------------------ End of Report -----------------------------



 F3=Exit   F11=Define field    F16=Delete field
 F22=Alternative keys          F24=More keys
```

The RLU Command Line

The command line that appears near the top of the RLU Design Report display allows the same commands as the SEU command line (e.g., FIND, SET, HIDE, TOP, BOTTOM). For more information, see the discussion of the SEU command line in Chapter 15 of this book (page 109). RLU supplies no additional commands — only those allowed in SEU.

Types of RLU Lines

Unlike SEU, RLU uses the sequence number area at the left side of the display to identify RLU line types. RLU uses four different types, as shown in Figure 26.5. The RLU line types are report lines, field lines, sample lines and filler lines. Certain RLU operations are only valid for certain line types. For example, you can only specify that you want to include the constants *DATESYS and *TIME on a field line. The sample line and field line have no effect on the DDS code that is generated by RLU, but are used instead to assist you in the report design process.

Figure 26.5 RLU Line Types

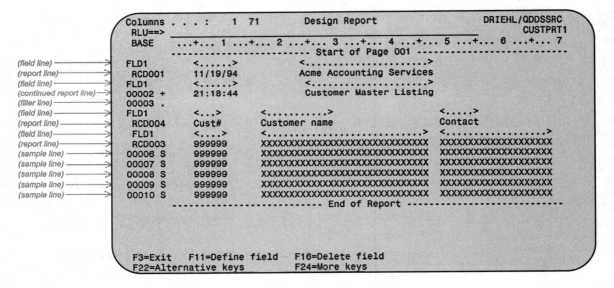

Report Line

The report lines identify data to include in the generated DDS for the printer file. RLU identifies the first report line in a group of report lines by the name of the record format (e.g., RCD001) that appears in the sequence number area. A + character in the sequence number area identifies subsequent report lines.

Field Line

RLU field lines contain the characters FLD in the sequence number area. A field line is an image of the way the record format might look when it is printed. You can modify the field line directly when you must modify fields within the record format. A field line is created and shown above a report line whenever a field is defined within a report line. If you find the field lines confusing, you can prohibit them from showing on the display by changing your RLU session defaults (discussed later). The contents of field lines do not affect the DDS generated by RLU.

Sample Line

Sample lines assist in the report design process, but do not affect the DDS generated by RLU. The first sample line in a group of sample lines is identified by the letter S that appears in the sequence number area. A + character in the sequence number identifies subsequent sample lines.

Filler Line

Filler lines have a period (.) in the sequence number area. You can use a filler line to separate one record format from another. When a filler line appears between two record formats, it causes the DDS keyword SPACEB(n) to be added to the second record format, where *n* is the number of filler lines appearing between the record formats, plus 1 (e.g., if one filler line exists, the result is SPACEB(2))

Using RLU Line Commands

Because RLU is so closely related to SEU, you can use SEU line commands for moving, inserting, copying, and deleting source lines within RLU. For example, you can copy an RLU line by placing the character C in the sequence number area of a report line and the character A in the sequence number area of another line. A summary of the SEU line commands appears in the SEU section of this book on page 53. In addition to using the SEU line commands, you can use special line commands that are only available within RLU. While we will discuss most of these line commands in detail, Figure 26.6 summarizes them for your reference.

Figure 26.6 Summary of Special RLU Line Commands

Command	Description
DR	Define a record format
CL	Change this line to a different line type
SD	Create sample data line(s)
VF	View the field line for this report line
NP	New page for prototype report
DC	Define fields on this line as constants
DF	Define fields on this line as named fields
CF	Center fields within the report margin
SP	Evenly space fields within the report margin

RLU Function Keys

RLU handles function keys differently than any other IBM application contained in ADTS/400. In RLU there are two distinct sets of function keys that you can use. You use the F22 key to toggle the RLU session between the two sets. You can determine which set of keys is active by looking at the RLU work display, just above the sequence line number area. If the word BASE appears, you can use the base set of RLU function keys. If the characters ALT appear, you can use the alternate RLU function keys. The purpose of the ALT set of function keys is to enable the SEU function keys within RLU. While some people may find this overloading helpful, I find little use for the SEU functions such as Browse/Copy, Find/Change, and so on when I'm working in RLU.

Figure 26.7 shows the RLU Design Report display for our sample report. You will notice that we are currently using the BASE set of function keys. Figures 26.8 and 26.9 list the BASE and ALT function keys available in RLU and a desciption of each.

Figure 26.7 BASE Function Keys

```
Columns . . . :    1  71       Design Report              DRIEHL/QDDSSRC
RLU==>                                                             CUSTPRT1
BASE      ...+... 1 ...+... 2 ...+... 3 ...+... 4 ...+... 5 ...+... 6 ...+... 7
          ------------------------- Start of Page 001 -------------------------
FLD1          <.....>           <....................>
RCD001     12/14/94          Acme Accounting Services
FLD1          <.....>           <....................>
00002 +    16:52:13          Customer Master Listing
00003 .
FLD1          <...>             <..........>
RCD004     Cust#             Customer name
FLD1          <....>        <....................>  <....................>
RCD003     999999        XXXXXXXXXXXXXXXXXXXXXXXXXXX  XXXXXXXXXXXXXXXXXXXXX
00006 S    999999        XXXXXXXXXXXXXXXXXXXXXXXXXXX  XXXXXXXXXXXXXXXXXXXXX
00007 S    999999        XXXXXXXXXXXXXXXXXXXXXXXXXXX  XXXXXXXXXXXXXXXXXXXXX
00008 S    999999        XXXXXXXXXXXXXXXXXXXXXXXXXXX  XXXXXXXXXXXXXXXXXXXXX
00009 S    999999        XXXXXXXXXXXXXXXXXXXXXXXXXXX  XXXXXXXXXXXXXXXXXXXXX
00010 S    999999        XXXXXXXXXXXXXXXXXXXXXXXXXXX  XXXXXXXXXXXXXXXXXXXXX
          ------------------------- End of Report -------------------------


 F3=Exit    F11=Define field    F16=Delete field
 F22=Alternative keys           F24=More keys
```

Figure 26.8 RLU BASE Function Keys

Key	Description
F1	Display help
F3	Exit RLU
F4	Show Work with Fields display
F5	Refresh display with original entries
F6	Show Condition Design Report display
F9	Retrieve last command
F10	Show Work with Database Fields display
F11	Show Define Field Information display
F12	Cancel split-screen display
F13	Mark and unmark data for ensuing operations
F14	Copy marked data to cursor location
F15	Move marked data to cursor location
F16	Delete field at cursor location
F17	Show Work with File Keywords display
F18	Show Work with Record Keywords display
F19	Scroll display to the left
F20	Scroll display to the right
F21	Show the CL command line window
F22	Toggle to ALTernate function keys
F23	Go to Work with Field Keywords display
F24	Display other available BASE keys

Figure 26.9 RLU ALTernate Function Keys

Key	Description
F1	Display help
F3	Exit RLU
F4	Prompt for line on which the cursor is located
F5	Refresh display with original entries
F6	Move split-screen line to cursor location
F9	Retrieve last command
F10	Toggle cursor position between command line and work area
F12	Cancel split-screen or prompt display
F13	Show Change Session Defaults display
F14	Show Find/Change Options display
F15	Show Browse/Copy Options display
F16	Repeat prior find operation
F17	Repeat prior change operation
F18	Perform DBCS conversion
F19	Scroll display to the left
F20	Scroll display to the right
F21	Show the CL command line window

Key	Description
F22	Toggle to BASE function keys
F24	Display other available ALTernate keys

Starting a Report Design

When you begin designing a new report, you can either start by copying an existing report to a new member and modifying that existing report format to meet the new requirements, or you can start from scratch with an empty source member. When you start from scratch, you specify the new member name on the STRRLU command. When you do, the Design Report display appears as shown in Figure 26.10.

Figure 26.10 Designing a New Report

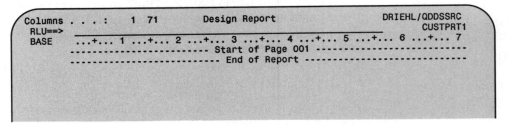

To begin adding constants and other data to the report, you first need to insert some blank lines. To do this, use the standard SEU command I, followed by the number of lines you want to insert. In Figure 26.11, we use the I5 command to insert five blank lines.

Figure 26.11 Using the SEU Insert Lines Command

```
Columns . . . :    1  71         Design Report                  DRIEHL/QDDSSRC
RLU==> _____             CUSTPRT1
BASE      ...+... 1 ...+... 2 ...+... 3 ...+... 4 ...+... 5 ...+... 6 ...+... 7
I5        ----------------------- Start of Page 001 -----------------------
          ----------------------- End of Report -----------------------
```

Adding Constants

You can add report constants in several different ways. You can use the SDA method of entering the constant enclosed in apostrophes, you can position the cursor to the desired location and press F11 (Define field), or you can use a third method outlined next. The method you use for adding constants is your choice; however, if you are familiar with SDA, you might prefer to use the SDA method.

Once the blank lines have been inserted, you can add constants to the report layout. First, enter the text for the constants as shown in Figure 26.12. Here, we add constants on two different lines.

Figure 26.12 Adding Constants

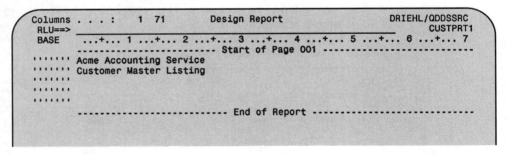

```
Columns . . . :    1  71         Design Report                  DRIEHL/QDDSSRC
RLU==> _____             CUSTPRT1
BASE      ...+... 1 ...+... 2 ...+... 3 ...+... 4 ...+... 5 ...+... 6 ...+... 7
          ----------------------- Start of Page 001 -----------------------
'''''''' Acme Accounting Service
'''''''' Customer Master Listing
''''''''
''''''''
''''''''
          ----------------------- End of Report -----------------------
```

Whenever new lines are added to the report layout, the lines are added as filler lines. In Figure 26.13, the sequence number area for the new lines contains a period (.) character. This indicates the lines are filler lines. Since filler lines do not generate DDS, we have to modify the lines somewhat to have them included in our finished report.

Figure 26.13 New Lines Added as Filler Lines

```
Columns . . . :    1  71        Design Report              DRIEHL/QDDSSRC
RLU==>                                                            CUSTPRT1
BASE    ...+... 1 ...+... 2 ...+... 3 ...+... 4 ...+... 5 ...+... 6 ...+... 7
                ---------------------- Start of Page 001 ----------------------
00001 . Acme Accounting Service
00002 . Customer Master Listing
                ----------------------- End of Report -----------------------
```

Defining a Record Format

Reports consist of record formats, which in turn are made up of constants and data fields. In Figure 26.14, the two filler lines are combined to form a record format, using the block form of the DR (Define Record format) command. Placing the block command DRR on the two lines tells RLU to create a record format that contains all the data on the included lines. If you needed a different record format for each line, entering the command DR on each line would create two different record formats.

Figure 26.14 Defining a Record Format

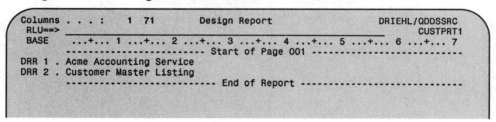

```
Columns . . . :    1  71        Design Report              DRIEHL/QDDSSRC
RLU==>                                                            CUSTPRT1
BASE    ...+... 1 ...+... 2 ...+... 3 ...+... 4 ...+... 5 ...+... 6 ...+... 7
                ---------------------- Start of Page 001 ----------------------
DRR 1 . Acme Accounting Service
DRR 2 . Customer Master Listing
                ----------------------- End of Report -----------------------
```

When a record format is defined, RLU assigns a name to the new record format in the form RCDnnn, where *nnn* is a sequential number starting with 001. As you can see in Figure 26.15, the record format RCD001 has been created and spans two report lines.

Figure 26.15 Record Format Report Lines

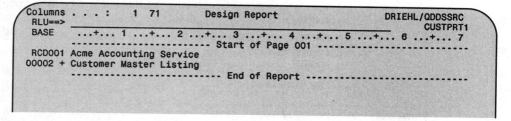

```
Columns . . . :    1  71          Design Report              DRIEHL/QDDSSRC
  RLU==>                                                          CUSTPRT1
  BASE      ...+... 1 ...+... 2 ...+... 3 ...+... 4 ...+... 5 ...+... 6 ...+... 7
            ----------------------- Start of Page 001 -----------------------
RCD001 Acme Accounting Service
00002 + Customer Master Listing
            ----------------------- End of Report -----------------------
```

To define the data on a line as a constant, use the DC (Define Constants) line command. The DC command will define a constant for each data element on the corresponding source line that is separated by two or more blanks. Figure 26.16 shows how you can define constants on two lines at the same time. Alternately, you could have used the block version of the DC command (DCC). You also could use the form DCn, where *n* is the number of lines to include in the DC operation. In this case, it would have been stated as DC2. If you wanted to define the fields as named fields instead of constants, you would use the line command DF (Define Fields) and/or its block forms DFF and DFn.

Figure 26.16 Defining Constants

```
Columns . . . :    1  71          Design Report              DRIEHL/QDDSSRC
  RLU==>                                                          CUSTPRT1
  BASE      ...+... 1 ...+... 2 ...+... 3 ...+... 4 ...+... 5 ...+... 6 ...+... 7
            ----------------------- Start of Page 001 -----------------------
DC D001 Acme Accounting Service
DC 02 + Customer Master Listing
            ----------------------- End of Report -----------------------
```

Once the constants have been defined, the field line is displayed for each line, as shown in Figure 26.17. The field line shows the representation of the fields using the characters <.>. When manipulation of a field or constant is required (e.g., moving, changing the format), the representation shown on the field line is used, not the field(s) shown on the report line.

Figure 26.17 The Field Line

```
Columns . . . :    1  71          Design Report              DRIEHL/QDDSSRC
  RLU==>                                                             CUSTPRT1
  BASE     ...+... 1 ...+... 2 ...+... 3 ...+... 4 ...+... 5 ...+... 6 ...+... 7
           ----------------------- Start of Page 001 -----------------------
FLD1       <....................>
  RCD001 Acme Accounting Service
FLD1       <....................>
  00002 + Customer Master Listing
           ----------------------- End of Report -----------------------
```

Centering Fields

You can use the RLU line commands to evenly space the fields across the report line, or to move a field to the center of the report. To evenly space fields, the RLU command is SP; to center a field on the report, the command is CF. In Figure 26.18, the CF command is being used to center the two heading fields within the report. Alternately, the block form of the CF command (CFF), or the form CFn (where *n* is the number of lines to center), could have been used. Here, the CFn would have been CF2.

Figure 26.18 Using RLU Line Commands To Center Fields

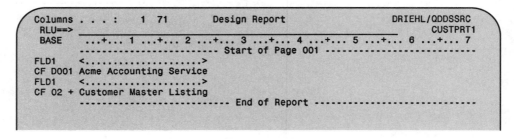

```
Columns . . . :    1  71          Design Report              DRIEHL/QDDSSRC
  RLU==>                                                             CUSTPRT1
  BASE     ...+... 1 ...+... 2 ...+... 3 ...+... 4 ...+... 5 ...+... 6 ...+... 7
           ----------------------- Start of Page 001 -----------------------
FLD1       <....................>
CF D001 Acme Accounting Service
FLD1       <....................>
CF 02 + Customer Master Listing
           ----------------------- End of Report -----------------------
```

Figure 26.19 shows the report heading, consisting of two constants. The constants are both contained in the same record format named RCD001. To add additional constants or data fields, you can insert additional lines where they are needed in the report by using the SEU I (Insert) command.

Figure 26.19 The Defined Constants and Record Format

```
Columns  . . . :    1  71         Design Report                DRIEHL/QDDSSRC
   RLU==>                                                              CUSTPRT1
   BASE   ...+... 1 ...+... 2 ...+... 3 ...+... 4 ...+... 5 ...+... 6 ...+... 7
          ------------------------------ Start of Page 001 -----------------------
FLD1                              <.....................>
   RCD001                         Acme Accounting Services
FLD1                              <.....................>
   00002 +                        Customer Master Listing
          ----------------------------- End of Report -------------------------------
```

Adding the RLU Special Constants

RLU lets you include special constants within your report design. The four special constants that can be included are *DATE, *TIME, *DATESYS, and *PAGNBR. You can specify these special constants only on a field line.

Use the *DATE special constant to include the job date on the report. Use the *TIME special constant to include the system time on the report. Use the *DATESYS special constant to include the system date on the report. And use the *PAGNBR special constant to display the page number on the report. Figure 26.20 shows how you could include the date and time in the report.

Figure 26.20 Using Special Constants

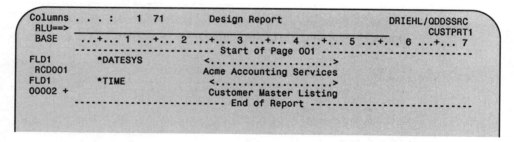

```
Columns  . . . :    1  71         Design Report                DRIEHL/QDDSSRC
   RLU==>                                                              CUSTPRT1
   BASE   ...+... 1 ...+... 2 ...+... 3 ...+... 4 ...+... 5 ...+... 6 ...+... 7
          ------------------------------ Start of Page 001 -----------------------
FLD1         *DATESYS             <.....................>
   RCD001                         Acme Accounting Services
FLD1         *TIME                <.....................>
   00002 +                        Customer Master Listing
          ----------------------------- End of Report -------------------------------
```

When you add the special constants, they already include editing characters, as shown in Figure 26.21.

Figure 26.21 Special Constants Added

```
 Columns  . . . :    1  71         Design Report              DRIEHL/QDDSSRC
  RLU==>                                                              CUSTPRT1
  BASE      ...+... 1 ...+... 2 ...+... 3 ...+... 4 ...+... 5 ...+... 6 ...+... 7
            ----------------------- Start of Page 001 ------------------------
 FLD1       <......>              <......................>
  RCD001    11/22/94              Acme Accounting Services
 FLD1       <......>              <......................>
  00002 +   12:18:44              Customer Master Listing
            ----------------------- End of Report ------------------------------
```

Defining Data Fields

RLU employs several methods to define a data field. You can place the cursor on the desired location and press F11 to define a field. You can also use the CF command to create named fields. But if you are familiar with SDA, you might appreciate the fact that you can define a data field using the SDA convention of entering the character + followed by the field designation, as in +OOOO, or +O(4). In Figure 26.22, three data fields are defined: a 6-digit numeric field, a 20-byte character field, and a 15-byte character field.

Figure 26.22 Defining Data Fields

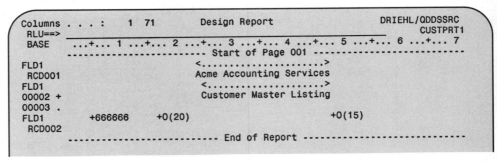

```
 Columns  . . . :    1  71         Design Report              DRIEHL/QDDSSRC
  RLU==>                                                              CUSTPRT1
  BASE      ...+... 1 ...+... 2 ...+... 3 ...+... 4 ...+... 5 ...+... 6 ...+... 7
            ----------------------- Start of Page 001 ------------------------
 FLD1                             <......................>
  RCD001                         Acme Accounting Services
 FLD1                             <......................>
  00002 +                         Customer Master Listing
  00003 .
 FLD1       +666666      +O(20)                           +O(15)
  RCD002
            ----------------------- End of Report ------------------------------
```

The resulting display in Figure 26.23 shows the definition of the new data fields.

Figure 26.23 Data Fields Defined

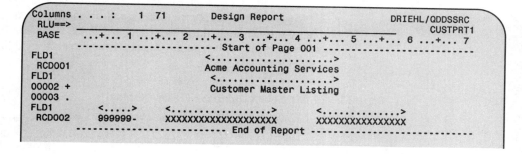

```
Columns . . . :    1  71        Design Report                    DRIEHL/QDDSSRC
   RLU==>                                                                CUSTPRT1
   BASE      ...+... 1 ...+... 2 ...+... 3 ...+... 4 ...+... 5 ...+... 6 ...+... 7
             --------------------- Start of Page 001 ----------------------
FLD1                            <.....................>
  RCD001                        Acme Accounting Services
FLD1                            <.....................>
00002 +                         Customer Master Listing
00003 .
FLD1        <.....>    <...................>      <...............>
  RCD002    999999-    XXXXXXXXXXXXXXXXXXXX       XXXXXXXXXXXXXXXX
            ----------------------- End of Report ----------------------
```

Adding Fields from Database Files

To add database fields to a report, follow the procedure outlined here.
First, from the Design Report display, press the F10 key. RLU then
shows you the Work with Database Fields screen shown in Figure 26.24.

Figure 26.24 The Work with Database Fields Display

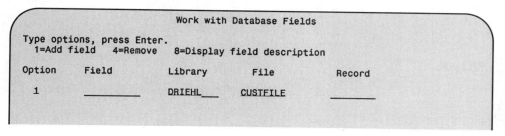

```
                        Work with Database Fields

Type options, press Enter.
  1=Add field    4=Remove    8=Display field description

Option     Field          Library       File        Record

   1       _____      DRIEHL___     CUSTFILE    _____
```

If you do not know the names of the fields or record formats you want to include, enter the file and library name, as shown here, and press F4 to get a list of the record formats and fields. Once you have selected a record format name, the Select Database Fields display in Figure 26.25 will appear. Here, you simply place a 1 next to each field that you want to include in the report.

Figure 26.25 The Select Database Fields Display

```
                          Select Database Fields
   File . . . . . . . . :   CUSTFILE       Record . . . . . . . :   CUSTREC
     Library  . . . . . :   DRIEHL

   Position to  . . . . .   _____     Field
   Subset . . . . . . . .   *ALL_____     *ALL, name, *generic*

   Type options, press Enter.
     1=Select    8=Display field description
                                                        Column
                                                        Heading
   Opt      Field      Length   Type                    CUSTAD
            CUSTAD         30   Character               CUSTCT
     1      CUSTCT         20   Character               CUSTNM
     1      CUSTNM         30   Character               CUSTNO
     1      CUSTNO        6,0   Zoned decimal           CUSTST
            CUSTST          2   Character               CUSTZP
     _      CUSTZP        9,0   Zoned decimal

                                                                     Bottom
   F5=Refresh    F11=Display unsorted    F12=Cancel
```

Once you have selected the fields that should be included on the report, you need to define the record format in which to place the fields. In Figure 26.26 we use the DR command to define a new record format. You will notice that the fields you selected from the database are listed at the bottom of the display.

Figure 26.26 Adding a Record Format for New Fields

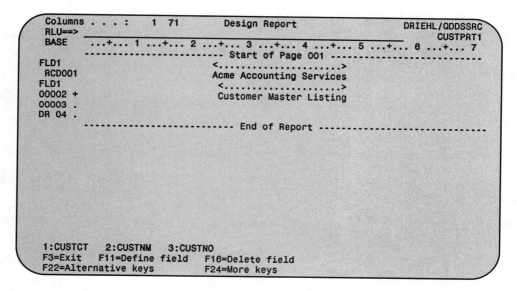

When you are adding database fields to a record format, RLU requires that you add the fields on a field line. However, RLU does not create a field line for a record format until a field has been defined within the format. To solve this problem, the RLU command VF allows you to view the field line for a report line even if no fields are yet defined for it. In Figure 26.27, we have used the VF (View Field line) command to cause RLU to display the field line.

Figure 26.27 Using the VF Command

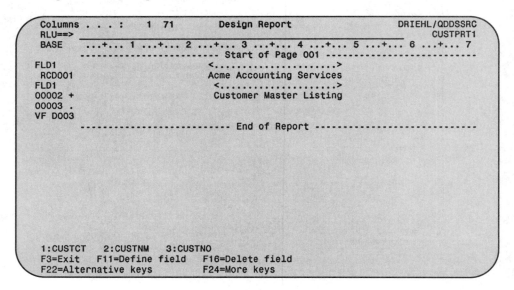

Now that the field line is displayed, as shown in Figure 26.28, you can use the SDA conventions for placing the database fields on the display. In this example, we use the command &3C to cause field number 3 at the bottom of the display to be placed at the location of the command; likewise with field 2 and field 1. Including the character C in the command &3C causes the column heading defined for the field to be included, centered above the field.

Figure 26.28 Placing Database Fields on the Report

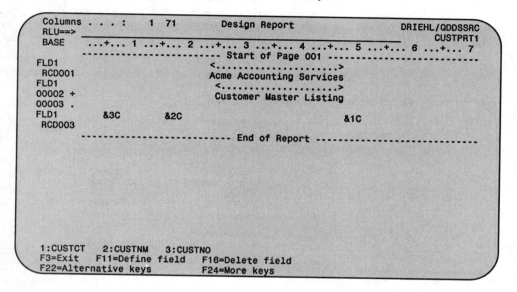

The & commands are the same as those used in SDA. Figure 26.29 is a summary of the valid & commands you can use in RLU.

Figure 26.29 Commands for Placing Database Fields on the Report

RLU Command	Function
&n (where *n* is the field number)	Place the field on the report
&nL	Place the field on the report with column heading at left
&nR	Place the field on the report with column heading at right
&nC	Place the field on the report with column heading above
&nP	Place the column heading for this field on the report, but not the field itself.

This procedure might seem to be a lot of trouble to go through, but because you can enter the & commands only on a field line, you first must get a new record format and field line created. Figure 26.30 shows the resulting display after the database fields have been added. You will notice that the column headings appear in a new record format (RCD004) that was created when RLU copied in the column headings.

Figure 26.30 The Resulting Display

```
Columns . . . :    1  71         Design Report              DRIEHL/QDDSSRC
RLU==>  _____          CUSTPRT1
BASE      ...+... 1 ...+... 2 ...+... 3 ...+... 4 ...+... 5 ...+... 6 ...+... 7
         ------------------------ Start of Page 001 ------------------------
FLD1                                <.....................>
RCD001                              Acme Accounting Services
FLD1                                <.....................>
00002 +                             Customer Master Listing
00003 .
FLD1      <....>                     <....>                      <....>
RCD004    CUSTNO                     CUSTNM                      CUSTCT
FLD1      <....>      <.........................>  <...................>
RCD003    999999      XXXXXXXXXXXXXXXXXXXXXXXXXXXX  XXXXXXXXXXXXXXXXXXXX
         ------------------------- End of Report -------------------------
```

Moving Fields

You can move fields in several different ways in RLU:

- Use the SEU line commands R and L to shift the entire line left or right.

- Press F4 to go to the Work with Fields display and change the relative position.

- Mark a field or group of fields using F13, then move the cursor to the desired location and press F14 to copy the marked field(s), or press F15 to move the marked field(s).

- Use the Insert and Delete keys on a field line.

Figure 26.31 shows the Work with Fields display that results when you press the F4 (Work with fields) key while the cursor is within the RCD003 record format area of the previous display. As you can see, all fields within the record format are displayed. Using the options available, you can change the field, delete the field, or work with the field keywords.

Figure 26.31 The Work with Fields Display

```
                              Work with Fields
      Record format  . . . . :  RCD003

      Type options, press Enter.
        2=Change    4=Delete    5=Work with keywords


      Opt  Field                  Line   Position   Length    -Indicators--
      2_   CUSTNO                            5
      __   CUSTNM                           +6
      __   CUSTCT                           +2




                                                                    Bottom
      F3=Exit    F5=Refresh    F11=Display interpreted values   F12=Cancel
```

When you place option 2 (change) beside the CUSTNO field, as shown in Figure 26.31, you are presented with the Specify Field Information screens in Figure 26.32a and 26.32b. On these screens you can specify a new field name, option indicators, line, and position of the field within the record format. You can also specify the data type and length for the field, and whether or not you want to reference a file for the desciption of this field.

Figure 26.32a Specify Field Information, Screen 1

```
                        Specify Field Information
        Edited length . . . . . . . . . . . . . :    6
        Record format . . . . . . . . . . . . . :    RCD003
        Number of keywords  . . . . . . . . . :      1
        Number of indicators  . . . . . . . . :      0

        Type choices, press Enter.

          Field . . . . . . . . . . . . . . .      CUSTNO____     Name
          Option indicators . . . . . . . . . .    ___ ___ ___    O1-99, NO1-N99
             More indicators . . . . . . . . .        N          Y=Yes, N=No
          Starting line . . . . . . . . . . . .     ___          1-255
          Starting position . . . . . . . . . .      _5          1-255, +nn
          Length of data  . . . . . . . . . . .     ___          1-378, +nn, -nn
          Data type . . . . . . . . . . . . . .      _           1=Character
                                                                 2=Zoned
                                                                 3=Floating point
          Decimal positions . . . . . . . . . .      __          0-31, +n, -n

                                                                          More...
        F3=Exit   F5=Refresh   F11=Convert to constant field   F12=Cancel
```

Figure 26.32b Specify Field Information, Screen 2

```
                        Specify Field Information
        Edited length . . . . . . . . . . . . . :    6
        Record format . . . . . . . . . . . . . :    RCD003
        Number of keywords  . . . . . . . . . :      1
        Number of indicators  . . . . . . . . :      0

        Type choices, press Enter.

          Reference a field . . . . . . . . . .      Y          Y=Yes, N=No
             Use referenced values . . . . . . .     N          Y=Yes, N=No






                                                                          Bottom
        F3=Exit   F5=Refresh   F11=Convert to constant field   F12=Cancel
```

Adding Sample Lines

You can add sample lines to your design layout by entering the SD (Sample Data) command. In Figure 26.33, we use the form SDn, where *n* indicates the number of sample lines to include. Here, we use SD5 to display five sample lines.

Figure 26.33 Including Sample Data

```
Columns . . . :    1  71          Design Report               DRIEHL/QDDSSRC
  RLU==>                                                                CUSTPRT1
  BASE        ...+... 1 ...+... 2 ...+... 3 ...+... 4 ...+... 5 ...+... 6 ...+... 7
             -------------------------- Start of Page 001 ----------------------
FLD1          <......>              <.....................>
  RCD001      11/19/94          Acme Accounting Services
FLD1          <......>              <.....................>
00002 +       21:18:44          Customer Master Listing
00003 .
FLD1          <....>               <....>                        <....>
  RCD004      CUSTNO                CUSTNM                        CUSTCT
FLD1          <....>      <.............................>  <..................>
SD5 003       999999      XXXXXXXXXXXXXXXXXXXXXXXXXXXXXXX  XXXXXXXXXXXXXXXXXXXX
             -------------------------- End of Report -----------------------
```

Figure 26.34 shows the resulting display with the five sample lines.

Figure 26.34 Sample Lines

```
Columns . . . :    1  71          Design Report               DRIEHL/QDDSSRC
  RLU==>                                                                CUSTPRT1
  BASE        ...+... 1 ...+... 2 ...+... 3 ...+... 4 ...+... 5 ...+... 6 ...+... 7
             -------------------------- Start of Page 001 ----------------------
FLD1          <......>              <.....................>
  RCD001      11/19/94          Acme Accounting Services
FLD1          <......>              <.....................>
00002 +       21:18:44          Customer Master Listing
00003 .
FLD1          <....>               <....>                        <....>
  RCD004      CUSTNO                CUSTNM                        CUSTCT
FLD1          <....>      <.............................>  <..................>
  RCD003      999999      XXXXXXXXXXXXXXXXXXXXXXXXXXXXXXX  XXXXXXXXXXXXXXXXXXXX
00006 S       999999      XXXXXXXXXXXXXXXXXXXXXXXXXXXXXXX  XXXXXXXXXXXXXXXXXXXX
00007 S       999999      XXXXXXXXXXXXXXXXXXXXXXXXXXXXXXX  XXXXXXXXXXXXXXXXXXXX
00008 S       999999      XXXXXXXXXXXXXXXXXXXXXXXXXXXXXXX  XXXXXXXXXXXXXXXXXXXX
00009 S       999999      XXXXXXXXXXXXXXXXXXXXXXXXXXXXXXX  XXXXXXXXXXXXXXXXXXXX
00010 S       999999      XXXXXXXXXXXXXXXXXXXXXXXXXXXXXXX  XXXXXXXXXXXXXXXXXXXX
             -------------------------- End of Report -----------------------
```

RLU Session Defaults

When you select the ALT set of function keys on the RLU Design Report display, you can press the F13 key to display and/or change the

RLU session defaults. Figures 26.35a and 26.35b show the RLU defaults that can be changed.

Figure 26.35a Changing RLU Session Defaults, Screen 1

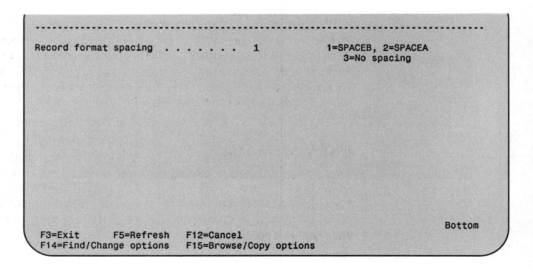

```
                      Change Session Defaults
Type choices, press Enter.

   Amount to roll . . . . . . . . . . .    H__      H=Half, F=Full
                                                    C=Cursor, D=Data
                                                    1-999
   Uppercase input only . . . . . . . .    N        Y=Yes, N=No
   Show all field lines . . . . . . . .    Y        Y=Yes, N=No
   Full screen mode . . . . . . . . . .    N        Y=Yes, N=No

   Insert marked data . . . . . . . . .    N        Y=Yes, N=No
   Replace marked data  . . . . . . . .    N        Y=Yes, N=No
   Semantic checking:
     When added/modified  . . . . . . .    Y        Y=Yes, N=No
     From page number . . . . . . . . .    ___      000-999
       Line number  . . . . . . . . .     _____    00000-32767
     To page number . . . . . . . . . .    ___      000-999
       Line number  . . . . . . . . .     _____    00000-32767
   Printer device type  . . . . . . . .    1        1=SCS, 2=IPDS, 3=AFPDS
                                                              More...
```

Figure 26.35b Changing RLU Session Defaults, Screen 2

```
   Record format spacing  . . . . . . .    1        1=SPACEB, 2=SPACEA
                                                     3=No spacing

                                                              Bottom
   F3=Exit       F5=Refresh    F12=Cancel
   F14=Find/Change options    F15=Browse/Copy options
```

Amount to roll

This attribute determines how RLU will process the Page Up/Page Down keys. F (Full) specifies that the Design Report screen will roll a full screen when you press Page Up/Page Down. H (Half) specifies a half-screen roll. C (CSR) rolls the screen so that the line where the cursor is currently positioned will be at the top of the screen when you press Page Down (or at the bottom of the screen when you press Page Up). D (Data) rolls the screen so that the last line of one screen will be the first line of the next screen. You can also specify an exact number of lines to roll in the range 1-999.

Uppercase input only

This attribute is used to determine whether or not lowercase characters can be entered into the report layout and on the FIND/CHANGE options display. To enable lowercase entry, specify 'N'. To disable lowercase entry, specify 'Y'.

Show all field lines

With this attribute you can determine whether or not field lines are displayed for each report line that contains at least one constant or data field. Enter a 'Y' if you want to display all field lines. Enter 'N' if you do not want field lines displayed. Even if you specify 'N', you can use the RLU command VF (View Field line) when you want a field line.

Full-screen mode

RLU uses this attribute to determine whether or not it will present displays in full-screen mode. Full-screen mode, also known as expert mode, presents more report lines on the Design Report display, but does not display the function keys and other useful information. To enable full-screen mode, specify 'Y'; for normal mode, specify 'N'.

Insert marked data

This attribute determines how the field-copy and field-move operations are performed when you use the F14 (Copy marked data) or F15 (Move marked data) key. If you specify 'Y', the marked data is inserted at the cursor location. If you specify 'N', the copied data overwrites any data already in that position.

Replace marked data

This attribute affects what happens to the empty space left when marked data is moved to another location when you use the F15 (Move marked data) key. If you specify 'Y', all data to the right of the empty space is shifted left to fill in the empty space. If you specify 'N', the data is not shifted.

Semantic checking when added/modified

This attribute determines whether or not semantic checking will be performed when data is added to the Design Report display. The semantic checking facility checks the Design Report display to ensure that the data adheres to the rules of RLU, and that RLU will be able to correctly generate the DDS for the printer file. To enable semantic checking for added or modified data, specify 'Y'; to disable the checking, specify 'N'.

Semantic checking; From page number/line number To page number/ line number

You can use this attribute to check the semantics of report lines when they are not being added or modified. Specify the from and to page numbers, and the from and to line numbers where semantic checking should begin and end.

Printer device type

This attribute determines the printer device type for which you are designing the report. Enter option 1 for an SCS (SNA Character Stream) printer, 2 for an IPDS (Intelligent Printer Data Stream) printer, and 3 for an AFPDS (Advanced Function Printing Data Stream) printer

Record format spacing

This attribute controls the DDS keyword that filler lines generate within the RLU Design Report display. If you prefer to use SPACEB (Space before), specify option 1. If you want to use SPACEA (Space after), use option 2. To specify no spacing keyword, use option 3.

Section 5

File Compare and Merge Utility (FCMU)

The CMPPFM Command

Chapter 27

When Version 3 Release 1 of the Application Development Toolset/400 licensed program product became available, IBM included in the base product a new tool called the File Compare and Merge Utility (FCMU). FCMU incorporates two new CL commands: CMPPFM (Compare Physical File Member) and MRGSRC (Merge Source). These two commands work independently of one another and perform distinct functions.

The CMPPFM command generates a listing of the differences between two physical or source physical file members. The MRGSRC command generates a listing of the differences between two source physical file members and, optionally, merges the changes together. Both commands are packed with features and allow for a high degree of user control over the compare and merge operations.

The CMPPFM Command

The CMPPFM command compares physical files, including source
physical files, and generates comparison reports based upon options that
you select. You can execute CMPPFM from a command line, include it
in a program, or use option 54 on the Work with Members Using PDM
display. Figure 27.1 shows the command prompt for the CMPPFM
command.

Figure 27.1 CMPPFM Command Prompt Display

```
                   Compare Physical File Member (CMPPFM)

 Type choices, press Enter.

 New file . . . . . . . . . . . . . > QCLSRC        Name
   Library . . . . . . . . . . . . > DANR          *LIBL, name, *CURLIB
 New member . . . . . . . . . . .    *FIRST        *FIRST, name, generic*, *ALL
               + for more values
 Old file . . . . . . . . . . .      *NEWFILE      *NEWFILE, name
   Library . . . . . . . . . . .     *LIBL         *LIBL, name, *CURLIB
 Old member . . . . . . . . . . .    *NEWMBR       *NEWMBR, name, *FIRST
               + for more values
 Compare type . . . . . . . . . .    *LINE         *LINE, *FILE, *WORD
 Report type . . . . . . . . . .     *DIFF         *DIFF, *SUMMARY, *CHANGE...
 Output . . . . . . . . . . . . .    *             *, *PRINT, *OUTFILE

                        Additional Parameters

 Select source type . . . . . . .    *ALL          *ALL, name

                                                                   More...
 --------------------------------------------------------------------------
```

```
 --------------------------------------------------------------------------
 Statement file . . . . . . . . .    _____      Name
   Library . . . . . . . . . .       *LIBL         *LIBL, name, *CURLIB
 Statement member . . . . . . . .    *FIRST        *FIRST, name









                                                                   Bottom
 F3=Exit   F4=Prompt   F5=Refresh   F12=Cancel   F13=How to use this display
 F24=More keys
```

CMPPFM Command Parameters

NEWFILE(*LIBL, *CURLIB, library-name/file-name)

The qualified name of the physical or source physical file containing the member(s) to compare against the file specified on the OLDFILE parameter.

NEWMBR(*FIRST, *ALL, generic-member-name, member-name)

The name of the member(s) to compare against the member(s) in the OLDMBR parameter. The default value is *FIRST, indicating that the first member in the NEWFILE will be compared against the member(s) specified in the OLDMBR parameter. You can also specify a generic member name (e.g., MBR*), the special value *ALL, or up to 25 member names.

OLDFILE(*LIBL, *CURLIB, library-name/*NEWFILE, file-name)

The qualified name of the physical or source physical file that contains the member(s) that will be used as the basis, or starting point, for the comparison. The default value is *LIBL/*NEWFILE, which specifies that you want to use the same file name here as was specified on the NEWFILE parameter, and that you want to use the job's library list to locate the file. You will almost always need to override the default value with the qualified name of the old file.

OLDMBR(*NEWMBR, *FIRST, member name(s))

The member(s) that will be used as the basis for the comparison. The default value is *NEWMBR, which specifies that you want to use the same member or list of members specified on the NEWMBR parameter. In addition to specifying up to 25 member names, you can also use the special value *FIRST to specify that only the first member in the OLDFILE will be used.

CMPTYPE(*LINE, *FILE, *WORD)

The type of comparison that you want to perform. The default value is *LINE, which specifies that the members are to be compared on a line-by-line (i.e., record-by-record) basis. Changed, inserted, and deleted records are reported.

If you specify the value *FILE, a summary report is generated that lists the file's members and indicates which members contain differences. This summary also identifies any members that do not exist in both the NEWFILE and OLDFILE.

You can also specify the value *WORD when you want to compare members on a word-by-word basis. A word in this context is defined as a character string delimited either by a blank or the end of a line.

RPTTYPE(*DIFF, *SUMMARY, *CHANGE, *DETAIL)

The type of comparison report to generate. The default value is *DIFF, indicating that a detailed report on the differences between members is to be produced.

If you specify *SUMMARY, a report is generated showing a comparison summary for each member.

If you specify *CHANGE, a detailed report similar to the *DIFF report is produced. However, in the *CHANGE report, 10 lines before and after any difference are also listed. This allows you to view any differences in their immediate context.

If you specify *DETAIL, a complete listing of the NEWMBR is produced that identifies any changed, deleted, or inserted lines.

OUTPUT(*, *PRINT, *OUTFILE)

The output option for the comparison report. The default value is *, which indicates that the report will be displayed interactively at the workstation. You can specify OUTPUT(*PRINT) to create a spooled output file, which can then be printed. You can also store the result in a physical file member by specifying the value *OUTFILE; if you specify OUTPUT(*OUTFILE), you must also specify a value for the OUTFILE parameter.

OUTFILE(*LIBL, *CURLIB, library-name/file-name)

The qualified name of the physical file that is to receive the output of the command. This parameter can only be specified if the OUTPUT parameter specifies the value *OUTFILE.

OUTMBR(*FIRST, member-name   *REPLACE, *ADD)

This parameter has two elements. The first specifies the member within the physical file named on the OUTFILE parameter that is to receive the output of the command. The default value of *FIRST specifies that the first member in the physical file will be used.

The second element of the parameter is used to specify whether the output of the command should be appended to data already in the member (*ADD), or that data in the member should be replaced with the output (*REPLACE). The default value is *REPLACE.

SRCTYPE(*ALL, member-type)

Specifies the type of source members to be compared. The default value is *ALL, but you can optionally specify a source type (e.g., CLP). Specifying a source type effectively delimits the scope of the comparison to members of source physical files with the corresponding source type.

OPTION(Process-options)

This parameter allows you to customize the compare process to suit your particular requirements. You may specify up to 10 options selected from the table in Figure 27.2. A given process option may be invalid, depending upon the comparison type specified in the CMPTYPE parameter. The table lists which CMPTYPE parameter values are valid for each process option.

Figure 27.2 Process Options

Process Option	Valid w/CMPTYPE	Purpose
Options to compare only certain columns based upon source type:		
*CBLSRCCOL	*LINE, *WORD	Compare only columns 7-72 of the source member. These are the standard COBOL source columns.
*RPGSRCCOL	*LINE, *WORD	Compare only columns 6-74 of the source member. These are the standard RPG source columns.
Options to filter out comments and blank lines:		
*OMTBASCMT	*LINE, *WORD	Exclude BASIC comments from the comparison.
*OMTBLANK	*LINE, *WORD	Exclude blank lines.
*OMTCBLCMT	*LINE, *WORD	Exclude COBOL comments and blank lines.
*OMTCCMT	*LINE, *WORD	Exclude C comments and blank lines.
*OMTCLCMT	*LINE, *WORD	Exclude CL comments and blank lines.
*OMTCMDCMT	*LINE, *WORD	Exclude CMD comments and blank lines.

Process Option	Valid w/CMPTYPE	Purpose
*OMTDDSCMT	*LINE, *WORD	Exclude DDS comments and blank lines.
*OMTPASCMT	*LINE, *WORD	Exclude Pascal comments and blank lines.
*OMTPLICMT	*LINE, *WORD	Exclude PL/I comments and blank lines.
*OMTRPGCMT	*LINE, *WORD	Exclude RPG comments and blank lines.

Options that affect the width of the report:

Process Option	Valid w/CMPTYPE	Purpose
*LONGLINES	*LINE	Create 198-column report. This option displays up to 176 positions from the compared members.
*NARROW	*LINE	Create 132-column report. This option allows only 55 columns, which are shown in a side-by-side format for each inserted and deleted record.
*WIDE	*LINE, *WORD	Create 198-column side-by-side report. This option displays up to 80 columns per side.

Other miscellaneous process options:

Process Option	Valid w/CMPTYPE	Purpose
*CHANGES	*LINE, *FILE, *WORD	List only changes in the report summary.
*CHGFLGS	*LINE, *WORD	Show changes using > symbol.
*CMPSEQDAT	*LINE, *WORD	Compare SEQ and DATE fields within the source file member.
*COUNT	*LINE	Include the number of source lines from both unpaired members.
*COUNTREFMT	*LINE, *WORD	Reformatted lines are counted in summary.

Process Option	Valid w/CMPTYPE	Purpose
*IGNORECASE	*LINE, *WORD	Ignore the case (upper, lower) of characters when determining differences.
*FLGMOVLIN	*LINE	Flag moved lines in the detail listing.
*OMTDUP	*LINE	Duplicate lines in the new member and the old member are not shown on the side-by-side listing.
*OMTREFMT	*LINE	Omit reformatted lines in the old member from the listing. Reformatted lines in the new member are listed. If this option is not specified, the reformatted lines from both the new and old member are listed.

STMTFILE(*LIBL, *CURLIB, library-name/ file-name)

Specifies the qualified name of a source physical file that stores special process statements that will be used in the comparison process.

STMTMBR(*FIRST, member-name)

Specifies the member within the source physical file in which special process statements are recorded. The default value is *FIRST.

Using Process Statements

With process statements you can predefine comparisons that enhance or override the parameters specified on the CMPPFM command. Process statements provide a more precise level of control over the comparison process than is available from the CMPPFM command's parameters.

You enter process statements into a source file member using a source editor such as SEU. When completed, the statements can be used in the comparison process by entering the name of the source file in the STMTFILE parameter and entering the member name in the STMTMBR parameter of the CMPPFM command.

Once the process statements have been entered into a source member, you can modify or reuse them as needed for other comparison operations. Since there is no IBM-supplied source file or source type for process statements, you may want to store them as source type TXT, in a source file named QTXTSRC. If you create several process statement members, you may want to create a new source physical file name, such as QPRCSRC, QPROCSRC, or QCMPSRC to hold the source members.

When entering process statements into a source member, you first enter the statement, followed by its operands. Both the statement and its operands must be fully contained on one source line. The length of a statement's operands must be less than 70 characters.

Process statements to specify the column numbers to include in the comparison

When only certain columns are to be compared, you can limit the comparison using the process statements CMPCOLM, CMPCOLMN, and CMPCOLMO. CMPCOLM specifies the included column positions in both the old and the new file. CMPCOLMN specifies the included column positions in only the new file; CMPCOLMO specifies columns in only the old file. For example, to compare columns 1 through 50 in both the old and the new member, you would use the statement

```
CMPCOLM 1:50
```

Rules of usage:

- CMPCOLMN and CMPCOLMO must be specified in the same source member.
- If CMPCOLM appears in a source member, CMPCOLMN and CMPCOLMO cannot be specified.
- When you enter column numbers and column ranges, enter them in ascending order by column.

When you enter one of the CMPCOLMx commands, you can specify either individual column numbers to compare, a range of column numbers, or a combination of the two forms. To specify a range of columns, you use a colon between the FROM column number and the TO column number, as in the above example. If more than one range of columns is required, separate the ranges using a comma. For example, to compare columns 1 through 50 and columns 72 through 75 in both the old and new member, you use the statement

```
CMPCOLM 1:50,72:75
```

If you must specify a single column, or a group of single columns, separate the column numbers with a comma. For example, to compare columns 5, 13, and 71 in both the new member and the old member, use the statement

```
CMPCOLM 5,13,71
```

If a range and a single column must be compared, the colon and comma must be used. For example, to compare columns 7 through 50 and column 72 in both the new and old member, use the statement

```
CMPCOLM 7:50,72
```

You specify the column positions for the CMPCOLMN and CMPCOLMO statements in the same way you do in the CMPCOLM statement. For example, to compare columns 10 through 50 in the new member with columns 30 through 70 in the old member, use the statements

```
CMPCOLMN 10:50
CMPCOLMO 30:70
```

Process statements to specify the member sections to include in the comparison

The CMPSECT statement is used to identify sections of the source members that should be included in the comparison. Section boundaries are identified and set using either character strings or line numbers. The CMPSECT statement is only valid when a single new member is being compared to a single old member (i.e., it is not valid when a list of members or *ALL is specified on the NEWMBR or OLDMBR parameters). You can identify as many sections within the source members as you want. The format of the CMPSECT statement is as follows:

```
CMPSECT  section-id  start-end-specifier  section-marker
```

The *section-id* is an arbitrary name that you assign to the section. It must be 1-8 characters long and cannot contain embedded blanks.

The *start-end-specifier* indicates whether you are defining the top or the bottom of the section, and whether the section is being defined in the new member or the old member. The allowable values are

TOP   Beginning of section in both the old member and the new member.

BTM   End of section in both the old member and the new member.

OTOP   Beginning of section in the old member.

OBTM   End of section in the old member.

NTOP   Beginning of section in the new member.

NBTM   End of section in the new member.

If you define a TOP, NTOP, or OTOP for a section but no BTM, NBTM, or OBTM, the section is assumed to end at the last line of the member.

The *section-marker* specifies the line number or the character string that must be found in the member to set the top or bottom of the section. The simplest form of the section marker specifies the line number. For example, to set the beginning of a section named HEADING in both the old and the new member at the first line in the member, you can use the statement

```
CMPSECT  HEADING  TOP  1
```

Here, the line number 1 is the section marker. Instead of specifying a line number, you may find it useful to set the top or bottom of a section based upon the occurrence of a character string. For example, the following statement will set the beginning of a section named HEADING in both the old and the new member at the first occurrence of the character string 'PROCESS':

```
CMPSECT  HEADING  TOP  'PROCESS'
```

To further identify the correct occurrence of the string 'PROCESS', you can optionally specify a starting and ending column in which the string must be found. Here, the beginning of the section named HEADING will be identified only when the string 'PROCESS' starts in column 8 through 11 of the member:

```
CMPSECT  HEADING  TOP  'PROCESS',8:11
```

The CMPSECT statement, to mark the end of the section to be compared, uses the same syntax except the start-end-specifier is BTM instead of TOP. To mark the sections in the old member only, you use the start-end-specifier OTOP and OBTM; to mark the sections in the new member, use the start-end-specifier NTOP and NBOT.

To see the usefulness of this section concept, consider an RPG source member where each section of code can be identified by the RPG specification identifer contained in column 6. Here, we can define some meaningful sections using a character string and a column position:

```
CMPSECT  CSPECS  TOP  'C',6
CMPSECT  CSPECS  BTM  'O',6
CMPSECT  OSPECS  TOP  'O',6
```

We defined a section called CSPECS that starts at the first line where a C is found in column 6 and ends at the first line where O appears in column 6. We also defined another section named OSPECS that starts at the first occurrence of O in column 6 and ends at the end of the member. It ends at the end of the member because we did not specify a BTM for the OSPECS section.

In a COBOL source member, we could limit the comparison of the old and new member to the Procedure Division only by specifying the following:

```
CMPSECT  PROCDIV TOP   'PROCEDURE DIVISION',8
```

Process statements to specify lines that are excluded from the comparison

The OMTLINE and OMTLINEC statements are used to identify lines that should be excluded from the comparison based upon the occurrence of one or more character strings within the line. For example, to exclude all lines that contain the character string 'PIC', you could use the statement

```
OMTLINE  'PIC'
```

Use the OMTLINE statement when one character string is enough to satisfy the exclusion condition. If you need to specify two or more character strings as the exclusion condition, you must use the OMTLINEC continuation statement in conjunction with the OMTLINE statement. For example, to exclude all lines that contain the character string 'PIC' and the character string 'VALUE', you would specify the following statements:

```
OMTLINE  'PIC'
OMTLINEC 'VALUE'
```

The OMTLINEC statement marks the continuation of the OMTLINE statement. In the preceding case, both character strings must be found on the same line for that line to be excluded from the comparison.

The OMTLINE and OMTLINEC statements let you specify a column position or range of column positions. For example, if you wanted to exclude all lines that contain the string 'C' in column 6, and the string 'JOE' if it begins in columns 70 through 80, you could use the following statement:

```
OMTLINE  'C',6
OMTLINEC 'JOE', 70:80
```

The OMTLINEC statement also lets you specify a relative column number. Consider the following statements:

```
OMTLINE  '#include'
OMTLINEC '<', +10
```

Here, the +10 is used to specify that the character string < must be found 10 columns after the string #include is found in the line.

Using the OMTLINE or OMTLINEC statements, you can also exclude lines based upon the occurrence of a hexadecimal code. In the following example, all lines containing the hexadecimal code X'32' in columns 1 through 5 are excluded from the comparison:

```
OMTLINE X'32',1:5
```

Process statements to modify the member text before the comparison

The NCHGT and OCHGT statements are used to modify the text of the member before the comparison takes place. These statements do not actually change the text stored in the member; instead, they change a temporary copy of the member used by the comparison process. One situation in which this facility is useful is when you have changed a field name in the new version of a member and do not want that field name change reflected in the comparison report. Consider the following statement:

```
NCHGT 'ACTNUM','CUSNUM'
```

This statement will cause all occurrences of the string ACTNUM to be changed to CUSNUM in the new member before the comparison takes place.

Alternately, if you wanted to change the temporary image of the old member instead of the new member, you could specify

```
OCHGT 'CUSNUM','ACTNUM'
```

With the NCHGT and OCHGT statements, you can also specify a column number or a range of columns, as in the following examples:

```
NCHGT 'ACTNUM','CUSNUM',24
OCHGT 'CUSNUM','ACTNUM',30:50
```

The first example changes the temporary image of the new member only if the string ACTNUM starts in column 24. The second will change the image only if the string CUSNUM starts in column 30 through 50.

In addition to specifying a string to modify before the comparison, you can also specify a string-mask. You specify a mask by including the wildcard character ? in the first character string. Consider the following statement:

```
NCHGT 'ACT?','ACT#'
```

This statement will change the image of the new member before the comparison so that every time the characters ACT appear, the character following ACT will be changed to the character #.

As in the OMTLINE command, you can specify a hexadecimal character string, as in the following example:

```
OCHGT X'32',X'20',1:5
```

This statement will change the temporary image of the old member so that any occurrence of the hexadecimal character X'32' will be changed to X'20' before the comparison takes place.

A Process statement to override the file members being compared

The SELECTF process statement is used to specify the names of the file members being compared. When the SELECTF statement is used, the file names specified on the CMPPFM command are ignored. One requirement of using the SELECTF process statement is that the file names entered must be fully qualified. For example,

```
SELECTF    TESTSRC/QCLSRC(MEMBER1):PRODSRC/QCLSRC(MEMBER1)
```

This statement makes TESTSRC/QCLSRC(MEMBER1) the new member in the comparison and makes PRODSRC/QCLSRC(MEMBER1) the old member in the comparison. You can specify multiple SELECTF statements within a process statement source member.

Process statements that affect the comparison report format

Until now, we have dealt with process statements that affect the comparison process itself. In addition to these, a few process statements are provided to affect the output format of the comparison report. These statements are LNCT, LSTCOLM, and SLIST.

The LNCT statement is used to specify the number of comparison report lines that appear on a page. This statement is only valid when the OUTPUT(*OUTFILE) parameter is used on the CMPPFM command. Because the report will be written to a physical file, you can use this statement to specify that report headings only appear in the *OUTFILE for the first page of the report. This ensures that, after the first page, you do not have to account for page headings when you are reading the *OUTFILE. To specify that headings are to appear only in the outfile for the first page, use the statement

```
LNCT 999999
```

If you want to include report headings in the *OUTFILE, you can specify a LNCT value of from 15 to 999,999.

The LSTCOLM statement is used to specify what columns of the source members should be listed in the report. This does not affect the comparison, but only the columns listed on the comparison report. When the LSTCOLM statement is used, you specify a range of columns to include. In the following example, the comparison report will list columns 30 through 80 of the source members:

```
LSTCOLM 30:80
```

The SLIST statement is used to specify whether or not the process statements used should be listed on the comparison report. The SLIST statement has two options: SLIST ON and SLIST OFF. If all process statements should be listed on the comparison report, specify SLIST ON as the first statement in your process statement source member. If you want to specify that only certain process statements should be listed on the comparison report, use a combination of SLIST ON and SLIST OFF statements. In the following example, only the OMTLINE and OMTLINEC statements will be included in the comparison report:

```
SLIST    ON
OMTLINE  'C',6
OMTLINEC 'JOE', 70:80
SLIST    OFF
LNCT     999999
LSTCOLM  30:80
```

Sample of the Comparison Reports

Figure 27.3 shows the report generated by the comparison of two CL source members. You will notice that the first page of the report lists the command parameters and any process options that were used. This report is a line comparison report (CMPTYPE(*LINE)), listing in detail the new member (RPTTYPE(*DETAIL)) and reporting the similarities and differences between the source members. No process options are used, and no statement file is specified.

You can see that all lines that have been inserted are marked with an I in the left-hand margin. Deleted lines are indicated by the letter D, and reformatted lines are listed from both the old (RO) and new (RN) member.

On the right side of the report are listed the Type, Length, N-LN num, and O-LN num. The type field indicates such things as inserted lines (INS=), matching lines (MAT=), and reformatted lines (RFM). The Length column indicates the number of lines for which the Type is used. For example, INS=4 indicates that the four lines starting here are inserted lines. Finally, the N-LN Num and O-LN Num show the new and old line numbers within the source members.

Following the detail listing is a comparison summary, followed by an explanation of the abbreviations used in the report.

Figure 27.3 Sample of Detail Comparison Report

```
IBM COMPARE V3R1MO  940909                    10/27/94        13:35          PAGE              1

New file..............................: QCLSRC
  Library.............................:   DANR
New member............................: MYPROGRAM2
Old file..............................: QCLSRC
  Library.............................:   DANR
Old member............................: MYPROGRAM
Compare type..........................: *LINE
Report type...........................: *DETAIL
Output................................: *PRINT
File to receive output................: QSYSPRT
  Library.............................:   *LIBL
Select source type....................: *ALL
Process option........................:
Statement file........................:
  Library.............................:
Statement member......................:
```

```
. . . . . . . . . . . . . . . . . . . . . . . . . . . . . . . . . . . . . . .

IBM COMPARE V3R1MO  940909                    10/27/94        13:35          PAGE              2
NEW:    DANR/QCLSRC(MYPROGRAM2)                         OLD:   DANR/QCLSRC(MYPROGRAM)

              LISTING OUTPUT SECTION (LINE COMPARE)

                                                                        N-LN  O-LN
ID         SOURCE LINES                                        TYPE LEN NUM   NUM
----+----1----+----2----+----3----+----4----+----5----+----6----+----7----+----8
I -/* PROGRAM NAME: MYPROGRAM                                */ INS=    4 00001
I -/* DATE:  10/25/94                                        */         00002
I -/* PURPOSE: COUNTS OBJECTS IN A LIBRARY                   */         00003
I -/*====================================================== */         00004
              PGM PARM(&LIBRARY)                              MAT=   21 00005 00001
                                                                        00006 00002
              DCL      VAR(&LIBRARY) TYPE(*CHAR) LEN(10)                00007 00003
                                                                        00008 00004
              DCL      VAR(&FILES) TYPE(*DEC) LEN(5 0)                  00009 00005
              DCL      VAR(&PGMS) TYPE(*DEC) LEN(5 0)                   00010 00006
              DCL      VAR(&DTAARAS) TYPE(*DEC) LEN(5 0)                00011 00007
              DCL      VAR(&JOBDS) TYPE(*DEC) LEN(5 0)                  00012 00008
              DCL      VAR(&OTHERS) TYPE(*DEC) LEN(5 0)                 00013 00009
                                                                        00014 00010
              DCL      VAR(&FILEX) TYPE(*CHAR)  LEN(5)                  00015 00011
              DCL      VAR(&PGMX) TYPE(*CHAR) LEN(5)                    00016 00012
              DCL      VAR(&DTAARAX) TYPE(*CHAR) LEN(5)                 00017 00013
              DCL      VAR(&JOBDX) TYPE(*CHAR) LEN(5)                   00018 00014
              DCL      VAR(&OTHERX) TYPE(*CHAR) LEN(5)                  00019 00015
                                                                        00020 00016
              DCL      VAR(&MSGID) TYPE(*CHAR) LEN(7)                   00021 00017
              DCL      VAR(&MSGDTA) TYPE(*CHAR) LEN(128)               00022 00018
              DCL      VAR(&MSGF) TYPE(*CHAR) LEN(10)                   00023 00019
              DCL      VAR(&MSGFLIB) TYPE(*CHAR) LEN(10)               00024 00020
              DCLF     QADSPOBJ                                         00025 00021
I -                                                           INS=    1 00026
              MONMSG   MSGID(CPF0000) EXEC(GOTO CMDLBL(ERROR)) MAT=   30 00027 00022
                                                                        00028 00023
              DSPOBJD  OBJ(&LIBRARY/*ALL) OBJTYPE(*ALL) +             00029 00024
                       OUTPUT(*OUTFILE) OUTFILE(QTEMP/QADSPOBJ)       00030 00025
                                                                        00031 00026
              OVRDBF   FILE(QADSPOBJ) TOFILE(QTEMP/QADSPOBJ)          00032 00027
                                                                        00033 00028
READLOOP:     RCVF                                                     00034 00029
              MONMSG CPF0864   EXEC(GOTO EDF)                         00035 00030
                                                                        00036 00031
              IF (&ODOBTP = '*PGM')  DO                              00037 00032
                CHGVAR &PGMS (&PGMS + 1)                             00038 00033
              ENDO                                                    00039 00034
              ELSE  +                                                00040 00035
                  IF (&ODOBTP = '*FILE') DO                          00041 00036
                      CHGVAR &FILES (&FILES + 1)                     00042 00037
              ENDDO                                                   00043 00038
              ELSE  +                                                00044 00039
              IF (&ODOBTP = 'DTAARA') DO                             00045 00040
                CHGVAR &DTAARAS (&DTAARAS + 1)                       00046 00041
              ENDDO                                                   00047 00042
```

```
. . . . . . . . . . . . . . . . . . . . . . . . . . . . . . . . . . . . . . .

IBM COMPARE V3R1MO  940909                    10/27/94        13:35          PAGE              3
NEW:    DANR/QCLSRC(MYPROGRAM2)                         OLD:   DANR/QCLSRC(MYPROGRAM)

              LISTING OUTPUT SECTION (LINE COMPARE)

                                                                        N-LN  O-LN
ID         SOURCE LINES                                        TYPE LEN NUM   NUM
----+----1----+----2----+----3----+----4----+----5----+----6----+----7----+----8
```

```
                    ELSE   +
                        IF (&ODOBTP = '*JOBD') DO                                      00048 00043
                            CHGVAR &JOBDS (&JOBDS + 1)                                 00049 00044
                        ENDDO                                                          00050 00045
                        ELSE CHGVAR &OTHERS (&OTHERS + 1)                              00051 00046
                                                                                       00052 00047
                                                                                       00053 00048
                    GOTO READLOOP                                                      00054 00049
            EOF:                                                                       00055 00050
                                                                                       00056 00051
RN-             CHGVAR    VAR(&FILEX)    VALUE(&FILES)              RFM=    5 00057 00052
RO-             CHGVAR    VAR(&FILEX) VALUE(&FILES)
RN-             CHGVAR    VAR(&PGMX)     VALUE(&PGMS)                         00058 00053
RO-             CHGVAR    VAR(&PGMX) VALUE(&PGMS)
RN-             CHGVAR    VAR(&DTAARAX)  VALUE(&DTAARAS)                      00059 00054
RO-             CHGVAR    VAR(&DTAARAX) VALUE(&DTAARAS)
RN-             CHGVAR    VAR(&JOBDX)    VALUE(&JOBDS)                        00060 00055
RO-             CHGVAR    VAR(&JOBDX) VALUE(&JOBDS)
RN-             CHGVAR    VAR(&OTHERX)   VALUE(&OTHERS)                       00061 00056
RO-             CHGVAR    VAR(&OTHERX) VALUE(&OTHERS)                MAT=   25 00062 00057
                                                                                       00063 00058
                SNDPGMMSG  MSG('There are' *BCAT &FILEX *BCAT 'files in +     00064 00059
                           library' *BCAT &LIBRARY)                          00065 00060
                SNDPGMMSG  MSG('There are' *BCAT &PGMX *BCAT 'programs +      00066 00061
                           in library' *BCAT &LIBRARY)                       00067 00062
                SNDPGMMSG  MSG('There are' *BCAT &DTAARAX *BCAT 'data +       00068 00063
                           areas in library' *BCAT &LIBRARY)                 00069 00064
                SNDPGMMSG  MSG('There are' *BCAT &JOBDX *BCAT 'job +          00070 00065
                           descriptions in library' *BCAT &LIBRARY)          00071 00066
                SNDPGMMSG('There are' *BCAT &OTHERX *BCAT 'other +            00072 00067
                           objects in library' *BCAT &LIBRARY)               00073 00068
                GOTO DONE                                                              00074 00069
        /*----------------------------------------------------------*/       00075 00070
        /* Error routine                                            */        00076 00071
        /*----------------------------------------------------------*/        00077 00072
            ERROR:    RCVMSG     MSGTYPE(*EXCP) MSGDTA(&MSGDTA) MSGID(&MSGID + 00078 00073
                                 MSGF(&MSGF) SNDMSGFLIB(&MSGFLIB)             00079 00074
                      MONMSG     MSGID(CPF0000)                              00080 00075
                      SNDPGMMSG  MSGID(&MSGID) MSGF(&MSGFLIB/&MSGF) +          00081 00076
                                 MSGDTA(&MSGDTA) MSGTYPE(*ESCAPE)            00082 00077
                      MONMSG     MSGID(CPF0000)                              00083 00078
        /*----------------------------------------------------------*/        00084 00079
            DONE:                                                              00085 00080
                      RMVMSG     CLEAR(*ALL)                                  00086 00081
                      MONMSG     MSGID(CPF0000)                  RPL=    1 00087 00082
I -                   RETURN
D -                                                               MAT=    1 00088 00083
                      ENDPGM
```

- -

IBM COMPARE V3R1M0 940909   10/27/94   13:38   PAGE   4

NEW: CANR/QCLSRC(MYPROGRAM2)   OLD: DANR/QCLSRC(MYPROGRAM)

LINE COMPARE SUMMARY AND STATISTICS

```
NUMBER OF LINE MATCHES...........................................:      77
TOTAL CHANGES (PAIRED+NONPAIRED CHNG)............................:      11
REFORMATTED LINES................................................:       5
PAIRED CHANGES (REFM+PAIRED INS/DEL).............................:       6
NEW FILE LINE INSERTIONS.........................................:       6
NON-PAIRED INSERTS...............................................:       5
OLD FILE LINE DELETIONS..........................................:       1
NON-PAIRED DELETIONS.............................................:       0
NEW FILE LINES PROCESSED.........................................:      88
OLD FILE LINES PROCESSED.........................................:      83
```

LISTING-TYPE = DETAIL   SOURCE COMPARE COLUMNS =   1:80   LONGEST LINE - 80
PROCESSING OPTIONS SPECIFIED : NONE

- -

IBM COMPARE V3R1M0 940909   10/27/94   13:38   PAGE   5

NEW: DANR/QCLSRC(MYPROGRAM2)   OLD: DANR/QCLSRC(MYPROGRAM)

ABBREVIATIONS DESCRIPTION

```
    ID SECTION
I    - Line inserted in the new file
D    - Line deleted in the new file
RN   - Reformatted line in the new file
RO   - Line from the old file reformatted in the new file
IM   - Line moved in the new file that also appears in the old file
DM   - Line moved in the old file that also appears in the new file

    TYPE OF DIFFERENCES
MAT= Matched lines
RFM= Reformatted lines
RPL= Replaced lines
INS= Lines that are in the new file, but missing in the old file.
```

238 • The CMPPFM Command   Desktop Guide to AS/400 Programmers' Tools

```
DEL= Lines that are in the old file, but missing in the new file.
IMR= Lines reformatted in the new file.
DMR= Lines reformatted in the old file.
IMV= Lines moved in the new file from the old file.
DMV= Lines moved in the old file from the new file.

   COLUMN HEADINGS
N-LN - Lines in the new file.
O-LN - Lines in the old file.
NUM  - Line number
INS  - Inserted
DEL  - Deleted
PROC - Processed
CHNG - Changed
REFM - Reformatted
```

`* * * * * *` E N D   O F   L I S T I N G `* * * * * *`

Figure 27.4 shows how the report would look if the RPTTYPE parameter specified to list the differences only (RPTTYPE(*DIFF)). You can see that the report is considerably shorter since only the differences between the members are listed.

Figure 27.4 Sample of Differences Comparison Report

```
IBM COMPARE V3R1MO  940909                 10/27/94        13:35         PAGE                    1

New file..................................:  QCLSRC
  Library.................................:    DANR
New member................................:  MYPROGRAM2
Old file..................................:  QCLSRC
  Library.................................:    DANR
Old member................................:  MYPROGRAM
Compare type..............................:  *LINE
Report type...............................:  *DIFF
Output....................................:  *PRINT
File to receive output....................:  QSYSPRT
  Library.................................:    *LIBL
Select source type........................:  *ALL
Process option............................:
Statement file............................:
  Library.................................:
Statement member..........................:


. . . . . . . . . . . . . . . . . . . . . . . . . . . . . . . . . . . . . . . . . .

        IBM COMPARE V3R1MO  940909           10/27/94        13:35        PAGE                   2
NEW:    DANR/QCLSRC(MYPROGRAM2)                         OLD:         DANR/QCLSRC(MYPROGRAM)
                                 LISTING OUTPUT SECTION (LINE COMPARE)

                                                                                 N-LN  O-LN
ID        SOURCE LINES                                                 TYPE LEN  NUM   NUM
  ----+----1----+----2----+----3----+----4----+----5----+----6----+----7----+----8
I -/* PROGRAM NAME: MYPROGRAM                                          INS=   4 00001
I -/* DATE:  10/25/94                                          */             00002
I -/* PURPOSE: COUNTS OBJECTS IN A LIBRARY                     */             00003
I -/*=========================================================*/             00004
                                                                      MAT-  21
I -                                                                   INS-   1 00026
                                                                      MAT-  30
RN-            CHGVAR      VAR(&FILEX)    VALUE(&FILES)           RFM=   5 00057 00052
RO-            CHGVAR      VAR(&FILEX) VALUE(&FILES)
RN-            CHGVAR      VAR(&PGMX)     VALUE(&PGMS)                      00058 00053
RO-            CHGVAR      VAR(&PGMX) VALUE(&PGMS)
RN-            CHGVAR      VAR(&DTAARAX)   VALUE(&DTAARAS)                  00059 00054
RO-            CHGVAR      VAR(&DTAARAX) VALUE(&DTAARAS)
RN-            CHGVAR      VAR(&JOBDX)     VALUE(&JOBDS)                    00060 00055
RO-            CHGVAR      VAR(&JOBDX) VALUE(&JOBDS)
RN-            CHGVAR      VAR(&OTHERX)    VALUE(&OTHERS)                   00061 00056
RO-            CHGVAR      VAR(&OTHERX) VALUE(&OTHERS)

I -            RETURN                                                 MAT=  25
D -                                                                   RPL=   1 00087 00082

                                                                      MAT=   1

. . . . . . . . . . . . . . . . . . . . . . . . . . . . . . . . . . . . . . . . . .

        IBM COMPARE V3R1MO  940909           10/27/94        13:35        PAGE                   3
NEW:    DANR/QCLSRC(MYPROGRAM2)                         OLD:         DANR/QCLSRC(MYPROGRAM)
```

```
                    LINE COMPARE SUMMARY AND STATISTICS

NUMBER OF LINE MATCHES...............................:      77
TOTAL CHANGES (PAIRED+NONPAIRED CHNG)................:      11
REFORMATTED LINES...................................:       5
PAIRED CHANGES (REFM+PAIRED INS/DEL)................:       6
NEW FILE LINE INSERTIONS............................:       6
NON-PAIRED INSERTS..................................:       5
OLD FILE LINE DELETIONS.............................:       1
NON-PAIRED DELETIONS................................:       0
NEW FILE LINES PROCESSED............................:      88
OLD FILE LINES PROCESSED............................:      83

LISTING-TYPE = DIFF    SOURCE COMPARE COLUMNS =   1:80      LONGEST LINE = 80
PROCESSING OPTIONS SPECIFIED : NONE


    - - - - - - - - - - - - - - - - - - - - - - - - - - - - - - - - - - - -


IBM COMPARE V3R1MO  940909           10/27/94        13:35              PAGE            4
NEW:     DANR/QCLSRC(MYPROGRAM2)                OLD:        DANR/QCLSRC(MYPROGRAM)

        ABBREVIATIONS DESCRIPTION


   ID SECTION
I    - Line inserted in the new file
D    - Line deleted in the new file
RN   - Reformatted line in the new file
RO   - Line from the old file reformatted in the new file
IM   - Line moved in the new file that also appears in the old file
DM   - Line moved in the old file that also appears in the new file

   TYPE OF DIFFERENCES
MAT= Matched Lines
RFM= Reformatted lines
RPL= Replaced Lines
INS= Lines that are in the new file, but missing in the old file.
DEL= Lines that are in the old file, but missing in the new file.
IMR= Lines reformatted in the new file.
DMR= Lines reformatted in the old file.
IMV= Lines moved in the new file from the old file.
DMV= Lines moved in the old file from the new file.

   COLUMN HEADINGS
N-LN - Lines in the new file.
O-LN - Lines in the old file.
NUM  - Line number
INS  - Inserted
DEL  - Deleted
PROC - Processed
CHNG - Changed
REFM - Reformatted      * * * * * *  E N D   O F   L I S T I N G  * * * * * * *
```

Figure 27.5 lists the abbreviations used in the comparison reports and a description of their meaning.

Figure 27.5 Summary of Codes Used in Comparison Reports

Codes	Description
MAT=	Matching lines. Line in old and new member match.
I, INS=	Line inserted. Occurs in the new member, but not in old member.
D, DEL=	Line deleted. Occurs in the old member, but not in the new member.
RN,RO, RFM=	Line reformatted. Occurs in both the old and new member, but with different spacing.
MC	For *WORD comparisons only, line contains words that match.

Codes	Description
IC	For *WORD comparisons only, line contains words in the new member that did not appear in the old member.
DC	For *WORD comparisons only, line contains words in the old member that are not found in the new member.
IM,DM, IMV=, DMV=	Line moved. The line appears in both the old and new member, but has been moved.
IMR=, DMR=	Line moved and reformatted. The line appears in both the old and new member, but has been moved and reformatted.
>	Line or word inserted or deleted. This code is only used if the *CHGFLGS process option is specified.

The MRGSRC Command

Chapter 28

The MRGSRC command is used to print a report containing the differences between source members; it also can be used to merge two different versions of a source member into a new version. The MRGSRC command is especially well suited to a situation in which you have customized a purchased software package which is then updated by the software vendor. You can use the MRGSRC command to merge your changes with the vendor's changes. This can be a very labor-intensive, time-consuming, and error-prone process without a tool like MRGSRC.

You can execute the MRGSRC command from a command line, include it in a program, or execute it from the PDM Work with Members Using PDM display using option 55. Figure 28.1 shows the command prompt for the MRGSRC command.

Figure 28.1 Command Prompt Display for the MRGSRC Command

```
                            Merge Source (MRGSRC)

 Type choices, press Enter.

 Target file  . . . . . . . . . . > QCLSRC       Name
   Library  . . . . . . . . . . . >   NEWSRC     Name, *LIBL, *CURLIB
 Target member  . . . . . . . . . > PROGRAM1     Name, *ALL
 Maintenance file . . . . . . . .   QCLSRC       Name, *TARGET
   Library  . . . . . . . . . . .     CUSTSRC    Name, *LIBL, *CURLIB
 Maintenance member . . . . . . .   *TARGET      Name, *TARGET
 Root file  . . . . . . . . . . .   QCLSRC       Name, *MAINT
   Library  . . . . . . . . . . .     VENDSRC    Name, *LIBL, *CURLIB
 Root member  . . . . . . . . . .   *MAINT       Name, *MAINT
 Select updates . . . . . . . . .   *YES         *YES, *NO
```

In this example, a software vendor's new version of the source code for PROGRAM1 is in library NEWSRC, the old version of the vendor's source is in library VENDSRC, and your customized version of the vendor's old version is in library CUSTSRC. When the MRGSRC command is executed, your changes in library CUSTSRC will be merged with the vendor's new version in library NEWSRC.

The vendor's old version in library VENDSRC is used by MRGSRC as a basis (or *root*) to determine what changes have been made by both you and the vendor. If you have made changes that conflict with those of the vendor, MRGSRC alerts you to the fact and does not attempt to merge that portion of the source code.

MRGSRC Command Parameters

TGTFILE (*LIBL, *CURLIB, library-name/source-file-name)

The qualified name of the source physical file into which the source updates will be merged. This file is considered as the *target* file for the merge operation.

TGTMBR(*ALL, source-member-name)

The source member(s) into which the updates are to be merged. In addition to specifying the name of a single source member, you can specify the special value *ALL. This allows you to perform a merge operation for all members within the target source file, based upon the updates in corresponding members in the maintenance file.

MAINTFILE(*LIBL, *CURLIB, library-name/*TARGET, file-name)

The qualified name of the source physical file with the member(s) that contain the updates to be merged into the target file member. The default value is *LIBL/*TARGET, which specifies that you want to use the same file name here as was specified on the TGTFILE parameter and use the job's library list to locate the file. You will almost always need to override the default value with the qualified name of the maintenance file.

MAINTMBR (*TARGET, source-member-name)

The source member(s) that contains the updates to merge into the target file member. The default value is *TARGET, which means that you want to use the same member name(s) as you specified on the TGTMBR parameter. Optionally, you can specify a single source member name. If the MAINTMBR parameter contains the value *TARGET, and the TGTMBR parameter contains the value *ALL, each member in the MAINTFILE that has a member of the same name in the target file will be merged with its corresponding member.

ROOTFILE(*LIBL, *CURLIB, library-name/*MAINT, source-file-name)

The qualified name of the source physical file that contains the member(s) to be used as the basis of the merge operation. The default value is *LIBL/*MAINT, which specifies that you want to use the same file name here as was specified on the MAINTFILE parameter, and you want to use the job's library list to locate the file. You will almost always need to override the default value with the qualified name of the root file.

ROOTMBR(*MAINT, source-member-name)

The source member(s) that is (are) the basis for the merge operation. The default value is *MAINT, which means that you want to use the same member name(s) as you specified on the MAINTMBR parameter. Optionally, you can specify a single source member name.

SELECT (*YES, *NO)

Specifies whether you want to manage the merge process using the SEU split-screen display and approve or disapprove all the source updates individually — SELECT(*YES) — or whether you want the command to execute all merge operations without intervention — SELECT(*NO). If you specify *NO, the merge operation will proceed without any intervention, and a merge report will print. If you run the MRGSRC command in a batch job, the SELECT parameter is ignored, and the merge procedure will occur. If you specify SELECT(*YES), you cannot specify RPTONLY(*YES).

RPTONLY (*NO, *YES)

Specifies whether you want to perform the merge operation — RPTONLY(*NO) — or simply print a merge report without performing the actual merge operation — RPTONLY(*YES). The default value is *NO. You would typically print the merge report first before performing the actual merge procedure. You can then check the report before proceeding to the actual merge process. If you specify RPTONLY(*YES), you cannot specify SELECT(*YES).

Using the SEU Split-Screen Merge Display

When you specify SELECT(*YES), MRGSRC presents the SEU split-screen merge display (Figure 28.2). This is a new type of split-screen display not available on previous releases of the SEU product. The top portion of the display is used to present the merge's target member. The lower portion of the split screen contains the maintenance member. The root member is not shown on this display, but is used as the basis of the merge operation. The root member helps determine how updates are displayed on the split-screen merge display — for example, inserted, changed, or deleted lines found in the maintenance member or target member when compared to the root member are presented with the characters >>>>>>> in the sequence number field. Additionally, when a line exists in the maintenance or base member, but does not exist in the target member, a dashed line is shown to indicate the omission. If the updates from the base, maintenance, and target members are in conflict, the characters ******* appear in the sequence-number area of the target and maintenance members.

Figure 28.2 The SEU Split-Screen Merge Display

```
Columns  . . . :   1  71            Target             DRNEWS/QCLSRC
MRG==>                                                    MYPROGRAM
BASE     ...+... 1 ...+... 2 ...+... 3 ...+... 4 ...+... 5 ...+... 6 ...+... 7
         *************** Beginning of data ****************************************
>>>>>>>          PGM    PARM(&library)
0002.00          DCL    &library  *CHAR    10
>>>>>>>   -------------------------------------------------------------
0003.00          DCL    &msgid    *CHAR     7
0004.00          DCL    &msgf     *CHAR    10
0005.00          DCL    &msgdta   *CHAR   512
0006.00          DCL    &msgflib  *CHAR    10

Columns  . . . :   1  71          Maintenance          DRPROD/QCLSRC
MRG==>                                                    MYPROGRAM
         *************** Beginning of data ****************************************
>>>>>>>          PGM    PARM(&library &file)
0002.00          DCL    &library  *CHAR    10
>>>>>>>          DCL    &file     *CHAR    10
0003.00          DCL    &msgid    *CHAR     7
0004.00          DCL    &msgf     *CHAR    10
0005.00          DCL    &msgdta   *CHAR   512
0006.00          DCL    &msgflib  *CHAR    10
F2=Reject       F14=Accept all    F15=Accept    F16=Next
F17=Previous    F22=Alternative keys            F24=More keys
Showing maintenance update 1 of 3.
```

The merge operation in split-screen mode displays each member update in order, and lets you accept the update or ignore it. In the previous figure, you can see from the message at the bottom of the screen that you are currently working with update number 1 of 3. On a color display, the current maintenance update is shown in white. The first update is a change to the first line of the program. Another parameter has been added to the PGM command. To accept this update, press the F15 (Accept) key — to reject it, press F2 (Reject). You will then be shown the next update, highlighted with white. If you want to accept all updates for the member, press F14 (Accept all). You can easily move through the member's updates by pressing F16 (Next update) or F17 (Previous update).

You can use most normal SEU line commands and function keys, such as Find/Change operations and moving, inserting, and copying lines, on the SEU merge display. In a merge session, the SEU command-line label is MRG==>. However, you use the same commands on the MRG==> line as you would on the SEU==> line in a normal SEU editing session. Also, as in a normal SEU split-screen session, you can modify only the member on the top portion of the display.

Section 6

Interactive Source Debugger (ISDB)

Introduction to Interactive Source Debugger (ISDB)

Chapter 29

Version 3 Release 1 of the Application Development ToolSet/400 (ADTS/400) licensed program product includes the new Interactive Source Debugger (ISDB) utility. This utility is an aid for debugging RPG/400, COBOL/400, and CL programs. The ISDB utility is used strictly with OPM (Original Program Model) programs; you cannot use it to debug ILE modules or programs, which use a separate ILE source-level debugger, included in the operating system.

Historically, IBM has not supplied very good debugging tools on the AS/400. Debugging commands such as STRDBG (Start Debug), ADDBKP (Add Breakpoint), ADDTRC (Add Trace), and so on are useful, but not very user friendly. Because IBM didn't provide good tools for debugging, several third-party developers joined in the fray of providing source-level debuggers for the AS/400. The typical cost for one of these third-party debuggers has ranged from $1,500 to $8,000, depending on the AS/400 size or the number of concurrent users. *News 3X/400* magazine also published two versions of a source-level debugging tool that proved to be very popular — first, because it worked reasonably well; and second, because it was free to anybody who wanted to use it. Finally, in ISDB, IBM has a very good offering that will improve AS/400 programmers' productivity with OPM programs written in RPG/400, COBOL/400, and CL.

A source-level debugger such as ISDB lets you view the source code of the program being debugged as it executes. You can easily set breakpoints, add watches for variables, work in step-by-step mode, and display or change program variable values as the program executes. Many AS/400 programmers have used PC-based debuggers for languages such as BASIC, C, or PASCAL. The ISDB utility, as indicated by the features listed in Figure 29.1, is designed in the form of those easy-to-use debuggers.

Figure 29.1 Facilities of ISDB

— Debug RPG/400, COBOL/400, and CL programs (OPM code only)

— Debug up to 10 programs at once

— Set up to 50 breakpoints for each program being debugged

— Source code is displayed as program executes

— Step-by-step mode available

— Pull-down menus for ease of use

— Command logging facility that allows you to create and store program test scripts

— Debug programs running in either interactive or batch jobs

— Special ISDB commands to customize the debug environment

Note: To debug COBOL/400 programs using ISDB, the programs must be compiled with the *SRCDBG option.

The STRISDB Command

Chapter 30

To start a debug session using the ISDB utility, you enter the command STRISDB (Start Interactive Source Debugger). You can press F4 and prompt for the command parameters. Figure 30.1 shows the command prompt for the STRISDB command.

Figure 30.1 The STRISDB Command Prompt

```
                          Start ISDB (STRISDB)

Type choices, press Enter.

Program . . . . . . . . . . . > MYPROGRAM    Name
  Library . . . . . . . . . . >   DRIEHL     Name, *CURLIB, *LIBL
Update production files . . . .  *NO         *YES, *NO
Invoke program . . . . . . . . >  *YES       *YES, *NO, *CMD
Parameters for call . . . . . .              _____

                     + for more values    __


                         Additional Parameters

Source member . . . . . . . . .  *PGM        Name, *PGM
Source file . . . . . . . . . .              Name
  Library . . . . . . . . . . .              Name, *CURLIB, *LIBL
Job to service . . . . . . . . .  *          *, *SELECT

                                                                  Bottom
F3=Exit   F4=Prompt   F5=Refresh   F12=Cancel   F13=How to use this display
F24=More keys
```

STRISDB Command Parameters

The parameters for the STRISDB command are pretty straightforward to those who have used the old STRDBG command. Only one parameter is required: the name of the program to debug. Let's take a good look at each parameter of the STRISDB command.

PGM(*LIBL, *CURLIB, library-name/program-name)

This required parameter specifies the qualified name of the program to be debugged. You can use the special values *LIBL and *CURLIB as the library, or you can specify an explicit library name.

UPDPROD(*NO, *YES)

This parameter specifies whether or not production files will be updated during the debug session. The default value of this parameter is *NO, which means that files existing in a production library (type *PROD) cannot be updated during the debug session. Alternately, you could specify *YES if you want to be able to update production files. You can override the value of this parameter once the debug session is started using a menu option on the debug pull-down menu.

INVPGM(*YES, *NO, *CMD)

This parameter specifies how you want to start the program to be debugged. ISDB can invoke your program, with or without parameters, or you can invoke it yourself from a special command entry screen provided by ISDB. You can also specify that a command is to be executed, which in turn will invoke the program to be debugged. The default value of this parameter is *YES, which means that ISDB will call the program specified on the PGM parameter. If the program requires parameters, you enter them into the PARM parameter.

If you specify the value *NO, a command entry screen is provided for you to perform any set-up work and then place a call to the program to be debugged. When you are debugging programs that are running in other jobs, such as debugging a batch job where the job must be serviced, this is the correct option to use.

You can use the value *CMD if you have a command definition that will call the program to be debugged. This is particularly useful when you are debugging command-processing programs and the programs that they call.

PARM(parameter-list)

When you are using the parameter INVPGM(*YES), this parameter specifies any parameters that must be used on the call to the program.

CMD(CL-command)

When you are using the parameter INVPGM(*CMD), this parameter specifies the command to execute that will in turn invoke the program to be debugged.

SRCMBR(*PGM, source-member-name)

This parameter specifies the name of the source member that was used to create the program being debugged. This is the source member that will be displayed in the debug session. The default value is *PGM, which means that the system should determine the name of the source member. Use the default value *PGM except in cases where you have moved or renamed the source member since the program was compiled. In these instances, enter the current member name.

SRCF(*LIBL,*CURLIB, library-name/ source-file-name)

You need to specify this parameter only if the source file and library have changed since the program was last compiled. It identifies the qualified name of the source file in which the program's source code resides.

SRVJOB(*, *SELECT)

This parameter specifies whether you want to debug a program running in the current interactive job, or you need to debug a program running in another job. If you are debugging a program running in another job, such as a batch job or another user's interactive job, you must first start a service function for that job. The SRVJOB parameter lets you select which job to service.

The default value is *, which means that the debug session will only debug programs running in the current interactive job. You can also use the value *SELECT, in which case you will be presented with a list of the active jobs on the system from which you can select the one to debug. If you use SRVJOB(*SELECT), you must also use INVPGM(*NO).

In addition to entering the STRISDB command on a command line, you can simply select option 34 from the PDM Work with Objects display (Figure 30.2). V3R1 added option 34 to PDM to provide immediate access to the source debugger.

Figure 30.2 Starting ISDB from PDM

```
                         Work with Objects Using PDM                    S999999

   Library . . . . .   DRIEHL____      Position to . . . . . . . .  _____
                                       Position to type  . . . . .  _____

   Type options, press Enter.
     26=Create program              27=Create service program
     34=Interactive source debugger 54=Compare ...

   Opt   Object      Type      Attribute   Text
   34    MYPROGRAM   *PGM      CLP         CL program to count up the objects in
   __    QCLSRC      *FILE     PF-SRC
   __    QRPGSRC     *FILE     PF-SRC




                                                                      Bottom
   Parameters or command
   ===>_____
   F3=Exit           F4=Prompt           F5=Refresh         F6=Create
   F9=Retrieve       F10=Command entry   F23=More options   F24=More keys
```

Understanding the Debug Display

Once you have invoked the program to be debugged, ISDB presents the Debug display (Figure 30.3). The top of the display consists of a group of pull-down menus. These menus are labeled *Debug, Goto, Program, Options,* and *Help*. Following the pull-down menus is the heading line, which lists the name of the program being debugged and the internal statement number of the breakpoint. Next is the listing from the source member associated with the program.

Figure 30.3 The Debug Display

```
Debug           Goto          Program          Options          Help
DRIEHL/MYPROGRAM:/0056              ISDB/400                    More:    +    >
   001000
   001100            DCL        VAR(&FILEX) TYPE(*CHAR)  LEN(5)
   001200            DCL        VAR(&PGMX) TYPE(*CHAR) LEN(5)
   001300            DCL        VAR(&DTAARAX) TYPE(*CHAR) LEN(5)
   001400            DCL        VAR(&JOBDX) TYPE(*CHAR) LEN(5)
   001500            DCL        VAR(&OTHERX) TYPE(*CHAR) LEN(5)
   001600            MONMSG  CPF0000 EXEC(GOTO ERROR)
   001700
   001800            CHKOBJ     OBJ(&LIBRARY/&FILE)
   001900            MONMSG   CPF9801   EXEC(DO)
   002000               CRTPF FILE(&LIBRARY/&FILE) RCDLN(180)
   002100            ENDDO




 ISDB ===>
 F3=Exit     F5=Step   F6=Break   F11=Display variable
 F12=Cancel  F17=Run              F23=Change variable   F24=More keys
 Stopped at statement 1800.
```

You can scroll through the source member using Page Up and Page Down keys. You can set breakpoints by positioning the cursor on the correct line and pressing a function key. You can display and change the value of a program variable simply by placing the cursor on the variable and pressing a function key.

Toward the bottom of the Debug display is the ISDB command line, identified by ISDB==>. This line is used to enter special ISDB commands that can affect the debug environment. Following the ISDB command line is a partial listing of valid function keys. Figure 30.4 contains a complete listing of the valid function keys.

Figure 30.4 Function Keys for the Debug Display

Key	Purpose	Cursor-Sensitive Selection
F1	Show Help display	YES
F3	Exit	NO
F4	Show current breakpoint line	NO
F5	Toggle Step-by-step mode on/off	NO
F6	Add or Remove breakpoint at cursor position	YES
F7	Page Up	NO
F8	Page Down	NO
F9	Retrieve previous command	NO
F10	Go to menu bar	NO
F11	Display variable at cursor position	YES
F12	Cancel	NO
F13	Run to location of cursor	YES
F14	Display program list	NO
F15	Display the previous screen	NO
F16	Repeat the Find operation from cursor position	YES
F17	Run the program	NO
F19	Move to the leftmost position of the source	NO
F20	Move to the rightmost position in the source	NO
F21	Show OS/400 command line window	NO
F22	Display variable at cursor position in hex format	YES
F23	Change variable at cursor position	YES
F24	Show additional F-keys that may be used	NO

The ISDB Command Line

The command line shown at the bottom of the Debug display is used to enter special ISDB commands. You can also enter CL commands on the ISDB command line as long as the command is preceded by the string SYS, (e.g., SYS WRKACTJOB). If you want to be prompted for the parameters of a CL command, use the string SYS followed by the CL prompting character ? (e.g., SYS ?WRKACTJOB).

Figure 30.5 presents a listing of the ISDB commands that can be entered on the ISDB command line. You will notice that there are two versions of each command: a standard version and an abbreviated version.

Figure 30.5 Summary of ISDB Command-line Commands

Command	Abbreviation	Purpose
ADDISDBPGM	AP	Add a program to the debug environment
BACKWARD *n*	BA *n*	Page backward in the source member *n* pages
BOTTOM	BOT	Go to end of source member
BREAK	B	Set a breakpoint
CHG	C	Change the value of a variable
CHGISDBPGM	CP	Change a program in the debug environment
CLEAR	CLR	Clear breakpoints
DEBUG	DE	Expand the Debug pull-down menu bar
DOWN *n*	DN *n*	Roll the source member down *n* lines
DSP	D	Display the value of a variable
DSPHEX	DH	Display the value of a variable in hex format
EQUATE	EQ	Assign or unassign a name to a command string
FIND	F	Find a character string
FORWARD *n*	FO *n*	Page forward in the source member *n* pages
GO	GO	Expand the Goto pull-down menu
GOTO	G	Go to a label in the source member
LABEL	LBL	Create a label name and associate the label with a source line
LEFT	L	Show the leftmost portion of the source member
nnnn	*nnnn*	Go to a line or statement number
OPTIONS	O	Expand the Options pull-down menu bar
PROGRAM	PR	Expand the Program pull-down menu bar
PRT	P	Print the value of a variable

Command	Abbreviation	Purpose
PRTHEX	PH	Print the value of a variable in hex format
QUIT	Q	Quit the debug session with confirmation
QQUIT	QQ	Quit the debug session without confirmation
RESTART	RST	Restart a program in debug mode
RFIND	RF	Repeat the previous find operation
RIGHT	R	Show the rightmost portion of the source member
RMVISDBPGM	RP	Remove a program from the debug environment
RUN	RUN	Run the program
SCREEN	SCR	Display the previous screen
SET BREAK	SET B	Set options for the breakpoint display
SET COLOR	SET COLOR	Set colors for source lines on the display
SET CURSOR	SET CUR	Set the cursor position on a breakpoint
SET FLOW	SET FLOW	Display logic flow arrows in RPG source
SET LOG	SET LOG	Record all actions and commands to log file
SET ROLL	SET ROLL	Set the number of lines to roll
STEP	STEP	Activate or de-activate step-by-step mode
SYS	SYS	Execute a CL command
TOP	T	Go to the beginning of a source member
UNWATCH	UW	End the watch process for a variable
UP *n*	UP *n*	Roll the source member up *n* lines
USE	USE	Execute commands contained in a file
WATCH	W	Monitor and report on changes to a variable's value
WATCHHEX	WH	Monitor a variable for value changes and report changes using hex format

Creating Your Own ISDB Commands with EQUATE

In addition to using the ISDB commands listed in Figure 30.5, you can create your own commands using the EQUATE command. When entering the EQUATE command, you specify the name of the command that you are creating, followed by the command string. For example, the following statement would create an ISDB command named DJ that would execute the CL command DSPJOB.

```
EQ  DJ  SYS  DSPJOB
```

Once you have created a command using the EQUATE command, you can delete that new command by issuing another EQUATE command, in which you specify the name of the command but do not specify a command to execute. The following statement would delete the command named DJ:

```
EQ  DJ
```

When the current debug session ends, all commands created using EQUATE commands are deleted.

If you want to save your EQUATE commands for later use, you must enter them into a source member. You can then make the stored EQUATE commands available in your debugging session through the USE command:

```
USE  library-name  file-name  member-name
```

The following command would make available all EQUATE commands in a member named DANGEN residing in source file QEQSRC in library DRIEHL. (*Note*: I used the name QEQSRC as a standard source file in which to store EQUATE statements for the debugger. This is my standard, but it might not be yours.)

```
USE  DRIEHL  QEQSRC  DANGEN
```

To customize your debugger session defaults, you can store ISDB commands in a special file that is executed every time you start a debugging session. The source file QIXAPROF stores a member containing the debugger profile that will be used when you start debug sessions. You should create your own copy of the QIXAPROF file and place it in a library high on the library list. Check to make sure that your copy of the file is the first in the library list for your job. A sample debugging profile is included in the member named PROFILE in the IBM-supplied source file QIXA/SAMPLES.

The Debug Log

When you begin a debugging session, all ISDB commands that you execute, and all the function keys you used that affect the debug environment, are recorded in a debug session log file. The log file is

---

named QIXALOG in library QTEMP. Using the debug log facility, you can create simple test scripts for your programs, so that after each program modification you can ensure that the program still passes all tests correctly. Because the log file QIXALOG exists only in library QTEMP, you need to copy it to another library to store it permanently. Each time a debug session is started, the log file is cleared. When you want to run the commands from the log file, you use the USE command, as demonstrated in the previous examples.

It might be useful to create several test scripts for one program. These scripts can contain commands such as CHG to change the value of a variable PRTHEX to print hex reports on variables, and so on. You can record and reuse your debugging and testing criteria in these log files. Using SEU, you can edit the log file to provide even more control.

Adding and Removing Breakpoints

There are a few different ways to set breakpoints within ISDB. First, you can simply position the cursor on a source line, and press the F6 key. This sets a breakpoint on that line. You can set breakpoints for up to 50 lines in this way. Another way to set breakpoints is to use the ISDB command BREAK. For instance, to set a breakpoint on lines 1100, 1200, 1300, and 1400, you simply enter the command

```
BREAK   1100   1200   1300   1400
```

Using the BREAK command, you can also specify conditional breakpoints. The debug session only stops at a conditional breakpoint if a specified condition is true. For instance, the following command would set up a conditional breakpoint for line 55500, the condition being if RRN > 500.

```
BREAK 55500 WHEN RRN > 500
```

Figure 30.6 shows a list of the allowable relational operators that can be used in the BREAK WHEN command.

Figure 30.6 BREAK/WHEN Relational Operators

Value	Symbol	Meaning
*EQ	=	Operands are equal
*LT	<	Operand 1 less than operand 2
*NG	not>	Operand 1 is not greater than operand 2
*NE	not=	Operand 1 is not equal to operand 2
*GE	>=	Operand 1 is greater than or equal to operand 2
*GT	>	Operand 1 is greater than operand 2
*NL	not<	Operand 1 is not less than operand 2
*CT		Operand 1 contains operand 2

Another form of the BREAK command lets you indicate that you want to skip the breakpoint a specified number of times. For example, if you are debugging a read loop in a program, you may not want to have the program stop at a breakpoint for each record that is read. Instead, you may want to skip the breakpoint for the first 500 records. The following example would set a breakpoint on line 55600 and would ignore the breakpoint until line 55600 has been executed 500 times:

```
BREAK 55600 SKIP 500
```

When you decide that you want to remove a breakpoint from the debug environment, you can simply position the cursor on that line and press F6. If you want to remove the breakpoint for several lines, you can use the CLEAR command, as in the following example. This will remove the breakpoints for all of the listed lines.

```
CLEAR   1200 1300 1400 1500 1600
```

If you want to clear all the breakpoints in a program, use the command CLEAR *. You can also perform some breakpoint management from the Debug pull-down menu.

Viewing RPG Indicators

When you are debugging an RPG program and you want to see all the RPG indicators displayed at once, use the command

```
DSP *RPGIND
```

This will result in the display shown in Figure 30.7. The indicators that are in the ON condition are screened and in bold type.

Figure 30.7 RPG Indicator Display

```
 Debug          Goto        Program         Options         Help
 DRIEHL/MYPROGRAM:/0458 _____ISDB/400_____More:_-_+___>
 002000   C        MAIN     BEGSR
 002100   C                 Z-ADDO          TOTAL
 002200   C        ...............................................
 002300   C        :     RPG Indicators 1 - 99, L1 - L9      :
 002400   C        :                                         :
 002500   C        : 01  02  03  04  05  06  07  08  09  10 :
 002600   C        : 11  12  13  14  15  16  17  18  19  20 :
 002700   C        : 21  22  23  24  25  26  27  28  29  30 :
 002800   C        : 31  32  33  34  35  36  37  38  39  40 :
 002900   C        : 41  42  43  44  45  46  47  48  49  50 :
 003000   C_       : 51  52  53  54  55  56  57  58  59  60 : _____
 003100   C        : 61  62  63  64  65  66  67  68  69  70 :
 003200   C        : 71  72  73  74  75  76  77  78  79  80 :
 003300   C        : 81  82  83  84  85  86  87  88  89  90 :
 003400   C        : 91  92  93  94  95  96  97  98  99     :
 003500   C        : L1  L2  L3  L4  L5  L6  L7  L8  L9     :
 003600   C        :                                         :
 003700   C        : Press Enter to continue.               :
 ISDB ===>         :.......................................:
 F3=Exit      F5=Step   F6=Break   F11=Display variable
 F12=Cancel   F17=Run              F23=Change variable   F24=More keys
```

Displaying Variables

When your program reaches a breakpoint, you can display the value of a variable simply by placing the cursor on the variable name and pressing the F11 key. If you want to view the value in hex format, you can press F22. Alternately, you can use the ISDB command DSP to display the values of several variables at once. For example, the following command will display the value of four variables at once:

```
DSP    TOT1  TOT2  TOT3  TOT4
```

To display the same variables in hex format, the command is

```
DSPHEX    TOT1  TOT2  TOT3  TOT4
```

Using the DSP command also lets you display a substring of a character variable. For example, the following command would display 75 characters from the variable LDA starting at position 1000:

```
DSP  (1000,75)LDA
```

You can view individual elements within tables and arrays by using the subscript form of the DSP command. For example, the following command will display the second element within the array named KEY:

```
DSP   KEY(2)
```

Changing Variables

When your program reaches a breakpoint, you can change the value of a variable simply by placing the cursor on the variable name and pressing the F23 key. Alternately, you can use the ISDB command CHG, which gives you more options for how the variable is changed. As a simple example, the following command will change the value of variable CITY to St. Louis:

```
CHG   CITY  'St. Louis'
```

When using the CHG command, you can use the same substring facility as that shown with the DSP command. For example, the following command will change the first three characters in the variable NAME to LOU:

```
CHG   (1,3)NAME   LOU
```

You can change individual array elements using the form

```
CHG   KEY(2)   956
```

Watching Variables

Many times you will want to monitor a particular program variable. For instance, if you are loading a subfile in your program, you may want to keep an eye on the variable that controls the subfile record number; we'll assume the variable's name is RRN.

To watch the variable RRN as it changes, use the following command:

```
WATCH   RRN
```

You can use the substring and subscript forms discussed earlier when you are using the WATCH command. When a watch is added for a variable, the current value of the variable is listed near the top left-hand side of the Debug display. Then any time the variable value changes, it is reflected in the Debug display. To stop the watch process for a variable, use the command

```
UNWATCH RRN
```

If you are watching several variables and want to end the watch operation for all of them, enter the command

```
UNWATCH  *
```

Ending a Debug Session

You can end a debug session when the program is stopped at a breakpoint, or when the program has finished execution. When a program is at a breakpoint, press F12 or F3 to end the debug session. As another option, you can use the ISDB command line to enter the command QUIT or QQUIT. When a program has finished execution, ISDB presents the Program Termination display.

To end a debug session for a serviced job, such as a batch job, you enter the command ENDISDB on the command line. This ends the service function and releases all locks held by the debugger.

Restarting a Debug Session

To restart the debugger when your program is at a breakpoint, use the ISDB command line to enter the RESTART command. If the program has finished execution, the Program Termination display lets you specify an option to restart the debug session.

Other Books in the Technical Reference Series:

Desktop Guide to CL Programming
by Bryan Meyers, a *NEWS/400* technical editor
ISBN: 1-882419-07-3

Desktop Guide to Creating CL Commands
by Lynn Nelson
ISBN: 1-882419-56-1

Desktop Guide to DDS
by James Coolbaugh
ISBN: 1-882419-15-4

Desktop Guide to OPNQRYF
by Mike Dawson, a *NEWS/400* technical editor,
and Mike Manto
ISBN: 1-882419-57-X

Desktop Guide to RPG/400
by Roger Pence and Julian Monypenny,
NEWS/400 technical editors
ISBN: 1-882419-18-9

Desktop Guide to SQL
by James Coolbaugh
ISBN: 1-882419-33-2

For more detailed information about these books and the more than 40 other
AS/400 books available from Duke Press, or to place an order, visit our Web site at

www.dukepress.com

or contact

NEWS/400
Duke Communications International
221 E. 29th Street • Loveland, CO 80539
(800) 621-1544 • (970) 663-4700 • Fax: (970) 669-3016